RESTORE

A modern guide to sustainable eating

GIZZI ERSKINE

RESTORE

A modern guide to sustainable eating

My darling Rose

I can't take full credit for this book, or anything I do if we're entirely honest. You have been standing by my side in everything I do and in the last five years your investment and talent have become invaluable. I joke that we've become like the Elton and Bernie of food, and I guess I want the rest of the world to know that behind all good cookery writers there's often a team of writers and food assistants, but with you and me it's just us, but our 'us' is so synchronised, strong, and such a slick operation, that we've not needed anyone else. This book is called *Restore*, and I thank you for taking on a bigger role and doing more than anyone's ever done for me and restoring me. I'm ever-concerned about sling-shotting you into all of the life-consuming projects we do, and I'm eternally grateful to you for taking each of them on as your own; working the same hours, with the same dedication, while I get all the glory! Everything is better in my life with you in it, and even in real life you are my best friend. I fear that I am Samson, and without you I would lose my powers. Fuck it! At this stage I'm kind of ready for our *Grey Gardens* premonition. Love you in a way that's inexplicable.

Gizzi x

Contents

Introduction   6

Ferments and Pickles   8

Vegetables: *Spring to Summer*   36

Vegetables: *Autumn to Winter*   72

Fruit   98

Pulses, Beans and Grains   112

Sugar, Flour, Fat, Eggs and Milk   142

Poultry and Game   174

Meat and Offal   190

Fish   234

Essentials   258

Cook's Notes   273

Index   276

Acknowledgements   287

INTRODUCTION
A MODERN GUIDE TO SUSTAINABLE EATING

As I'm writing this, the COVID-19 pandemic is in full swing. The world has ground to a halt, we have lost loved ones and businesses, and the global economy is experiencing its biggest crash in history. It's a catastrophic moment.

When I started writing this book, over a year ago, the world felt like a very different place. Brexit was an undone deal. Boris Johnson was not our Prime Minister (who could have predicted that?), and the potential of leaving Europe only to trade more heavily with America seemed much more distant than it does today. I was already in something of a tizz about the state of the world, both agriculturally and environmentally, and was finding the mixed messaging – and the fact that no one was taking responsibility for the real cause of all this damage done to the planet – maddening. I was horrified at the implications of Brexit in terms of trade deals and the future of farming in the UK. The possibility of closed borders and a distancing in our relationship with the EU, hand in hand with the climate crisis, were bringing us ever closer to the kind of dystopian future so far brought to life only on screen and in books. And this made me realise I had to re-evaluate how I approach my use of imported ingredients – ingredients I truly cannot live without. I needed to teach myself how to adapt. And now I want to share everything I've learnt.

Our food story starts at home but it feeds into a bigger narrative – one of consumption and destruction on a massive scale.

We are in a global crisis. Scientists and environmentalists are suggesting that we are at the early stages of the sixth mass extinction event. So what exactly does this mean?

And how can changing the way we eat alter this trajectory? I'm first going to give you the briefest, but most shocking of breakdowns.

Since the first industrial revolution, we have been taking fossil fuels from the Earth. Through every modern human activity that requires energy (which, let's face it, is most things these days, as fossil fuels are not just used for energy, but also in our building materials, foods, packaging, pharmaceuticals, clothes and beauty products… essentially the entire infrastructure that we've created on this planet) these fossil fuels then convert this energy into CO_2, methane and nitrous oxide. These gases have slowly created a barrier in the atmosphere which means the Earth is heating up at an exponential rate. Every 1°C rise in temperature equates to 7 per cent more precipitation, which is leading to the continually increasing violent weather events we're witnessing.

Most alarming are the fresh water melts in the Arctic and Antarctic, which are happening at a far more rapid rate than scientists previously predicted, leading to extreme changes in the global currents, which in turn affects the global weather systems even further. It is predicted that within the next seven decades we will see an extinction of over half of the species of life on Earth.

The reason we're experiencing a pandemic is a direct result of the extensive deforestation of the world's rainforests in order to create more land for agriculture, which is putting people and livestock in closer and closer contact with wildlife and their otherwise harmless and dormant viruses: consumption of bush meat such as pangolins and bats has been confirmed as the likely source of human transmission.

Some people, when they engage with the reality of our planet's condition, decide to stop eating meat and dairy products. I fully accept that the meat and dairy industry is problematic, but I don't accept that this black and white approach is necessarily the right way forward. It's more complex than we think, and prominent films such as *What The Health* and *Gamechangers*, which suggest that veganism is the only answer to saving the planet, are extremely misleading and one-sided.

The whole thing is terrifying and when you start to read more into it, it only gets more overwhelming, as it only opens up an even bigger and more complex can of worms. While we are slowly catching on, we are still very much living the capitalist dream of consume, consume, consume. I have a lot of opinions about this, many of them social and economic, and with this book I'm attempting to debunk some of these highly complex issues to help provide a down-to-earth guide to shopping, eating and cooking for now.

Corporations are slowly accepting the terrifying realisation that we are at a critical juncture in history where drastic changes need to be made to preserve our planet and made quickly; it seems that real change has to come from the individual at home, as it's us who drive the market and have the potential to start this revolution with our own actions.

To me, the word 'restore' has several meanings. First of all, I want to help you understand what it takes in modern farming practices to restore the pH balance and equilibrium of the soil, how we can restore the balance of human impact on the world, and how we can restore

our own bodies with the food we consume in the process. To 'restore' ourselves is not how we live any more. Imbalance is rife. Most people's modern mode of living involves excessive calorie consumption, wildly beyond what's essential for our survival. Accepting that change starts at home can be overwhelming, devastating and depressing for anyone with any joie de vivre, but it doesn't mean that we have to live this incredibly staunch, colourless or bland life. If anything, it's the opposite: when we look into food production and the reality of what it means to eat sustainably we are in fact offered a pretty bountiful plate. There are some incredible food producers in this country, and our seasons deliver an abundance of wonderful ingredients. Yes, eating in a 'restorative' way takes consideration, forming new habits, and stepping away from conveniences, but it can also be creative, fun and delicious.

I want this to be a cook's companion full of practical steps and advice that can help push you towards living and eating more sustainably. I've investigated the real carbon footprint of food and looked at the reality of what we need to do to support our environment, our agricultural industry and the health of our bodies and I want to use this information to inform accessible and attainable recipes – a handbook on how to shop, eat and cook, full of recipes that are a celebration of life.

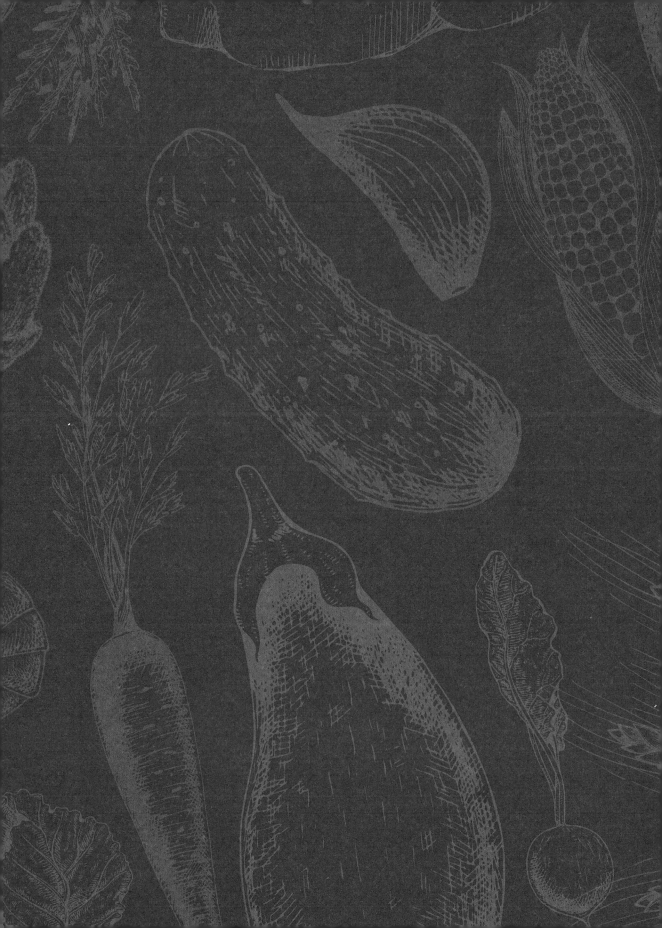

FERMENTS & PICKLES

FERMENTING AND PRESERVING

Assuming that you've read my introduction, you will know that the motivation for me writing this book was the enormous impact food production, and how we trade and transport produce, has on the health of our planet. It made me ask myself, what would I do if I couldn't get my hands on some of the most critical international ingredients I use for cooking every day? Asian food is one of my favourites, but many of the ingredients I use in these dishes – particularly the fermented condiments – are imported. For me, life without soy sauce, fish sauce, miso and gochujang isn't a life I want to be a part of. So what can we do?

If you're into cooking, there is nothing more satisfying than the process of creating a meal, from buying your ingredients, to preparing them, then the metamorphosis of the cookery process and finally placing the dish in front of someone you love and watching it be devoured. You know the amount of love you've put into it. Realising there are people out there who specialise in making some of the ingredients you've used, who have the same passion and consideration as you've put into making that meal, makes me want to scoop up all the good producers in the world and hold them to my breast in gratitude! I wanted to learn how to make some of these products.

How fermenting works

The Asian condiments I love all look and taste different, but they share the same foundation – one of the most uncontrollable ingredients in cookery: bacterial cultures. These cultures require regulated temperature (as opposed to heat) and time. Fermenting is about enabling these bacteria to impart life into food. Bacteria are what change milk into yoghurt and cheese, turn pieces of meat into charcuterie, a cabbage into kraut or kimchi, and a bean into miso or soy sauce.

Fermenting is a complex process and fermented foods vary widely based on the key ingredients, how much salt is added, what temperature the ferment is left at and for how long. Flavour notes can range from tangy to savoury umami and salty, a spectrum of taste that brings a depth and roundness that is almost impossible to define but is addictively satisfying. Soy and fish sauces require years of fermenting to turn into the rich, salty full-bodied sauces that are packed full of umami. To get that flavour requires understanding, time, energy and real commitment. Then there's fizzy, light and tangy kimchi, vinegar or yoghurt, quicker ferments that are ready within a week or two but that – even though they are speedier to make – still contain the umami backbone.

The most magical thing for me is that fermentation stems from the basic need, before the world of refrigeration, to preserve food and make it safe to eat. The fact that fermented foods were stored in the ground near biodiverse soil and that the initial process of fermenting owed itself to this very same biodiversity is one of the most beautiful examples of how nature interacts with humanity.

With age, bacterial cultures become more powerful and can change the structure of a food, transforming it into something new. You need to create a selective environment for the fermentation process. Take kimchi, for example. Kimchi is cabbage that has been wedged into a jar with salt and aromatics and essentially left to rot, but managing the good bacteria and keeping the bad bacteria at bay results in something delicious. When the right environment has been created to harvest and promote the growth of good bacteria, they grow to be so potent that they become hugely beneficial to the human body, but in order to get there and fully understand this, you have to approach fermentation less like cookery and more like a science lesson.

The most important ingredient in fermentation is salt. Salt draws out liquids by osmosis. A vegetable ferment with a small amount of salt retains the structure of the vegetables by reinforcing the pectin in the vegetable's cell walls, whereas higher salt levels will slow down the fermentation process, break down the structure of the food and allow it to age for flavour, letting the sugars develop and helping the food keep for longer.

The other key factor is temperature. Heat above 70°C kills bacteria and yeasts. Anything between room temperature (about 20°C) and 50°C is a really fertile space for bacteria. At cooler temperatures, right down to fridge temperature (about 4°C), bacterial growth is slower, and fridge temperature inhibits bacteria growth and helps keep it stable. Freezing fully inhibits the growth of bacteria, keeping it dormant until it warms up again and comes back to life. This is a good way to understand how quickly things ferment. Products like fish sauce are fermented at about 40°C, whereas kimchis can be slow-fermented in fridges. For home cooking, I simplify the temperature factor by fermenting foods at room temperature until required fermentation is desired, then transferring them to the fridge.

Why fermented foods are good for your health

The modern western diet, typically high in fat and sugar, attacks the delicate balance of essential microbiota in our digestive system, which affects everything, particularly obesity levels and mental health. This, combined with depleted nutrients in the soils our food is growing in (and therefore less-nutritious food), means that our guts are seriously deficient in bacterial diversity. Fermented foods restore this diversity.

If you get bitten by the bio-culture bug, there are great books out there such as *The Noma Guide to Fermentation* by René Redzepi and David Zilber, and *The Art of Fermentation* by Sandor Ellix Katz, which delve far deeper, but I want to show you that it is possible to get into the world of fermenting and preserving in a practical and realistic way, with delicious results.

Quick Ferments

Accelerated Gochujang

MAKES 1.1 litres
Preparation time 5 minutes
Fermenting time 5 weeks

120g rice flour
120g fine sea salt
800ml water
250g fine Korean red pepper flakes
70g sweet white miso

AFTER 2 WEEKS
8 tbsp rice or barley malt syrup
2 tbsp salt

You will need a sterilised 1.5-litre
preserving jar.

Gochujang, a Korean red hot pepper paste, is at the foundation of so many Korean dishes. It's an effort to make (trust me, I've been to South Korea's Sunchang region and made it properly), but I really wanted to include it in the book. It's usually activated with a special soy bean, however to speed things up here I've used miso in its place, which is already fermented; I'm not normally one to cut corners but this recipe is genuinely surprising. The Korean pepper is what makes this special. It's roughly ground (even the 'fine' stuff), it's very hot and is naturally sweet (having originated from the Spanish peppers) and bright, bright red! You can buy it on the internet or in Asian supermarkets.

Mix the rice flour, sea salt and water together well in a bowl, then stir through the Korean red pepper flakes and miso until evenly distributed into a thickish paste. Transfer to a sterilised 1.5-litre preserving jar and seal tightly. (You need the jar to be a bit bigger than the volume of the gochujang as the paste will need room to expand as it ferments.)

Set aside in a cool, dry place (out of direct sunlight) and leave to ferment for 1 week. Once this time has passed, you will start to see some little bubbles forming on the surface. Now it's time to add a final hit of flavour and balance out the spice of the gochujang, so a hit of sugar from the rice or barley malt syrup and some more salt is just the ticket. The salt will also inhibit the gochujang from fermenting too much, too fast. Mix both thoroughly into the paste, then clean the inner walls of the jar with a cloth dipped in vodka to keep the inside of the jar sterile. Place a cellophane jam seal on the gochujang, seal tightly and put it in the fridge to continue slow fermenting for another month. As ever, it will only deepen in flavour the longer it ferments.

Cheats' Activated Kimchi

**MAKES enough to fill a 3-litre
preserving jar**
Preparation time 30 minutes, plus
1 hour minimum brining time
Fermenting time 2 days

50g salt
300ml water
2 heads of Chinese napa cabbage,
    outer leaves removed, cabbages
    quartered lengthways
300g Accelerated Gochujang (see
    opposite)
80g fresh ginger, peeled and cut into
    thin matchsticks
6 spring onions, julienned into 4mm-
    thick strips
2 apples, cut into thin matchsticks
    (with skin intact)

You will need some kitchen gloves
and a sterilised 3-litre preserving jar.

**I've been making kimchi for years, the recipe for which I've already posted online,
but when I made the gochujang (opposite) I was playing around with things to do
with it. The fact that the gochujang is full of live bacteria means that it starts the
process of fermentation really quickly and you will have decent kimchi within a day
or two rather than a few weeks. This kimchi is also vegan.**

Begin by giving the cabbage a quick brine. To make the brine simply dissolve the salt
in the 300ml of water in a saucepan over a medium heat. Pour it into a non-reactive
container which the cabbage will fit into. Once the water has completely cooled, add
the cabbage, pour over enough cold water on top to ensure the cabbage is submerged,
and allow to brine for a minimum of 1 hour.

Once the time has passed, remove the cabbage from the brine and dry it thoroughly.
You'll need to get in between every leaf to make sure it's as dry as possible. (Over the
course of fermentation the cabbage will release lots of liquid and you don't want the
flavour to become too diluted, so it's good to eradicate as much water at the start as
you can.)

Wash the non-reactive container you brined the cabbage in and dry it very thoroughly.
Add the gochujang, followed by the ginger, spring onions and apples. You'll want
to wear gloves for this next part of the process: once you've donned your gloves, use
your hands to mix the ginger, spring onion and apples thoroughly with the gochujang
until combined. Take your dried cabbage quarters and spread a little of the gochujang
marinade between each cabbage leaf so that it is really well rubbed into the cabbage.

Wrap each cabbage quarter around itself to create a tight parcel and wedge into a
sterilised 3-litre preserving jar. It will start fermenting pretty much immediately,
and you'll be able to tell by the level of liquid that leaches out of the cabbage that it's
starting to ferment.

Within two days, it's good to go, or you can store it in the fridge. It will deepen in
flavour the longer it ferments.

MAKES 350g
Preparation time 15 minutes
Fermenting time 2–3 weeks

finely grated zest of 16 limes
2 tbsp finely grated lemon zest
2 tbsp finely grated pink grapefruit
  zest
1 tbsp finely grated clementine zest
1 tbsp salt
juice of 2 fresh limes
2 tbsp grapefruit juice
2 tbsp fresh clementine juice
3 green finger chillies, very finely
  chopped
pinch of sugar

You will need a sterilised 500g
preserving jar.

Fauzu Kosho

My favourite ingredient in the world is yuzukoshō. Yuzu, a Japanese citrus fruit, has a flavour that sits somewhere between a lime, mandarin and grapefruit; 'kosho' describes the part where the rind and juice of the fruit are fermented with very spicy green chillies and salt. NamaYasai, a brilliant farm in Lewes, in the south of England, grows yuzu, but whether you buy UK-grown or imported fruit, they are still quite expensive, and here you need quite a lot of fruit, so I go for a combination of limes and other citrus fruits. This recipe's great because it's a really quick ferment, and you can use up all the limes in my Lemon and Lime Pickle (page 25). It's fantastic in everything from mayonnaise with fried chicken or tofu, to a margherita (though use it sparingly). Use unwaxed fruit and wash them thoroughly before grating the zest.

Mix all of the citrus zests in a small bowl with the salt using the back of a spoon until you have a coarse paste. Mix in the lime juice, grapefruit juice, clementine juice and green chillies until well combined. Transfer to a sterilised 500g preserving jar and seal tightly.

Leave to ferment at room temperature (out of direct sunlight) for 1–2 weeks. Once it starts to look fizzy you will know it has begun fermenting. At this stage transfer it to a food processor and blitz until smooth. Return to the jar and leave to ferment at room temperature for 1 more week.

Once this time has passed it's ready to eat, and should be kept in the fridge.

Fermented Fruit Vinegar

MAKES 1 litre
Preparation time 10 minutes
Fermenting time 3–4 weeks

scraps of 10 apples (or whichever fruit
   you decide to use), including cores,
   stalks and peel (about 450g)
50g granulated sugar
850ml lukewarm water
splash of cider vinegar

You will need a sterilised 3-litre
wide-neck preserving jar or
glass bowl.

I've used apple scraps in this recipe, but the method can be easily adapted to use up other fruit you have such as pears, overripe plums, peaches or grapes.

Measure out the fruit scraps in a measuring jug. This method works on the principle of 1 part fruit to 2 parts sugar-and-water solution, so adjust the measurements according to how much fruit you have (e.g. for 500g of fruit you will need 1 litre of sugar-water solution). Put the fruit scraps in a large, clean glass bowl or 3-litre wide-neck preserving jar (glass is the best material to make it in as it is not reactive to high acidity levels, whereas some metals and plastics are). Stir the sugar into the lukewarm water until dissolved. Pour the solution over the fruit, making sure it is well submerged. Cover the bowl or jar with a sheet of muslin and secure with an elastic band or string. Leave the mixture to ferment in a dark cupboard for a week or so, swirling it every day to keep it well mixed and aid fermentation. Room temperature of 26–28°C is ideal – if it's colder, it will just take longer to ferment.

After about a week, you should see the mixture start to bubble, which means fermentation has begun. The bacteria and natural wild yeasts in the atmosphere will be eating the sugars, which produces carbon dioxide, and hey presto – you are fermenting! Strain the liquid through a muslin-lined sieve into a large jug or container. Clean the original bowl or jar and return the liquid to it, adding the cider vinegar to speed up the fermentation. Re-cover with the muslin and secure with the string or elastic band. Return it to the dark cupboard and leave for a further 2–3 weeks, giving it just the occasional gentle swirl so as not to disturb the growth too much. This bacterial growth is what is known as the 'mother', a thick film that's almost cotton-woolly. It is full of good bacteria so don't be put off! You can remove this easily, and if you rinse it gently under warm water and store it with a splash of your nice new vinegar, it will be a brilliant kick-starter for any vinegars you make in the future, and replace the need for cider vinegar. Store it covered with muslin.

Once you have removed the 'mother', strain the vinegar again, this time through a fine sieve lined with a double layer of muslin, to remove any sediment. Transfer to freshly sterilised, dry glass jars or bottles (the warmth will help promote further maturing). The vinegar will keep indefinitely in a cupboard, and only deepens in flavour as it matures.

Tepache

MAKES 2 litres
Preparation time 5 minutes
Fermenting time 3–4 days

2 ripe to overripe medium
    pineapples, skin washed and
    scrubbed
2 lemons, washed and thinly sliced
60g golden caster sugar
2 litres cold water

TO SERVE
ice
pineapple leaves or sprigs of mint
extra sugar (if liked)

My mum has been making this Mexican fermented pineapple skin 'beer' (or cooler) for years – that makes her cooler than anyone, in my opinion. It is the best summer drink ever! It's made from fermenting overripe pineapple skins and cores that would normally get thrown out. My mum's version is inspired by a Delia Smith recipe that has been bastardised throughout the years. It gets fizzy in about three days thus making it beer-like, and – served over ice, with mint or pineapple leaves – it's just magic. Add some dark rum to the equation for some real fun!

Cut the top off the pineapples with a sharp knife and discard for compost. Carefully cut away the skin in long strips, working your way around the whole fruit, then cut the fruit away from the core in quarters. Keep the pineapple flesh for eating.

Chop the skin and core into small pieces (about 2cm). Place in a bowl and add the sliced lemons and sugar. Mix everything with clean hands until well dispersed. Pour over the cold water, cover the bowl with a cloth, and leave at room temperature to ferment for 3–4 days, until the surface of the liquid is starting to bubble.

Strain the liquid into a clean jug, chill and serve within 2 days.

Serve poured over lots of ice and with pineapple leaves or sprigs of mint. You can add a bit more sugar if you prefer a sweeter drink.

MAKES about 1kg (enough to fill
a 1-litre jar)
Preparation time 20 minutes
Fermenting time 1–3 weeks

1 head of red or white cabbage (about
  1.4kg), washed and finely shredded
  (use a mandoline if you have one)
28g sea salt flakes

You will need a sterilised 1-litre
preserving jar.

Sauerkraut

For the uninitiated, this is perhaps the easiest entry point into lacto-fermentation. You don't need any special equipment, just a container to put it in. The lactobacillus bacteria that live on the surface of the cabbage convert the sugars within the cabbage into lactic acid when the cabbage is submerged in brine, and this acid acts as a natural preservative, prohibiting growth of any nasty harmful bacteria. This preserves the cabbage for months in a cool dark cupboard, and in the fridge for up to a year (if you don't devour it quicker). Sauerkraut is great cold from the jar with cured meats, but I also love it fried in butter, with German sausages and mustard.

Making sauerkraut couldn't be simpler. It works on the principle of salting the cabbage at a ratio of 2 per cent salt to the weight of the cabbage, so here the cabbage weighs 1.4kg, therefore you need 28g salt (1 per cent would be 14g).

Put the shredded cabbage in a large bowl and sprinkle over the salt. Massage it with your hands, kneading and squeezing the salt thoroughly into the cabbage for a good 10–20 minutes. You'll notice its liquid start to leach out, which is what you want to happen, as this is the first sign of the cabbage starting to break down. Keep massaging it until enough liquid has developed to cover the cabbage once it's compressed into the jar, as it's this liquid that will form the brining solution.

Transfer the cabbage and liquid to a sterilised 1-litre preserving jar and press the cabbage down so that the liquid rises to the surface. Seal tightly and leave to ferment at room temperature (out of direct sunlight) for at least a week. It's safe to eat at any stage of the process, and it will develop in sourness and flavour the longer it is left to ferment. Transfer to the fridge once it's fermented to your liking, to slow down the fermentation process.

Slow Ferments

MAKES about 1.45kg salty miso, and 1.65kg sweet miso

Preparation time 5 minutes, plus overnight soaking

Cooking time 4 hours

Fermenting time 6 months minimum

SWEET MISO

500g dried soybeans

10–20cm-long piece of kombu

500g white rice koji

60g fine sea salt

SALTY MISO

500g dried soybeans

10–20cm-long piece of kombu

250g white rice koji

100g fine sea salt

You will need 2 × 2-litre sterilised preserving jars.

White Miso

This is the grittiest of all of the recipes in this book, but every step is necessary. I suggest making it by hand to get a traditional chunky miso. If you prefer it smooth, just blend it once fermented before popping it in the fridge. I like sweet white miso for its taste and speed of fermenting, but this recipe provides ingredients and methods for both sweet or salty, so you can choose which one you want to make. The kombu (seaweed) adds an extra element of umami. Both types of miso take at least 6 months to ferment. White rice koji is available on the internet.

Rinse the soybeans under cold running water at least three times until the water runs clear, to remove any impurities. Transfer the beans to a large clean bowl and cover with fresh cold water so that the water sits 2cm above the beans. Leave to soak overnight in a cool place. Using filtered water at every stage here helps to maintain the purity of the miso.

The next day, drain the beans. They should have expanded and almost doubled in size and weight. Put the beans in a large saucepan and cover with more cold filtered water, so the water sits at least 3cm above the beans. Add the kombu and bring to the boil, skimming off any scum. Reduce the heat and simmer, uncovered, for 4 hours, skimming occasionally if any more scum appears on the surface and adding more water if necessary to keep the beans submerged. You know the beans are cooked when they are completely soft when squeezed between your finger and thumb. At this point, drain the beans, retaining the cooking liquid. Set aside to cool. You want the beans to be warm when you add the koji to activate it, but be aware that the enzymes in the koji will be inhibited at any heat over 60°C, so allow them to cool for at least 20 minutes, stirring occasionally so that any beans in the centre cool down too.

Once the beans have cooled, start mashing! I considered using my food processor for this, but it would probably have become like cement and jammed the machine. I also favour a slightly more textured miso, which is traditional, so that means mashing by hand, a task I find satisfyingly therapeutic. Pound them with the end of a rolling pin or a potato masher until they form a pale mush (the odd bit of bean is nothing to worry about). Split the mashed beans into equal halves and put them in separate bowls

CONTINUED ››

– the cooked weight of our soybeans when we tested this recipe totalled 2.2kg, so we split them into 1.1kg portions.

In *The Art of Fermentation* – my bible for understanding the process of miso making – author Sandor Ellix Katz suggests dissolving the salt in a couple of ladles of warm cooking water from the soybeans. I don't know if this is totally necessary, as the salt becomes well mixed when you combine it with the koji and soybeans, but perhaps it is reassuring to dissolve the salt first to ensure it is evenly distributed. Either way, you want a thick paste that is spreadable but not too liquid. Add 4 or 5 small ladles of cooking liquid to each miso mix to achieve the right consistency and, depending on your preference and whether you are making the salty or sweet miso, add the appropriate amount of salt and white rice koji. Knead the mixture thoroughly: you want the rice and salt to be well combined and the whole mixture to be amalgamated.

Ensure your jars are completely sterile: this is an essential first step in waging war against mould potentially forming while the miso ferments. Now start filling the jars with your miso: add small balls of miso to the jars gradually, packing them down tightly at each stage to eradicate any chance of air pockets. Allow for a 5cm gap at the top of each jar. Clean the inner walls of the jar with a cloth dipped in vodka to keep the inside of the jar sterile. Katz mentions that he likes to 'sprinkle salt on the moist internal surfaces of the crock before filling it with miso… to increase salt concentration at the edges', however he also happily says, 'I do it unless I forget: and when I have forgotten, I have never had a problem with contamination.'

Sprinkle salt on the flat, packed-down surface of the miso before weighing it down, to help inhibit mould bacteria, then place a layer of cling film or jam film on the surface of the miso to create an airtight seal. Push a sandwich bag or something similar into the remaining cavity of the jar and pour as much salt as you can fit into the bags to act as a weight. Seal tightly, label and put it in a dry place out of direct sunlight, preferably not too cool (an airing cupboard would be ideal).

The miso takes at least 6 months to ferment. Resist the temptation to open the jars and stir it, as once you expose it to air you invite trouble and the potential for mould. If you do detect any mould, don't panic, just carefully scrape it off with a knife and re-sterilise any exposed surfaces on the jar. You'll be able to taste when it's reached its prime: it will have that delicious well-rounded depth of flavour. Once opened, it will keep very happily in the fridge for weeks.

MAKES 300g
Preparation time 20 minutes
Cooking time 1 hour
Fermenting time 2 weeks to 2 months

40g dried shiitake mushrooms
400ml warm water
2 banana shallots or 5 round ones,
    peeled
100g fresh ginger, cut into chunks
3 red bird's-eye chillies, stalks
    removed
1 head of garlic, cloves peeled
2 large sheets of dried nori seaweed
150ml oil
200ml Shaoxing wine
2 rounded tbsp miso paste
3 tbsp sugar

You will need a sterilised 300g
preserving jar.

Vegan XO Sauce

XO sauce is a slow-fermented chilli, seafood and pork sauce from Hong Kong that is served all over China and Southeast Asia in seafood restaurants. London has been flooded with love for the sauce, almost to the point of annoyance, but I feel like the rest of the country hasn't quite got to grips with it. It has the deepest flavour and is fantastic over everything from veggies to fish. This vegan version uses umami-rich ingredients like seaweed and shiitake mushrooms: it makes a great base for vegan curries, as there's no need for fish sauce.

Put the shiitake mushrooms in a bowl with the warm water and set aside for about 10 minutes to rehydrate, then strain, retaining the soaking liquor.

Put the shallots, ginger, chillies, strained mushrooms, garlic and nori in a food processor and pulse so that everything is blitzed but still maintains some texture – you want a coarse paste.

Heat the oil in a medium saucepan over a medium-low heat and scrape the spicy paste into the pan. Pour the water you rehydrated the mushrooms with into the pan, being careful to leave the last little bit in the bowl as there will be some residual grit that has sunk to the bottom. Add the Shaoxing wine and mix in the miso and sugar. I go for a white miso, as I like its hint of sweetness, but any miso would work well.

Fry very gently for about 30 minutes, until everything has thoroughly sweated down, moving it around the pan occasionally to prevent it catching. Once the liquid has completely evaporated you will notice the paste will begin to brown and caramelise more rapidly, so for the next 30 minutes you will need to keep a more watchful eye on it, stirring it regularly to avoid it burning. Once you have a thick, fibrous, deeply caramelised tapenade-like paste, which is separating itself from its oil, the XO is done. Turn off the heat, transfer to a sterilised 300g preserving jar and seal. Leave it to ferment for anything from 2 weeks to 2 months. Once opened, it will keep in the fridge for months.

MAKES 1.5 litres
Preparation time 5 minutes
Cooking time 2 hours
Fermenting time 6 months

1kg mackerel and fish guts, roughly
    chopped
180g salt

You will need a sterilised 2-litre
preserving jar.

Fish Sauce

An absolute staple in my house, fish sauce is imperative to so much Asian cookery. It's sometimes called 'garam', depending on how it's made. I've discussed this recipe about a million times with chef and fermenting friends (I must give a shout-out to Andrew Clarke of chef's mental health charity Pilot Light, whose recipe this actually is, but also Andy Oliver of Som Saa, John Chantarasak of AngloThai and Glyn Gordon of Eaten Alive, who all helped). Andrew Clarke's recipe is the easiest I've found, and it makes incredible fish sauce, but I warn you, for two days you will wonder why on earth you bothered, because it reeks. Oh. My. God. It reeks.

For the best results, use a 15–20 per cent ratio of salt to fish (I've used 18 per cent below). I use a combination of fish guts I had left over from a previous dish and an extra couple of mackerel that I simply chopped into pieces.

Put the fish and salt in a blender or food processor, add enough water to cover, and blitz until smooth. Transfer the mixture to a saucepan and cover with cold water to a level 10cm higher than the fish. Bring to the boil, skimming off any scum on the surface as this will contain all the impurities, then reduce the heat and cook at a strong simmer (not quite boiling) for 2 hours, skimming again if necessary. The idea is for the fish and bones to break down into a slurry so you can just leave it bubbling away, as long as you keep the water level up. Your house will stink, but no pain no gain!

Remove from the heat and allow to cool, then pour into a sterilised 2-litre preserving jar and seal tightly. The optimum temperature for the sauce to ferment at is 40–60°C. Andrew Clarke recommends using a reptile heat pad (you can find these online; they're used to keep cold-blooded creatures like snakes and lizards warm), which you can place the jar on top of to keep it warm and help the process along (I keep mine next to my coffee machine). Alternatively, a warm airing cupboard would work.

It will need about 6 months fermenting until it's ready to use, there's no getting around this. After it has fermented for 6 months, strain it through a fine muslin cloth-lined sieve to remove any sediment or slurry, then either keep it in the jar or transfer it through a funnel (lined with more muslin) into a sterilised bottle. It will keep at room temperature, but I advise keeping home ferments in the fridge as they will then keep forever.

Brines and Pickles

MAKES 1kg
Preparation time 10 minutes
Cooking time 15 minutes
Fermenting time 2–3 weeks

1kg zested limes and/or thin-skinned
  lemons, cut into eighths, pith
  removed
120ml sunflower or organic rapeseed
  oil
30 fresh curry leaves
2 tsp mustard seeds
½ tsp fenugreek seeds
2cm piece of fresh ginger, peeled and
  grated
5 garlic cloves, thinly sliced
4 green finger chillies, sliced into
  thirds at an angle
1cm piece of fresh turmeric, peeled
  and grated
1½ tsp ground turmeric
35g sea salt
1 tbsp golden caster sugar
3 tsp Kashmiri chilli powder

You will need a sterilised 1-litre
preserving jar.

Lemon and Lime Pickle

What makes this a good saviour of the fruit basket is that so often with baking you need more citrus zest than juice. I often end up with some sorry-looking limes and lemons in my basket. Zested lime and unwaxed thin-skinned lemons make brilliant Indian pickle, as the zest of the types of limes and lemons available in this country can be a bit too intense and make a bitter pickle. I like using Kashmiri chilli powder to get that deep red colour and a more rounded and sweet flavour, but you can use a bog standard one too. This is an excellent condiment with any curry, such as my Sri Lankan Beetroot and Coconut Curry (page 87) or Tarka Dhal (page 125).

First, steam the limes. If you don't have a steamer, you can make one by simply bringing a saucepan of water to a rolling simmer over a medium heat, putting a colander or sieve on top, then covering the colander or sieve with a saucepan lid to keep the steam in. Sit a batch of lime and/or lemon pieces in one layer in the steamer and steam for 8–10 minutes, until tender. Remove and set aside and steam the remaining lime/lemon pieces.

Heat the oil in a frying pan over a medium heat. When hot, add the curry leaves, mustard seeds and fenugreek seeds. As soon as they start to crackle, add the ginger, garlic, green chillies, fresh and ground turmeric, salt, sugar and chilli powder and stir-fry for a couple of minutes to cook the spices, being careful they don't burn as this will make them acrid. Add the steamed limes and/or lemons and stir-fry for another couple of minutes, making sure they are well coated in the spicy oil, then take off the heat. Leave to cool, transfer to a sterilised 1-litre preserving jar and seal tightly.

Allow to ferment at room temperature (out of direct sunlight) for 2–3 weeks before eating. As with all fermenting, the speed at which it happens is temperature dependent (the warmer the environment, the faster it happens), so check that the limes/lemons have softened enough before you eat them. If they are still a bit hard you may want to leave it to ferment for another few days. Once opened, it will keep in the fridge for ages, as long as all the citrus is covered in oil (top up with more oil if necessary).

Wonderful watermelons

Looking around the world I see how valuable the watermelon is. It's not just about the fruit – there are loads of different methods for curing the skins for eating, too. Watermelon is in the same family as a cucumber, and the skin is there to keep the moisture in as it's one of the most hydrated of all fruits (hence 'water' in its name). We all know the fragrance and flavour of the flesh, but the best way to describe how the rind tastes is somewhere between the flavour of watermelon and cucumber. I've included two of my favourite recipes here: a pickle and a lacto-ferment. When pickling it with sugar it takes on the sweet edge of the fruit, and when lacto-fermented it becomes very cucumbery. I've also thrown in a little watermelon vinegar recipe for any leftover watermelon, as some of them are so monstrously big!

Mexican-spiced Pickled Watermelon Rind

MAKES enough to fill a 3-litre preserving jar
Preparation time 20 minutes
Pickling time 2 weeks minimum

850ml water
300ml apple cider vinegar
a combination of dried (preferably Mexican) chillies (I use 3 sweet ñora peppers and 2 hot guindilla chilli peppers)
75g sea salt
150g golden caster sugar
1.3–5kg watermelon rind, cut into shard-like strips

You will need a sterilised 3-litre preserving jar.

This is absolutely delicious with pork carnitas, hard cheese or fish tacos.

Put the water, vinegar, dried chillies, salt and sugar in a saucepan. Bring to the boil and give it a few stirs to make sure all the sugar and salt has dissolved, then add the watermelon rind, bring to the boil once more and take off the heat, to allow the flavours to infuse. Once it has cooled a little, transfer the whole lot to a sterilised 3-litre preserving jar and seal tightly.

You can eat these pretty much straight away once cooled, if you want, but they will improve with age and can be kept in the fridge for a long time.

Watermelon Juice Vinegar

Using this in a ceviche is really exceptional, especially with some finely chopped watermelon pickle.

MAKES 1 litre
Preparation time 10 minutes
Fermenting time 3–4 weeks

1.3kg watermelon flesh, juiced and sieved to remove pips
2 tbsp apple cider vinegar (with the 'mother')

You will need a sterilised 1-litre preserving jar.

Once you have juiced the watermelon flesh, put it in a sterilised 1-litre preserving jar with the vinegar. Cover the top of the jar with muslin and secure the muslin in place with string or an elastic band – the vinegar needs to be able to 'breathe'. Leave to ferment at room temperature (out of direct sunlight) for 3–4 weeks. Once it has reached the desired level of 'vinegary-ness' (keep tasting it), store it in the jar it was fermented in. It will stay 'shelf stable' in the cupboard indefinitely.

Lacto-fermented Watermelon Rind

Use this fermented rind in the same way you would cucumber pickles, in salads and alongside smoked fish. You want to use a 2 per cent ratio of salt to water.

MAKES enough to fill a 3-litre preserving jar
Preparation time 10 minutes
Fermenting time 2 weeks

28g sea salt
1.4 litres filtered water
1kg watermelon rind, green outer skin peeled off and cut into 15cm-long shards
handful of fresh dill
2 tbsp mustard seeds
5 bay leaves
1 tbsp black peppercorns
5 garlic cloves, peeled

You will need a sterilised 3-litre preserving jar.

Stir the salt into the water in a bowl or saucepan, until it has completely dissolved.

Put the watermelon rind, dill, mustard seeds, bay leaves, peppercorns and garlic in a sterilised 3-litre preserving jar. Fill the jar with the salt solution until it is full and the watermelon is submerged. Seal tightly and allow to ferment at room temperature (out of direct sunlight) for about 2 weeks. You can leave these in a cool place or in the fridge for months.

Preparation time 20 minutes
Cooking time 50 minutes
Maturing time 3 months minimum

FOR THE VEG AND FRUIT

juice of 1 lemon (for acidulating
   the water)
1 carrot, cut into 1cm dice
1 large courgette, cut into 1cm dice
200g cauliflower (about ½
   cauliflower), cut into 1cm dice
   (you can use leaves and stalk)
200g peeled and deseeded butternut
   squash (about ½ medium squash),
   cut into 1cm dice
½ cucumber, deseeded and cut into
   1cm dice
2 apples, peeled, cored and cut into
   small chunks
150g prunes, cut into small dice
200g dates, cut into small dice
5 large pickled gherkins, cut into
   1cm dice

FOR THE PICKLE

3 tbsp oil
3 onions, roughly chopped
1 head of garlic, cloves peeled and
   finely chopped
2 tsp black mustard seeds
1 tbsp chilli powder
1 tbsp freshly ground black pepper
1 tbsp ground coriander
1 tbsp ground cumin
1 heaped tsp ground allspice
1 tsp ground ginger
pinch of ground cloves
200ml water
400g soft dark brown sugar
30g sea salt
700ml malt vinegar
1 tsp cornflour
50ml Worcestershire sauce
50ml lemon juice

Fridge-raid 'not quite Branston's' Pickle

I consider myself quite the aficionado at recreating famous recipes, but there are some that are so hard to compete with that it's just not worth it. I've lost track of the number of times I've tried to recreate Branston pickle but not quite made it. Half of me is not sure why I bother: it's so accessible and, let's be honest here, it's more marmite than Marmite – you either love it or hate it! So many people have really un-fun memories of it. My friend at school used to have thickly-buttered chewy bread rolls filled with Marmite, a thick slice of Cheddar and Branston pickle that she'd never eat, so would give to me, and a love affair was born.

The reason I decided to bother this time is because I wrote this mid lockdown, and I had promised myself to not throw out a single thing during the COVID-19 pandemic. I was rummaging around my fridge and there were some vegetables and apples looking very sorry for themselves – I was pretty certain all these things are what go into Branston pickle, so I went to my last recipe (one that hadn't quite worked). It was looking good: technically, Branston pickle has swede in it and I only had butternut squash, but I searched the storecupboard and I had everything else. My notes from the last time I'd tried to make it were, 'stick to the dark brown sugar and malt vinegar – less cornflour', so I retested it and it's the closest to Branston's that I've got so far. I wanted to include it in this book as it's a really good way to use up things that are on their last legs, and refreshing everything in ice-cold water makes it spring back to freshness. Remember that dehydrated veg is just that – it's simply lost its water. More often than not, it has retained its nutrients (look at the nutritional content of a fresh grape compared to a raisin, for example). When you cook or salt something, generally this is to remove the water from it, so making chutneys is great for veg and fruit past their best that have already begun this process of dehydration.

So here's my most up-to-date 'Branston-style' pickle recipe. It's not quite Branston's, but it's bloody delicious and works marvellously in that very same buttered, Marmite, cheese and pickle sandwich!

Bear in mind it needs at least 3 months' maturing time before it's ready to eat, and that you need to sterilise your jars (enough jars for 3kg of pickle).

You will need a sterilised 3-litre jar or bottle, or several smaller jars.

First, take the biggest bowl or pan you can get your hands on. Fill it with cold water and a load of ice cubes, then add the lemon juice (this stops everything from browning). As you prep your vegetables, throw them into the ice-cold water and lay the fruits and diced gherkin on a plate next to it.

To make the pickling mixture, heat the oil in a large saucepan over a low-ish heat, add the onions and fry for 20 minutes, or until softened. Add the garlic and cook for another 5 minutes or until the garlic is soft and the onions start to tinge golden. Next, add the spices and cook for 30 seconds. Add the apples, half the prunes and dates and the water. Coat the fruits in the spicy onions then add the sugar, salt and vinegar and stir really well to incorporate. Cook for 15 minutes, stirring continuously, until the apples are cooked to a chunky puree and the prunes and dates are soft. Add the cornflour, transfer to a food processor and blitz until the mixture is very, very smooth (I blitz it for about 2 minutes). Return the mixture to the pan then add all the veg (drained of the ice-cold water), gherkins and the rest of the prunes and dates. Coat in the brown pickle puree and cook very gently for 10 minutes, or until the veggies start to soften. They will continue to soften while they mature in the pickle.

Transfer to sterilised jars while hot. I eat A LOT of pickle so I always put it into a sterilised 3-litre jar (I am a Kilner-jar person, as they never let me down), but you can split the 3kg between any amount of jars. Seal and leave to mature in a cool, dark place for at least 3 months. Once open, you can keep it in the fridge for ages. I have Piccalilli (overleaf) that's still going strong from last year!

Punchy Piccalilli

MAKES 3kg
Preparation time 15 minutes, plus
2 hours salting time
Cooking time 10 minutes
Pickling time about 1 month

1 cauliflower, florets trimmed and
stalk cut into bite-sized chunks
1 yellow and 1 green courgette, cut
into bite-sized chunks
1 green pepper, deseeded and cut into
bite-sized chunks
1 red pepper, deseeded and cut into
bite-sized chunks
3 small Lebanese cucumbers, cored
and cut into bite-sized chunks
300g green beans, cut into bite-sized
chunks
150g carrots, cut into bite-sized
chunks
300g silverskin or tiny pickling
onions (I use frozen)
35g fine sea salt

FOR FRYING
80ml sunflower oil
1 tbsp mustard seeds
2 tbsp English mustard powder
1 tsp ground turmeric
1 tsp curry powder
¼ tsp ground cloves
2 garlic cloves, crushed
4cm piece of fresh ginger, peeled and
grated
50g sugar
100ml water
750ml cider vinegar
1 tbsp plain flour
2 tbsp cornflour

You will need enough sterilised
preserving jars for 3kg piccalilli.

With this piccalilli, the flavour has been lifted with the addition of curry powder and more spice than is typically used. I love my piccalilli really pickly and although I don't usually cheat much when it comes to cooking, the addition of pre-peeled pickling onions saves on time and gives the piccalilli some extra va-va-voom! Piccalilli is the perfect partner for cheese, cold ham or pork pies, or whatever you fancy.

Mix the vegetables with the pickling onions in a large bowl. Sprinkle over the salt and mix thoroughly with your hands so the salt is evenly dispersed. Set aside at room temperature for 2 hours – this begins to break down the vegetables, ready for pickling.

After the 2 hours, rinse the vegetables under cold running water, drain and set aside.

Heat the sunflower oil in a large saucepan over a high heat. Once it's hot, add the mustard seeds and fry until they start popping, then add the rest of the dry spices and the garlic and ginger, and fry for another 30 seconds, stirring as you go. Add the drained vegetables and fry for 2 minutes, then add the sugar, water and cider vinegar and bring to the boil.

For a good piccalilli you need the spicy sauce to cling to the vegetables, so the next step is to thicken it. In a small bowl, mix together the plain flour and cornflour with a little water to make a paste. Spoon one ladles' worth of cooking liquor into the bowl and whisk until smooth. Pour this back into the pan of vegetables and cook for 2–3 minutes until it thickens and the vegetables are cooked through but still firm.

Remove from the heat and allow the mixture to cool slightly before carefully pouring into sterilised jars. Seal tightly and leave at room temperature to pickle for about a month. Once opened, it will keep in the fridge for at least a year.

Chilli Sauces

MAKES 500ml
Preparation time 10 minutes
Cooking time 10 minutes
Fermenting time 3–7 days

3–4 Scotch bonnet chillies
20g fresh turmeric
4 garlic cloves, peeled
350g pineapple, peeled, cored and
    chopped
2 tbsp English or American yellow
    mustard
250ml white wine or cider vinegar
40g caster sugar
2 tsp salt

You will need a sterilised 500g
preserving jar or bottle.

West Indian Hot Sauce

This is a quick chilli sauce that can be used fresh or left to ferment. It's completely essential with the Rice and Peas (page 268) and Allotment 'Ital-style' Stew (page 84).

Throw all of the ingredients into a food processor and blitz until smooth. Transfer the puree to a saucepan and cook over a medium heat for 8–10 minutes until it has begun to thicken and bubble. Take off the heat and immediately transfer to a sterilised 500g preserving jar or bottle and seal tightly. Leave at room temperature (out of direct sunlight) for a few days, until it has started to ferment, then pop it in the fridge to continue to age slowly. It will keep in the fridge for weeks and deepen in flavour as it ages.

Sriracha

MAKES 750g
Preparation time 10 minutes
Fermenting time 2 weeks

800g red chillies, stalks removed and
    chillies roughly chopped
50g bird's-eye chillies, deseeded and
    stalks removed
2 heads of garlic, cloves peeled
100g caster sugar
2½ tbsp tapioca or cornflour
250ml rice wine vinegar
3 tbsp table salt

You will need a sterilised 1-litre
preserving jar or bottle.

This may be the number one thing I can't live without. When I started experimenting with making my own, none of them had the right viscosity, until I did things a little differently. Normally, people ferment the chillies and then make the sauce, but I swapped the steps, cooking it, thickening it and then letting it ferment, which keeps the viscosity you would expect from a squeezy bottle of sriracha.

Put the chillies in a food processor with the garlic, sugar, tapioca or cornflour, vinegar and salt. Blitz on high speed for 3 minutes, or until it is as smooth as possible (I am lucky I have a really powerful Thermomix and Vitamix which processes in double time; the main thing is that you need to let it blitz for as long as it takes to get a smooth paste), then transfer the paste to a saucepan. Bring to the boil then reduce the heat and simmer for 5 minutes, until the sauce has reduced by about an eighth and the flour's thickening powers have engaged! Transfer to a hot, sterilised 1-litre preserving jar or bottle and seal tightly with a lid.

Allow the paste to sit at room temperature for 2–3 days, stirring it once a day.

After about 3 days you should see bubbles forming on the surface. This means fermentation has begun. Within 2 weeks it will have fully fermented. It will keep in the fridge for ages, and will continue to ferment slowly even when chilled. As is often the case with ferments, the flavour only gets better with age!

VEGETABLES:
SPRING TO SUMMER

FRUIT AND VEGETABLE AGRICULTURE

Since writing my last book, *Slow*, my perceptions and values regarding the way we eat have changed a little. *Slow* was written with idealist, virtuous intentions and I'd not taken into account the practical side of things, the social economics and the way most people shop and eat. My life is a privileged one: I am able to sample and afford some of the best produce in the world. I care not only about the ingredients, but also the producers who farm them and the soil in which they are farmed – I've become a soil geek. But I've had to confront my idealistic ambitions for agriculture: at the time of writing we're in the middle of a pandemic, poverty levels are reaching an all-time high and food banks and charities like The Trussell Trust are needed and used more than ever. I wince at conversations I've had at parties about my views and principles, because on face value, they may not seem so important right now. With this book, I want to approach these issues in a more nuanced way, giving you the science and facts so you can make your own informed choices.

As I write this in July 2020, The Vegan Society has announced that there has been a 20 per cent increase in people lowering their meat consumption and a 15 per cent increase in people lowering their dairy and egg consumption since COVID hit, while sales data from retail analyst Kantar suggests beef sales in the UK have increased by 26 per cent (minced beef by 34.5 per cent, and steaks by 43.9 per cent). These 'statistics' illustrate that the way the public are reacting to environmental and sustainability issues, and the way figures are being reported, is anything but clear cut. The ethics of being a responsible modern consumer who is eating more fruit and vegetables, and from sustainable sources is complex: what is the expenditure of resources and water required to grow these crops out of their natural environments? Are the rights of the growers, pickers and labourers fairly respected? How much plastic packaging is involved?

Waste

The Food and Agriculture Organization (FAO) estimates that one third of all food produced, amounting to a staggering 1.3 billion tons, is wasted every year globally. A large part of that can be attributed to fruit and vegetable production, with up to 40 per cent of vegetable crops being rejected simply because they do not meet the arbitrary but extremely stringent aesthetic requirements laid out by supermarkets. In this country, farmers are forced to throw away tons of perfectly good produce which the supermarkets deem to be unsellable, so constantly have to over-produce in order to meet targets. Not only is this a criminal waste of food, it's a catastrophic waste of the resources that go into growing them! However, there are some brilliant companies who are utilising waste produce: Oddbox delivers affordable wonky veg to your door; FeedBack's gleaning network rescues surplus produce from farms and distributes it to those in need; Rubies in the Rubble use wonky tomatoes to make the only ketchup that I've ever tried that rivals Heinz in taste (they make other sauces too); and Snact makes a chewy fruit 'jerky' from surplus fruit (think strawberry laces), Rejuce and Waste Not Juice make juices; and ChicP makes dips. This indicates that people are thinking about reducing food waste, but oddly, the level of waste is still on the rise.

When it comes to household waste, most councils provide food waste bins, and it's really important that we use them. It's an easy way to re-purpose what would otherwise go to landfill into something that can feed our soils.

Monoculture agriculture

The biggest problem we have right now in vegetable crop growing is single crop rotation. Particularly prevalent in industrialised regions, monoculture agriculture is useful for farmers because specialising in one crop helps cut down costs and increase yields in the short term. However, it can cause irreversible damage to the ecological system. The eradication of biodiversity and the stripping of soil's nutrients (which leads to an increased need for synthetic fertilisers and insecticides) only increases exponentially when land is farmed in this way. In contrast, permaculture (a system of crop rotation that utilises the patterns and resilient features of natural ecosystems, which some smaller-scale farmers are putting into practice) ensures the planting of a wide range of crops which work together to increase biodiversity and then by proxy increase the volume of different nutrients in the soils as they rotate around the land, maintaining and improving soil health (which impacts positively onto our foods and our gut and nutritional health). This is why it's hard for me to fully get behind a vegan diet, because animals are necessary in this cycle and it's erroneous to believe that eradicating animals from land management is the answer to our problems. See pages 192–198 on Ethical Meat Eating to read more.

Veganism and the soy industry

Many people are choosing a plant-based diet in response to the damning environmental science surrounding the global beef and dairy industry, and much of the new plant-based produce being sold to 'save the world' is made using the following crops: soy, corn and pea protein. Soy's reputation as a vegan and eco-friendly protein alternative has come under serious scrutiny recently. Soy and corn are not just farmed for human consumption: they are also grown for use as animal and fish feed and increasingly for use as a cooking oil and biodiesel/fuel, and pea proteins are quickly catching up. These crops are most responsible for single-crop monocultures, depleting the land of water and nutrients, and most have been genetically modified to such an extent (prior to GM foods being banned in this country) that they are genetically almost unrecognisable when compared to their heritage species. Soy production does require less water than cattle farming in the areas it's grown, but this is not the full story: soy is the second largest agricultural driver of deforestation. Eighty per cent of the world's soy is grown in Brazil, Argentina and North America. Over the past 20 years, over 300 million hectares of tropical forest have been felled to feed the voracious appetite for land to support vast soya plantations. The transformation of some of the most biodiverse habitats on the planet into bleak pesticide-fuelled monocultures is as depressing as it gets.

Huge global corporations such as Monsanto, Unilever and Carrefour have become equivalent to oil barons when it comes to their domination of soy agribusiness. The displacement of small farmers and indigenous peoples is just part of the human impact this monster of an industry is having. Soy production is only expected to increase, as the demand for meat and plant-based protein alternatives increases, especially in developing countries.

Be wary of the word 'natural' on soy product packaging. Often packaging neglects to mention that products were made using hexane, a neurotoxin petrochemical solvent. Nasty. Opting for organic soy helps avoid this. There are organic soy, pea and corn producers who are rebuilding their produce to be truer to its original genetic form.

I use British and French organic soybeans at Filth Foods, the sustainable nutritional burger company I founded with my good friend, nutritionist Rosemary Ferguson. Soybeans produced on a large scale, with fertilisers, normally hold little nutritional value, but organic beans are full of fibre, protein, iron and calcium.

Is organic best?

I support the ethos of organic farming, and biodynamic farming for that matter (my restaurant, The Nitery, was built on this ethos), but there is a lot of misleading information, and organic doesn't always guarantee the best produce. A lot of land certified as organic soil can retain synthetic chemicals that were applied for decades previously, meaning produce grown on that land will contain them too, but often regulations still allow the produce to be sold under the 'organic' banner. I look for producers who have slow-grown their foods.

Buy local

Importing and food miles is a huge issue. Having access to exotic fruits and vegetables is part of the joy of the modern world, but we should all aim to buy seasonal, locally sourced produce wherever possible. Buying our food this way should be cheaper, given the lower food miles and reduced storage times, and the abundance of a seasonal crop, but sadly, smaller-scale farmers have a hard deal competing with supermarkets that have an 85 per cent share of the grocery market and are constantly driving down prices. Supermarkets' commercial structure often means an abhorrent version of economic colonialism, that dominates other less affluent countries' agricultural industries, too. Looking beyond the supermarket is a great way to discover different varieties of fruit and vegetables: e.g. there are over 2,200 varieties of apples, and supermarkets usually only sell about five, with just one in three coming from the UK. That is crazy, especially considering that the UK has one of the oldest relationships with apple farming – we as consumers are missing out.

Shopping at local greengrocers and farmers' markets, growing your own or signing up for vegetable box schemes can help stem the supermarkets' tyrannical rule (and tends to involve less plastic packaging too), but for most of us, supermarkets are the most convenient and practical option for food shopping. I just can't, and won't, buy meat from a supermarket, especially as we're all cutting back now (*I'm eyeballing you all, because this is what has to happen*), but I do buy organic fruit and vegetables there, particularly from the frozen, dried and canned sections where it's cheaper than buying fresh.

Here is a guide to what's in season when:

January: apples, beetroot, Brussels sprouts, cabbage, cauliflower, celeriac, chicory, Jerusalem artichokes, kale, leeks, mushrooms, parsnips, pears, pomegranate, potatoes, rhubarb, spring onions, squash, swedes, turnips

February: Brussels sprouts, cauliflower, celeriac, chicory, Jerusalem artichokes, kale, kohlrabi, leeks, parsnips, potatoes, purple sprouting broccoli, rhubarb, salsify, shallots, swede, truffles (black), turnips

March: artichokes, beetroot, cabbage, cauliflower, chicory, cucumber, kale, leeks, oranges, parsnips, purple sprouting broccoli, radishes, rhubarb, sorrel, spinach, spring greens, spring onions, watercress, wild nettles

April: artichokes, beetroot, cabbage, chicory, kale, morel mushrooms, new potatoes, parsnips, rhubarb, rocket, sorrel, spinach, spring greens, spring onions, watercress

May: apricots, artichokes, asparagus, aubergine, beetroot, chicory, elderflowers, lettuce, marrow, new potatoes, nectarines, peas, peppers, radishes, rhubarb, rocket, samphire, spinach, spring greens, spring onions, watercress

June: apricots, asparagus, aubergine, beetroot, blackcurrants, broad beans, broccoli, carrots, cauliflower, cherries, chicory, courgettes, cucumber, elderflowers, fennel, globe artichoke, gooseberries, lettuce, marrow, new potatoes, nectarines, peas, peppers, radishes, raspberries, redcurrants, rhubarb, rocket, runner beans, spring greens, spring onions, summer squash, Swiss chard, turnips, watercress

July: apricots, aubergine, beetroot, blackberries, blackcurrants, blueberries, broad beans, broccoli, cauliflower, cavolo nero, cherries, chicory, chillies, courgettes, cucumber, fennel, French beans, garlic, globe artichoke, gooseberries, greengages, loganberries, new potatoes, onions, peas, potatoes, radishes, raspberries, redcurrants, rhubarb, rocket, runner beans, samphire, spring onions, strawberries, summer squash, Swiss chard, tomatoes, turnips, watercress

August: apricots, aubergine, beetroot, blackberries, blackcurrants, broad beans, broccoli, carrots, cauliflower, cavolo nero, celery, cherries, chicory, courgettes, cucumber, damsons, fennel, fig, French beans, globe artichoke, greengages, leeks, lettuce, mangetout, marrow, mushrooms, parsnips, peas, peppers, potatoes, plums, pumpkin, radishes, raspberries, redcurrants, rhubarb, rocket, runner beans, samphire, spring greens, spring onions, strawberries, squash, sweetcorn, Swiss chard, tomatoes, watercress

September: apples, apricots, aubergine, beetroot, blackberries, broccoli, Brussels sprouts, butternut squash, carrots, cauliflower, cavolo nero, celery, chicory, courgettes, cucumber, damsons, fennel, fig, globe artichoke, leeks, lettuce, mangetout, marrow, onions, parsnips, pears, peas, peppers, plums, potatoes, pumpkin, radishes, raspberries, rhubarb, rocket, runner beans, samphire, spinach, spring greens, spring onions, strawberries, squash, sweetcorn, Swiss chard, tomatoes, turnips, watercress, wild mushrooms

October: apples, aubergine, beetroot, blackberries, broccoli, Brussels sprouts, carrots, cauliflower, cavolo nero, celeriac, celery, chestnuts, chicory, courgettes, cranberries, cucumber, elderberries, fig, kale, leeks, lettuce, marrow, onions, parsnips, pears, peas, potatoes, pumpkin, radishes, rocket, runner beans, spinach, spring greens, spring onions, squash, summer squash, swede, Swiss chard, tomatoes, turnips, watercress, wild mushrooms

November: apples, beetroot, Brussels sprouts, butternut squash, cabbage, carrots, cauliflower, celeriac, celery, chestnuts, chicory, cranberries, Jerusalem artichokes, kale, leeks, onions, parsnips, pears, potatoes, pumpkin, squash, swede, Swiss chard, turnips, watercress, wild mushrooms

December: apples, beetroot, Brussels sprouts, cabbage, cauliflower, celeriac, celery, chestnuts, cranberries, Jerusalem artichokes, kale, onions, parsnips, pears, pumpkins, quince, radicchio, salsify, swede, sweet potato

English Garden Antipasto

I have vivid early memories of being eye-height to a glorious plethora of antipasti on display at Justin de Blank Provisions Ltd on Elizabeth Street, Belgravia, the delicatessen owned by the father of my future best friend, Martha Sitwell. He was a true pioneer both as a restaurateur and a food importer, bringing Italian, French and world foods to the streets of London back in the 1970s. I must have been two or three, and the myriad colourful produce glistening in oil made a big impression on me.

Traditionally served in Italy as the first course of a meal, antipasti can include anything from cured meats to olives or marinated anchovies, but here I want to focus on the vegetables. While the dish is associated with the south Mediterranean, we can grow the vegetables I've featured here in the UK and this is a great way of making the most of seasonal vegetables. Antipasto can be eaten in all kinds of ways, as a side to grilled meats or fish, or incorporated into other recipes, but this is such an impressive thing to bring to the table when you use a wide array of vegetables that it warrants being the main feature, perhaps with a simple green salad and crusty bread. Peppers, artichokes, aubergines and courgettes are classic summery choices, but this can work just as well in autumn and winter with young kale, mushrooms, leeks or squash. Roasting or grilling the vegetables intensifies their flavour, and the chilli and parsley in the dressing bring the whole thing together with an extra little kick. Use this as a guide to working with whatever's available and in season, picking and choosing from the ingredients here and on the following pages. Apart from the artichokes, which are slightly more complicated to cook, I've not provided quantities – just work with what you have available. The dressing recipe makes enough for a large, mixed platter of vegetables to serve 4–6 people.

All the vegetables keep well if submerged in oil and kept in a clean, airtight jar.

Roasted Violet Artichokes

1 tbsp sea salt, plus extra for sprinkling
2 lemons, halved, plus a little extra juice for the acidulating water
4 violet artichokes, trimmed
olive oil, for drizzling

Preheat the oven as hot as it can go (about 260°C/240°C fan/gas mark 10).

Bring a large pan of water to the boil. Add the salt and squeeze in the juice from both the lemons. Add the artichokes and par-boil for 6–7 minutes. Remove and place top down on a tray to drain. Once cool enough to handle, quarter lengthways and use an ice cream scoop, knife or metal spoon to remove the fibrous part of the heart. Set aside in a bowl of cold water with more lemon juice.

Peel off and discard the tougher outer leaves, then place the artichokes on a baking tray. Drizzle generously with olive oil and sprinkle with salt. Roast in the oven for 10 minutes, then turn over and roast for a further 10 minutes until the outer edges of the leaves are crisp.

Butternut Squash and Pumpkin

Peel the squash or pumpkin, remove the seeds and fibres and cut the flesh lengthways into roughly 6mm-thick slices. Heat a griddle pan over a high heat. Drizzle the squash or pumpkin slices with oil, season with salt, place on the griddle pan and grill until softened and charred,

CONTINUED ››

turning them to give them a criss-cross pattern if you wish – it may help to put some weight on the slices with another pan or baking tray.

Aubergines

Cut the aubergines lengthways into 8mm-thick slices. Heat a griddle pan over a medium-high heat. Drizzle the aubergine slices with olive oil and season with plenty of salt. Grill for a few minutes on each side until the flesh is charred and is becoming translucent – it may help to weight the aubergine slices down with another pan or baking tray. I lie the aubergine horizontally in the pan and then vertically on both sides to create a criss-cross pattern.

Courgettes

Cut the courgettes lengthways into 5mm-thick slices. Heat a griddle pan over a medium-high heat. Drizzle the courgette slices with olive oil and season generously. Grill for a few minutes on each side until charred and becoming translucent. I lie the courgettes horizontally in the pan and then vertically on both sides to create a criss-cross pattern.

Peppers

Preheat the oven as hot as it can go (about 260°C/240°C fan/gas mark 10). Put the whole peppers in the oven on a baking tray and roast for 20 minutes, shaking to turn the peppers a couple more times during cooking. (The same method applies to chillies, only roast them for half the time.) Once the skins are charred and the flesh is soft, remove the peppers from the oven and set aside to cool, covered with a clean tea towel (this helps to steam them, which makes removing the skins easier). When cooled enough to handle, pull out the stalks and the seeds, and gently peel off the skins revealing the soft flesh within.

Portobello Mushrooms

Preheat the oven to 240°C/220°C fan/gas mark 9. Put the mushrooms on a baking tray, drizzle with olive oil, season with salt and put in the hot oven for 10 minutes. Turn down to 200°C/180°C fan/gas mark 6 and cook for a further 10 minutes until the mushrooms are soft and starting to crisp at the edges.

Leeks

Preheat the oven to 240°C/220°C fan/gas mark 9. Prepare the leeks by cutting them in half lengthways and giving them a good wash under cold running water to ensure you've removed any grit from between the leaves. Place the whole leeks on a baking tray, drizzle with oil and season with salt. Roast for 20 minutes until charred.

Kalettes

Preheat the oven as hot as it can go (about 260°C/240°C fan/gas mark 10). Blanch the kalettes in a pan of salted boiling water for 30 seconds, then refresh in ice-cold water to maintain the vibrancy of the green leaves. Place the kalettes on a baking tray, drizzle with olive oil, season and roast for 5–7 minutes, until the edges of the leaves begin to become crisp.

Tomatoes

Preheat the oven as hot as it can go (about 260°C/240°C fan/gas mark 10). Place the tomatoes on a baking tray, drizzle with olive oil and add a good sprinkling of salt. Roast for up to 30 minutes, depending on their size (larger tomatoes will need longer). Remove from the oven when soft, yielding and the skins are beginning to split and char.

FOR THE DRESSING

700ml olive oil
2 heads of garlic, cloves peeled and thinly sliced
2–3 dried chillies, broken up
5 sprigs of rosemary
1 tsp salt
a decent grinding of black pepper
100ml red wine or sherry vinegar
large bunch of flat-leaf parsley, finely chopped

Put 200ml of the oil in a saucepan with the garlic, chillies, rosemary, salt and pepper, and cook slowly over a medium-low heat for 5–10 minutes, letting the garlic soften, become translucent and begin to colour, but not letting it get brown and crisp – be sure to keep an eye on it. Pour in the vinegar, increase the heat and allow to reduce until nearly all the vinegar has evaporated. Remove from the heat, pour in the remaining 500ml of oil, add the parsley, and stir to combine.

Ratatouille

SERVES 2 as a main course or 4 as a side dish

Preparation time 15 minutes, plus 1 hour 45 minutes for the tomato sauce

Cooking time 20 minutes

300g Slow Cooked Tomato Sauce (page 264)

1 large green courgette, thinly sliced widthways on a mandoline

1 yellow courgette, thinly sliced widthways on a mandoline

2 large tomatoes, thinly sliced on a mandoline

1 aubergine, thinly sliced widthways on a mandoline

2 tbsp extra-virgin olive oil, for drizzling

sea salt flakes

basil leaves (micro basil if you can find it), to serve

You will need a 2-litre gratin dish or 4 small 500ml gratin dishes, and a mandoline.

Ever since seeing the film *Ratatouille*, I haven't been able to get the image of the actual ratatouille out of my head, because of how neatly the character Remy presents his version of the dish in the film (I have the same thing when I think of oysters because of Disney's *Alice in Wonderland*). The flavours of ratatouille are quite simple, but what was it about the ratatouille in that film that made it scream out to me to be made? Well, firstly, it was based on a beautiful version of ratatouille made by the guy who held the title of best chef in the world for many years, Thomas Keller, and if this peasant dish screams out of the telly at me, even in a cartoon version, I know it's going to be good. What separates Keller's version from a classic ratatouille is that all the vegetables are very thinly sliced and are all pretty much the same size. If you can't find vegetables that are roughly the same diameter and there's a bit of haphazard variation in their size, it doesn't really matter: the main thing is that they are sliced to the same thickness. The best way to ensure uniformity is to slice everything on a mandoline. My French pastry chef says this dish is actually called a 'tian' of Provençal vegetables, but I argue that in this version the vegetables sit in a piquant tomato sauce (my Slow Cooked Tomato Sauce) and that makes it a ratatouille. Either way, the dish has been hijacked by a cartoon and I love this version of it. Serve it as it is, with a rice pilaf, or alongside simple grilled white fish.

Preheat the oven as hot as it can go (about 260°C/240°C fan/gas mark 10).

Pour the tomato sauce into a 2-litre gratin dish (or divide it among 4 small 500ml gratin dishes) in an even layer. Make two stacks of vegetables, alternating the slices in a pattern (or one stack if you are using smaller gratin dishes) – one slice of aubergine, then green courgette, then yellow courgette, then tomato – and repeat until you have used everything up. Carefully transfer the stacks of vegetables to the gratin dish (or dishes), lying them down so they are in two rows (or one), with each vegetable slice overlapping. Generously drizzle olive oil over the top and add a good sprinkling of salt.

Bake in the oven for 20 minutes until the veg have softened and are beginning to caramelise. Remove from the oven and serve straightaway, garnished with basil leaves.

AVOCADOS

Hailed as a superfood, avocados have become ubiquitous. You can't read a brunch menu anywhere without seeing them in some form, whether smashed, smoothied or sliced. As an excellent source of much sought-after, heart-healthy monosaturated fats (including oleic and linoleic acid, which are linked to preventing high cholesterol), not to mention vitamin E, soluble fibre, potassium, iron and the B vitamin folate, it certainly deserves its superfood status and it's no wonder that they have become so popular, especially among the more health-conscious younger generations. But the western world's insatiable appetite for this fruit comes at a heavy price.

Demand for the crop is off the charts, and it is putting unprecedented pressure on the avocado farmers. Avocados grow in tropical climates, with Mexico being the world's largest exporter, and the current booming market has seen avocados becoming more profitable to grow than most other crops in the region. This is leading to some farmers unlawfully felling mature, established pine forest in order to plant avocado trees, which require cyclical input of fertilisers and pesticides to deliver the highest yields. As with any monoculture, a lack of diversity strips the soil of fertility over time and devastates local wildlife and ecosystems. Much like almonds, avocados have a large water footprint, which puts huge pressure on water reserves in an increasingly hot and dry climate. Produce imported from far flung climes such as Central and South America is inevitably going to have a major carbon footprint due to the airfreighting, which is hard to justify when we are facing such an enormous climate crisis.

As with any farming, it's also important to consider the impact on the workers involved. Soaring prices of avocados in Mexico has led to drug cartels monopolising production, which means that any revenue may well be going to fund criminals who wreak fear and suffering among the communities they dominate (refusing to capitulate to these gangs will most likely have terrifying consequences). A crop once known by locals as 'green gold' is now referred to as 'blood guacamole'. The pesticides and chemicals used to grow avocados on such a large scale pollute water systems, which in turn impacts the health of the workers, who are often paid next to nothing.

Like with other tropical fruit, opting to buy certified Fairtrade avocados can mitigate against the negative environmental and ethical impact to some extent. If you really must eat them, buying Spanish-grown avocados means less air mileage, and more stringent EU regulations with regards to their production.

I truly believe that we need to seriously consider our level of avocado consumption. I don't see how, taking into account all the negative factors, we can include it as a staple food in our diets. I think we should only consume them as the occasional treat – it just simply isn't sustainable the way things stand.

Green Tomato Salsa

MAKES 600g
Preparation time 10 minutes
Cooking time 20 minutes

600g green tomatoes
1 large onion, peeled and quartered
2–3 fresh green jalapeños, stalks
    removed and cut in half (seeds
    or no seeds, depending on your
    preference)
1 head of garlic, cloves peeled
3 tbsp oil
juice of 3 big juicy limes
1 tsp salt
very large bunch of coriander, leaves
    picked

This might resemble the simple green salsa you get in burrito restaurants, but its heritage in Mexico is rich and varied. You can dress your tacos and dishes with a variety of salsas in Mexico and this one is prized for its clean green acidity. Green salsas are usually made with tomatillos, which are a variety of the deadly nightshade plant family (as aubergines, peppers and tomatoes also are) and they are prevalent in Mexico. They are green and unripe in flavour, and the green tomatoes that grow on our fair shores will do the job brilliantly. This recipe is smashing on so many things such as tacos with the Pumpkin Seed and Cocoa Mole Sauce (page 52) and Queso Fresco (page 161), or with fried battered fish in tacos, and it also makes a terrific base for my Green Shakshuka (overleaf).

Put the green tomatoes, onion, jalapeños and garlic in a food processor and blitz until smooth.

Heat the oil in a frying pan over a medium heat, pour in the tomato mixture and cook for 10 minutes, allowing it to reduce, then squeeze in the lime juice. Add the salt, then the coriander. Allow to cook for a further minute, return to the food processor and blitz again to achieve a really smooth sauce. Serve at room temperature.

The salsa will keep for up to 2–3 days in the fridge.

Green Shakshuka

SERVES 2
Preparation time 10 minutes
Cooking time 10 minutes

3 tbsp olive oil
1 tsp cumin seeds
400g Green Tomato Salsa (page 49)
1 tsp ground coriander
85g fresh spinach, washed, wilted in
   a pan for a minute and drained
80g green peppers, roasted (page 44)
   and sliced
4 free-range eggs
sea salt and freshly ground black
   pepper

TO SERVE
good handful of coriander leaves,
   chopped
a few dill fronds
a few mint leaves, shredded
2 tbsp sour cream
300g Queso Fresco (page 161),
   made to a firm and crumbly texture
3 tbsp toasted mixed seeds mixed
   with ½ tsp za'atar
freshly made Flatbreads (page 166)
   or grilled Turkish bread
extra-virgin olive oil, for drizzling

You will need 2 individual
22–25cm baking or gratin dishes.

I developed this recipe in the early days of Filth, with Rosemary Ferguson. Our mission was to get extra nutrition into everyday dishes. We wanted to make a healthy breakfast, both loved shakshuka and huevos rancheros, and thought we could somehow merge them. That week, I'd made a huge vat of Green Tomato Salsa that ended up being the base of this dish. We fried some cumin seeds in oil then added the salsa, before blending it with fresh spinach to an even more nutritious, virtually Hulk-green sauce, got some roasted green peppers into the dish and baked the eggs in this sauce instead of the usual red one. We finished it with a combo of Middle Eastern and Mexican toppings and served it with flatbreads or grilled Turkish breads with some good extra-virgin olive oil. It's a superb healthy weekend brunch dish and pretty fancy-pants in the impressiveness stakes, too.

Preheat the oven to 240°C/220°C fan/gas mark 9.

Heat the oil in a frying pan over a medium-high heat, add the cumin seeds and fry for a minute or two until toasted. Add the green tomato salsa, coriander and spinach and cook for a minute. Season with salt and pepper if necessary, then remove from the heat and blitz until smooth.

Divide the blitzed sauce between two individual (22–25cm) ovenproof baking or gratin dishes. Split the green peppers between the two dishes, then simply make two little holes in the top of the sauce in each dish and break an egg into each hole. Season each egg with salt and pepper and bake in the oven for about 8 minutes or until the egg whites are cooked through, but the eggs still have runny yolks.

Remove from the oven and top the two shakshukas with the chopped coriander, dill, mint, sour cream, queso fresco and seeds, and serve with toasted or warmed bread, drizzled with extra-virgin olive oil.

Pumpkin Seed and Cocoa Mole Sauce
for pumpkins, poultry and beans

MAKES 500g (200g is enough for tacos for 4–6 people and it freezes really well)
Preparation time 20 minutes
Cooking time 1 hour

3–4 tbsp oil
3 largish onions, thinly sliced
1 head of garlic, cloves peeled
600g tomatoes
2 dried Mexican chillies, such as ancho, mulato, ñora, guindilla, pasilla, chipotle, etc.
2 tbsp ground cumin
½ tsp ground cinnamon
¼ tsp ground cloves
generous grating of nutmeg
50g unsalted cashews
25g pumpkin seeds
6 prunes
500ml fresh chicken stock or poaching liquor
2 tsp cocoa powder
juice of 1 orange
juice of 1 lime
sea salt and freshly ground black pepper

Mole is a traditional Mexican sauce that generally contains a fruit, a chilli pepper, a nut, a seed, and spices like cinnamon, black pepper and cumin. The word 'mole' is an archaic word for 'mix', and some of the very traditional ones, like mole poblano, contain about 24 different ingredients. This recipe is a little simpler than that, but it's still deep and richly flavoured.

You can cook poultry pieces in the mole, but I prefer poaching a whole bird in a spiced broth made with onions, bay leaves, thyme, cinnamon, star anise and peppercorns, leaving the bird to cool, and using the poaching liquor in the mole sauce, in place of the chicken stock, then lacquering the cooked chicken meat with it. Another classic way to use mole is to roast large chunks of deseeded pumpkin or squash (see cooking method on pages 43–44) and serve them with the sauce.

To make a really phenomenal plant-based meal, serve this mole with Rye Tortillas (page 167), Queso Fresco (page 161) and Green Tomato Salsa (page 49), swapping the chicken stock in the mole for vegetable stock.

Heat about 2 tablespoons of the oil in a heavy-based casserole dish over a medium-low heat, add the onions and garlic and cook for a good 20 minutes until really soft and sweet, golden and just beginning to caramelise. Turn off the heat while you prepare the rest of the ingredients.

Next, you need to char the tomatoes. Traditionally, this is done over a naked flame, but if you whack your oven up as hot as it can go (to about 260°C/240°C fan/gas mark 10) and roast them in a roasting tray for 10–12 minutes, you can achieve a really good char and the tomatoes intensify in flavour. It's up to you, but ultimately you need to achieve burnt skins. Once you have done this, put them in a food processor (with their skins) and blitz until smooth.

Heat the remaining oil in a deep frying pan over a medium-high heat. Add the dried Mexican chillies, all of the spices, cashews and pumpkin seeds and fry for a few minutes until everything is toasty and brown, being careful not to scorch the chillies. Transfer the nuts, seeds, spices and dried chillies to the casserole dish with the onions and garlic, then pour in the blitzed tomatoes, add the prunes and chicken stock or poaching liquor and allow to reduce for 10 minutes.

Carefully transfer everything to a food processor and blitz for at least 2 minutes until you have a smooth sauce. Clean out the casserole dish and return the smooth mole to it. Now let it reduce over a medium heat for about 20 minutes, until it has the consistency of double cream. Finally, stir in the cocoa powder, check for seasoning and add the lime juice and orange juice.

Globe Artichokes with Real Salad Cream

SERVES 4
Preparation time 15 minutes
Cooking time 15 minutes

2 globe artichokes, washed and
   trimmed (outer woody leaves
   removed, stalks scraped clean)

FOR THE COURT BOUILLON
10 litres water
400ml white wine
200ml olive oil
150ml white wine vinegar
juice and pared rind of 4 lemons
½ bunch of thyme
5 bay leaves
2 tbsp white peppercorns
6 tbsp sea salt

FOR THE REAL SALAD CREAM
1 tbsp Dijon mustard
pinch of sugar
2 tbsp sherry vinegar
juice of ½ lemon
generous pinch of sea salt
good grinding of freshly ground
   black pepper
2 tbsp single cream
5 tbsp sunflower oil
1 tbsp extra-virgin olive oil

The moment that sticks in my memory where I really understood the beauty of this French classic was a few years ago in LA, at The Ivy. I was so impressed by the confidence of celebrating the simplicity of these beautiful big globe artichokes – they were brought to the table with just a bowl of vinaigrette and nothing more, for the diners to pull apart with their hands at the table. It just seemed so fresh and modern, even though it's an age-old dish. Peeling off the petals and scraping off the mellow flesh with your teeth is one of life's pleasures. Now, let's come to the 'salad cream'. I will eat anything, but commercial salad cream is one thing I cannot stand. This is world's apart, like a really well-rounded, creamy vinaigrette. As with everything, it's about the quality of the ingredients you put in and I am a believer that in this case, it's 100 per cent necessary to use Dijon mustard and sherry vinegar. Because the dressing has cream in it, it won't last long in the fridge (I wouldn't be surprised if you polished the lot off in one go anyway).

To make the court bouillon, bring all of the ingredients to the boil in the largest pan you've got and simmer for 10 minutes.

Cook the globe artichokes stem end down in the bouillon for 15 minutes. Once the time is up, carefully remove them from the bouillon and set aside to cool briefly while you whip up the salad cream.

Whisk together the mustard, sugar, vinegar, lemon juice, salt and pepper in a small bowl, then whisk in the cream until well combined. Combine the oils in a small jug, then, in a fine stream (much like when you make mayonnaise), slowly pour in the oil, whisking continuously until all the oil is combined and you have a thick, pale dressing. Check the seasoning.

Trim the artichoke stalks.

Serve the salad cream alongside the artichokes, pulling off the leaves and dunking them into the cream. When you get to the artichoke heart it will be covered in the fibrous 'choke'. Fear not – you can scrape it away really easily to reveal the best bit, the heart. Cut the heart through the stalk lengthways and dunk it into the salad cream.

Summer Salad Soup

SERVES 6

Preparation time 5 minutes, plus
optional overnight chilling
Cooking time 10 minutes

2 tbsp oil
bunch of spring onions (about 125g),
    roughly chopped
350g Lebanese cucumber, roughly
    chopped
500g fresh or frozen peas
750ml fresh chicken or vegetable
    stock
2 little gem lettuces, roughly
    chopped
10 mint sprigs, leaves picked and
    chopped
a decent pinch of white pepper
a decent pinch of celery salt
½ nutmeg
200g crème fraîche
juice of ½ lemon
sea salt flakes and freshly ground
    black pepper

TO SERVE (OPTIONAL)
deseeded and finely chopped
    cucumber, radishes, mint leaves,
    dill fronds, a lick of your favourite
    dressing oil, and crème fraîche

I know cold soups can be divisive, but I am a real backer of the chilled soup. I'm sitting editing this right now in the middle of a baking-hot heatwave and, honestly, there is nothing I would like more for lunch. We're really lucky in the UK that our seasons are so pronounced and that summer brings us classic British cold soups such as iced cucumber or chilled pea soup – here, I have hauled together all of our great summer salad vegetables to wave the flag for refreshing cold summer soups. And this one, unlike most gazpachos, it is equally delicious hot.

Ideally, make this soup the day before you're going to serve it, so it has time to get properly cold.

Heat the oil in a saucepan over a medium-high heat, add the spring onions and fry for 2–3 minutes, then add the cucumber and fry for a further 2 minutes, before adding the peas. Pour over the stock, bring to the boil and cook for 2 minutes. Add the lettuce and mint and cook for a further 2 minutes. Remove from the heat and carefully pour the mixture into a blender or food processor. Season with the white pepper and some black pepper, the celery salt, and a pinch of sea salt, grate in the nutmeg, add the crème fraîche and lemon juice, and blitz until smooth.

If you're planning on serving it cold, transfer to a container and allow to cool to room temperature before chilling it in the fridge, preferably overnight. I like to serve it with crème fraîche and some deseeded, finely chopped cucumber and radishes scattered on top.

Alternatively, serve the soup straight away, hot, with some crème fraîche swirled in and a few chopped mint leaves and dill fronds.

Greenhouse Romesco Sauce with Chargrilled Spring Onions

SERVES 4
Preparation time 10 minutes
Cooking time 25 minutes

2 red, orange or yellow peppers
75g tomatoes (whatever type you
    like)
30g blanched almonds
4 large overgrown spring onions
1 garlic clove, finely grated
3 tbsp sherry vinegar
1 tsp sea salt, plus extra to serve
generous ½ tsp smoked paprika
good pinch of cayenne
1 tbsp tomato puree
3 tbsp extra-virgin olive oil, plus
    extra for drizzling

There is a common misconception that we can't grow tomatoes, peppers and aubergines here in the UK like they do in the Mediterranean. Naturally, the history of us growing these ingredients differs from our European neighbours, due to the lack of hot weather, however a new breed of tomato growers on the Isle of Wight are growing superb tomatoes with a really strong end of season glut, and long and slow growth over our slightly colder summers makes world-class tomatoes. The horrifyingly hot summers of recent years have meant even better gluts. The same goes for peppers and chillies, and – flavourwise – some of the sweetest and most round-bodied chillies I've ever tasted have been grown here in Hackney, in local allotment greenhouses. If you're into growing your own veg, this vegetable is easy to grow and provides good yields. Classically, romesco sauce is made from red peppers, but I make it with whatever I can get my mitts on and, while paler, this sauce is punchier. I'm a vinegar fiend and this sauce is pokey, but that's how I love it! If you're a little less into acidic food, hold back a teaspoon or two of the vinegar. I serve this with large spring onions as I'm not able to find British-grown calçots that easily.

Preheat the oven as hot as it can go (about 260°C/240°C fan/gas mark 10).

Put the peppers and tomatoes on a baking tray and roast in the oven for about 15 minutes until they are soft and the skins are peeling away easily. Remove and leave until cool enough to handle so you can pull away the skins from both the tomatoes and the peppers (and the seeds from the peppers).

Put the almonds on a baking tray and toast in the oven for a few minutes until nice and brown, but be careful not to let them burn.

Classically, the onions would be barbecued, but you can get a good result by roasting them on a baking tray in the hot oven for 10 minutes until they start to char. Remove from the oven and once cool enough to handle, cut them in half lengthways.

Put the peppers, tomatoes, almonds, garlic, sherry vinegar, salt, paprika, cayenne, tomato puree and olive oil in a food processor and pulse until the mixture is well blended but still has texture from the almonds – you don't want this super smooth.

To serve, spread the sauce on a plate and lay the roasted onions on top, with an extra drizzle of olive oil and a little sprinkle of sea salt.

Peas, Broad Beans and Lettuce Gratin

SERVES 4 as a side dish
Preparation time 15 minutes
Cooking time 15 minutes

200ml white wine
300g shelled fresh or frozen peas
300g podded broad beans
500ml fresh chicken stock
300ml double cream
juice of ½ lemon
1 little gem lettuce, roughly
  chopped
10 sprigs of tarragon, leaves removed
  and roughly chopped
¼ nutmeg, grated
20g Parmesan, grated
sea salt and freshly ground black
  pepper

Gratins tend to be carby and rich, but on seeing chef Anthony Demetre's fricasée of English peas and broad beans, I was totally inspired to put my own spin on it. I started off by making a winey sauce, with a reduced chicken stock and lots of cream, and the flavours of tarragon and nutmeg running through it, before pouring it over peas and broad beans and baking. The result is an unusually fresh and light gratin that still has the richness of the cream, and works perfectly alongside roast chicken, or some sturdy collagen-rich fish such as hake or turbot.

I think freshly podded broad beans are the best, so do seek them out, especially when they are in season during summer. However, with peas, I have to admit to preferring frozen petits pois on the whole rather than fresh, as they are sweeter and less likely to be dry.

Preheat the oven as hot as it can go (about 260°C/240°C fan/gas mark 10).

Pour the wine into a saucepan, place it over a high heat and reduce the volume by two thirds. While this is on the go, blanch the peas and broad beans in a pan of salted boiling water for about 2 minutes, then drain and refresh in ice-cold water to halt the cooking process.

Once the wine has reduced, add the stock and the cream and reduce again over a medium-high heat until the sauce has emulsified and thickened. Squeeze in the lemon juice, add the chopped lettuce to wilt it slightly, then add the tarragon leaves and season with the nutmeg and a healthy pinch of salt and pepper.

Drain the peas and beans and transfer them to an ovenproof gratin dish. Pour over the cream and lettuce sauce and top with the grated Parmesan. Place in the scorching-hot oven for 15 minutes, until the cheese is gratinated and golden. Remove from the oven and serve.

Patlican Salata

SERVES 4 as part of a meze
Preparation time 10 minutes
Cooking time 30 minutes

2 red peppers
6 tbsp oil
2 aubergines, cut into 2cm-thick
    rounds
1 head of Confit Garlic (page 269),
    cloves finely chopped, plus 2 tbsp
    of the oil
½ garlic clove, grated
large handful of flat-leaf parsley,
    leaves finely chopped
40g ghee
150g Greek yoghurt
sea salt flakes and freshly ground
    black pepper
pinch of pul biber, to serve

A number of the recipes in this book have come about as a direct result of living in Hackney and absorbing the influence of the large local Turkish communities. This was not my intention, but more of a subconscious osmosis. There are so many ocakbasi restaurants in my area ('ocakbasi' means 'fireside' or 'stand by the grill') with huge charcoal barbecue grills on which all kinds of meat and vegetables are cooked, and the side dishes and meze are just as big a part of their offering as the grilled meat. My assistant, Rose, alerted me to patlican salata, a buttery smoked aubergine, red pepper, garlic and yoghurt salad and perhaps one of the lesser known gems, and I can't believe I've missed out on it all this time. Grill-roasted aubergines and peppers take on a delicious smokiness, and are then covered in a butter *and* yoghurt – it's damn delicious in its simplicity. None of us have enormous grills but you can still achieve that smoky charred flavour through aggressive cooking on the hob. This is ideal served as part of a meze, alongside my Broad Bean, Mint and Feta Salad (page 68).

Preheat the oven as hot as it can go (about 260°C/240°C fan/gas mark 10).

Place the peppers on a baking tray and roast for 20 minutes until the skins are nice and charred. Remove from the oven, set aside and leave until cool enough to handle, then pull away the skins (they should come off pretty easily) and pull out the seeds.

Heat 2 tablespoons of the oil in a frying pan over a high heat, add a third of the aubergine rounds and cook for a few minutes on each side until well blackened. Don't be scared: you need the aubergine to be a bit burnt to achieve a charred, smoky flavour. Lower the heat and fry for a further few minutes on each side until the aubergine is nice and soft. Do this in three batches, adding more oil to the pan as you go (the aubergines will soak it up like a sponge). Once all the aubergine is ready, chop it roughly as you want it to have a bit of texture. Do the same with the roasted red pepper and combine with the aubergine in a bowl. Mix in the confit garlic, fresh garlic and garlic oil, followed by the chopped parsley. Season generously.

If you work at the right pace this should all come together at the right time. Melt the ghee in a small saucepan over a low heat, being careful not to burn it. Spread the aubergine mixture on a plate, dollop the yoghurt in the centre and pour the ghee over the top. Finish with the pul biber. The salad doesn't have to be hot, but it's at its best when warm, so once the ghee hits the plate get it to the table pretty sharpish.

Egg and Bacon Potato Salad

SERVES 4
Preparation time 10 minutes
Cooking time 20 minutes

1kg purple potatoes, scrubbed clean
2 litres cold water
2–3 tbsp salt
3 free-range eggs
110g smoked streaky bacon, cut into
  thin lardons
2 spring onions, thinly sliced
3 tbsp pickled jalapeño slices, finely
  chopped
smoked salt or celery salt, to serve
  (optional)

FOR THE DRESSING
150g sour cream
150g mayonnaise
2 tbsp lemon juice
good pinch of salt
good grind of black pepper

Purple potatoes are a heritage potato variety from Peru, and Peruvians know how to cook them. Causa, their traditional cold potato salad, is made with lime juice and sour cream, and when I learnt about it I realised what a great addition the acidity of sour cream would be in a salad dressing. I created this potato salad recipe using classic American ingredients like bacon and jalapeños, but with causa in the back of my mind.

Put the potatoes in a large saucepan with the cold water and 2–3 tablespoons of salt. That might sound like lots of salt, but when cooking any potatoes it helps bring out their flavour. Bring to the boil and cook for 20 minutes, then drain and allow to steam dry.

Meanwhile, cook the eggs in a saucepan of boiling water for 8 minutes exactly, then place in a bowl of cold water to halt the cooking process. While the potatoes and eggs are cooking, fry the bacon in a frying pan until nice and crispy.

To make the dressing, simply mix the sour cream and mayonnaise together in a bowl with the lemon juice, salt and pepper.

When everything is ready, it's time to assemble the salad, beginning with the potatoes. Pull them apart into bite-sized pieces (I think it looks nicer than cutting them with a knife, and the rough edges hold the dressing better) and lay them out on a large plate or platter. Spoon the dressing over the potatoes and sprinkle half of the spring onions on top. Peel and roughly chop the eggs and sprinkle them in an even layer over the potatoes, followed by the bacon, the jalapeños and the rest of the spring onions. I like to sprinkle over a little smoked salt or celery salt if I have some to hand.

Braised Courgettes

SERVES 4 as a side dish or large salad
Preparation time 5 minutes
Cooking time 15 minutes

3 tbsp olive oil
1 dried chilli
4 courgettes (ideally a mixture of green, yellow and white)
½ tsp sea salt, plus extra to serve
100ml water
grated zest and juice of 1 lemon
handful of mint leaves, chopped

Who has braised a courgette or marrow before? Unlikely these days, as I figure most people assume this method of cooking will make them mushy and tasteless, but actually the opposite is true. I first came across courgettes cooked this way in an 'ingredients-led' Italian restaurant, served with nothing more than really good olive oil and salt. It was a revelation. Here, the courgettes hold their weight and stay firm, while retaining the added flavours of chilli, lemon juice and mint. I like to serve this with grilled fish or roast lamb as a side dish, or as a central salad in a multitude of ways, such as with crumbled feta and mint, ricotta and oregano, or burrata and basil.

Heat the olive oil in a wide lidded saucepan over a high heat. Crumble the chilli (you can leave out some of the seeds, depending on how hot you like it) and add it to the pan, allowing it to infuse in the oil for a minute or two. Now put the largest courgettes into the pan and cook for 2 minutes, followed by the smaller ones. Add the salt and water to the pan, cover with a lid and cook for a further 2 minutes. Turn the courgettes over with a pair of tongs, re-cover and braise for a further 2 minutes. Repeat this a few times, replacing the lid after each turn, until they are cooked but still firm – this will take about 15 minutes in total. You definitely don't want them to be mushy!

Remove from the heat and allow to cool a little so you can handle them. Cut them into 2–3cm-thick slices and place in a serving dish, squeeze over the lemon juice and sprinkle the lemon zest and mint leaves across the top. Season with a little more salt. These are equally delicious served hot or cold.

Stuffed Marrows and Tomatoes with Mushrooms and Orzo

SERVES 4
Preparation time 15 minutes
Cooking time 50 minutes

150ml olive oil, plus extra for
   drizzling
2 onions, finely chopped
4–6 garlic cloves, finely chopped
150g orzo
500g mixed mushrooms, such as
   oyster, king oyster, chestnut,
   shiitake and enoki, finely chopped
2 very large tomatoes, such as the
   'Rouge de Marmande' heirloom
   variety
300g tomatoes (including the innards
   of the large tomatoes)
250ml white wine
5 sprigs of oregano, leaves picked
grated zest of ½ lemon
good grating of nutmeg
small bunch of flat-leaf parsley,
   leaves picked and finely chopped
2 small marrows, seeds scooped out
sea salt and freshly ground black
   pepper

In the past I've made this dish with minced lamb, so by all means replace the mushrooms with minced lamb if you wish, but in a bid to cut down my meat intake and not sacrifice that same deep umami flavour, mushrooms are the obvious substitute. These are great served alongside a crisp green salad.

Heat 2 tablespoons of the oil in a large frying pan over a low heat, add the onions and cook them very slowly for about 30 minutes until soft and golden. After they've been cooking for about 15 minutes, add the garlic.

Meanwhile, cook the orzo in a saucepan of salted boiling water for 8 minutes until almost done (it will finish cooking in the mushroom ragu). Drain and set aside.

Preheat the oven as hot as it can go (about 260°C/240°C fan/gas mark 10).

Heat the rest of the oil (you can pour off excess oil at the end if you wish) in a separate frying pan over a medium heat and sweat the mushrooms in batches for about 15 minutes per batch: treat the mushrooms as if you're browning meat, taking your time to get a really good caramelisation.

Cut the tops off the 2 large tomatoes and scoop out the insides (retain the tops). Add the insides to the rest of the tomatoes to make the weight up to 300g and blitz in a food processor until smooth.

Once you've cooked all the mushrooms, add them to the onions. Deglaze the mushroom pan with the wine, let it bubble for a couple of minutes, then pour it over the mushrooms and onions. Add the oregano and blitzed tomatoes, then the orzo, lemon zest, nutmeg and parsley. Cook over a medium heat for about 5 minutes, then season liberally.

Season the cavities of the tomatoes and marrows, drizzle with olive oil, and gently spoon the filling in. You don't want to pack it in too tightly, but try to get as much in as you can, with a little mound on top. Use the tops of the tomatoes to form a lid, leave the filling in the marrows exposed, and bake in the oven on a baking tray for about 12 minutes, until the tomatoes and marrows are just cooked through.

Remove from the oven and serve.

Braised Flat Beans in Slow Cooked Tomato Sauce

SERVES 4 as a side dish

Preparation time 10 minutes, plus 1 hour 45 minutes for the tomato sauce

Cooking time 10 minutes

3 tbsp Confit Garlic oil (page 269) or regular oil
½ dried chilli
pinch of dried chilli flakes
1 sprig of rosemary, marjoram or oregano
400g Slow Cooked Tomato Sauce (page 264)
500g flat beans, stalk ends cut off
½ tsp sea salt flakes

TO SERVE

2–3 tbsp Greek yoghurt
½ tsp pul biber
good handful of a combination of chopped flat-leaf parsley, dill and mint leaves

I've seen variations of this dish all over the place, here in the UK, but also in Turkey, France and Italy, which to me is an exciting situation as no one has ownership over the recipe, and its ubiquitousness and longevity is a sure-fire sign that beans and tomatoes are a tried-and-tested combination. Traditionally, the beans are meant to be served a little more cooked than you might be used to seeing these days, and are as a result not as vibrant, but have the confidence to let them to lose some of their colour in order to achieve the right texture. Here, they are cooked for less than the standard 30 minutes, and are instead allowed to cook a little further in the residual heat of the pan once it's removed from the hob, to maintain some freshness and bite. This recipe requires some of my Slow Cooked Tomato Sauce on page 264 (about a quarter of the quantity). The beans can be braised in advance and reheated.

Heat the confit garlic oil or regular oil in a wide saucepan (one wide enough to fit the beans in whole) over a high heat, and add the dried chilli, dried chilli flakes and rosemary, marjoram or oregano. Allow to infuse the oil for a minute, then pour in the tomato sauce and lay the beans flat in the pan. Add the salt and a splash of water and cover with a lid. Reduce the heat to medium and cook for 10 minutes until the beans are tender but still retain a bit of bite. Check for seasoning, remove from the heat and set aside to cool (they will cook a little further in the sauce while they cool).

When ready to serve, spoon over the yoghurt, sprinkle over the pul biber and scatter the chopped herbs on top.

Linguine alla Courgette Aglio e Olio

SERVES 4
Preparation time 5 minutes
Cooking time 15 minutes

150ml extra-virgin olive oil
1 head of garlic, cloves peeled and
   thinly sliced
2 dried chillies, finely chopped
3 medium courgettes, coarsely grated
100g cooked linguine per person
   (and a few tbsp of the pasta cooking
   water)
juice of 2 lemons and grated zest of 1
sea salt and freshly ground black
   pepper
grated Parmesan, to serve

This is my take on the Italian classic *aglio e olio*, an incredibly easy pasta dish made with ludicrous amounts of garlic, chilli and olive oil, bound with starchy pasta water. A good-quality extra-virgin olive oil really lifts this dish as it's all about celebrating simple delicious flavours, and the courgette and lemon deliver extra vibrancy and freshness. Courgettes work well because of the water content, which helps to bring the sauce together, but the same is true of marrows, so feel free to use them instead.

Heat the oil gently in a large frying pan or wok over a low heat, then add the garlic and chillies and cook for a few minutes until the garlic starts to become soft and translucent but has only taken on a little colour. Keep an eye on it, as there is nothing worse than the flavour of burnt garlic. Once the garlic is cooked through, turn up the heat and add the grated courgettes. Fry for about 5 minutes, until the courgette is softened but still retains its brightness, season generously, then add the lemon juice and zest. Add the cooked pasta with a couple of tablespoons of the pasta cooking water and stir through thoroughly. Check for seasoning (this dish really can take quite a lot of salt, so don't be shy) and serve immediately with a good grating of Parmesan.

Broad Bean, Mint and Feta Salad

**SERVES 4 as part of a meze
or starter**
Preparation time 20 minutes
Cooking time 5 minutes

about 1kg whole broad bean pods,
   podded (to yield 350–400g podded
   beans)
1 head of Confit Garlic (page 269),
   cloves chopped
2 tbsp Confit Garlic oil
1 sprig of rosemary, leaves finely
   chopped

Mint is an ideal companion for broad beans, just as it is for peas. This is an excellent addition to a meze and would sit perfectly alongside my Patlican Salata (page 61) and my Flatbreads (page 166).

First, remove the tough, pale skins from the podded broad beans. Yes this is a bit of a faff, but it's a strangely satisfying job and is really worth it, as removing the skins reveals the lovely bright green beans within. The best way to do this is to push your thumbnail lightly through the pale skin to make a little hole, then peel the rest of the skin off. Try to keep the peeled beans whole if you can (they have a habit of splitting in half – don't worry if a few do). Bring a pan of salted water to the boil then blanch

juice of ½ lemon
50g Greek yoghurt
150g feta cheese
handful of chopped mint leaves
1 tbsp extra-virgin olive oil or extra
    Confit Garlic oil, to serve
good pinch of sumac
good pinch of pul biber
salt

the podded beans for just 3 minutes, drain, transfer to a bowl of ice-cold water and set aside.

Put the garlic, oil and rosemary leaves in a small frying pan, place over a medium heat and fry for about 1 minute (being careful not to burn the garlic). Remove from the heat and put in a bowl. Add the lemon juice, yoghurt and feta and mash together with a fork so everything is well combined. It's nice to retain a bit of texture, so it doesn't have to be super smooth. Gently stir in the beans and mint (being careful not to mash the beans up too much), taste and adjust seasoning if necessary. Before serving, drizzle over the oil, and lastly sprinkle over the sumac and pul biber.

Elote

SERVES 4
Preparation time 5 minutes
Cooking time 5 minutes

4 corn on the cob, with husks intact
4 tbsp sour cream or mayonnaise
4 tbsp grated Parmesan
pinch of your choice of chilli powder
lime wedges, to serve

FOR THE HONEY BUTTER
60g butter, at room temperature
¾ tbsp runny honey
1 tsp your favourite hot sauce
pinch of salt

Even the fussiest vegetable eater loves corn on the cob. It grows in the UK for a short season in late summer, and at its peak it's super sweet and juicy. I first had it in this incarnation at La Esquina in Soho, New York, about 15 years ago and it was a real revelation. There's no way to eat this elegantly, you've just got to get stuck in.

To prepare the corn in the traditional way, you need to plait the husk. Peel off a couple of the outer leaves and set aside. Pull the rest of the leaves away from the kernels and fan them out around the base. Group them into three bunches then plait them together tightly. Tie up the end with one of the leaves you removed, to help keep it together.

Bring a large lidded saucepan of salted water to the boil and plunge the corn into it. Cover and cook for 5 minutes until the kernels are beginning to soften. Remove from the water and set aside.

Meanwhile, mix the butter, honey, hot sauce and salt in a bowl until well combined. With a pastry brush, brush about a tablespoon of the honey butter across each cob, followed by the same amount of sour cream or mayonnaise. Sprinkle the Parmesan all over, followed by a dusting of chilli powder. Serve with lime wedges to squeeze over.

Nam Prik Ong with Allotment Vegetables

SERVES 6 as a starter
Preparation time 30 minutes, plus chilli soaking time
Cooking time 30 minutes

3 tbsp lard or sunflower oil
300g pork mince
500g tomatoes, crushed in batches in a pestle and mortar
30g dehydrated tamarind block, rehydrated in hot water and sieved to make 50ml tamarind
1 tbsp fish sauce
1 tbsp light brown muscovado sugar
2–3 tbsp soy sauce
a few spring onions, shredded, to garnish

FOR THE PASTE

5 dried red chillies, soaked for 15–30 minutes, drained, deseeded and roughly chopped
1 tbsp chopped lemongrass
100g shallots, roughly chopped
1 head of garlic, cloves separated and roughly chopped
4 lime leaves, stalks removed and leaves shredded
1 tsp shrimp paste

SERVE WITH YOUR CHOICE OF:

½ butternut squash, peeled, deseeded, sliced into 1–2cm-thick shards and steamed for 8–10 minutes
1 aubergine or leek, halved lengthways and barbecued, wood-fired or roasted with a bit of oil and salt until dark and soft
large handful of raw green beans, trimmed
¼ white cabbage, leaves separated
½ cucumber, sliced
radishes
cherry tomatoes
spring onions

Northern Thailand is famous for its food. The mountainous landscape of the region is mostly jungle and it is absolutely beautiful. People who spend their Thai holidays travelling between Bangkok and the Islands often miss out on the best food in Thailand, and the more authentic and laidback cities. I love the city of Chiang Mai. It's a cultural melting pot of the most brilliant people and the place is filled with kiln and barbecue foods. The city is most famous for its sausages, but the most enlightening dish I discovered there was nam prik ong. It's a pork relish into which you can plunge anything from steamed or crunchy fresh vegetables to sausages, eggs and crackling! It's rich, sweet, sour, delicious and has an ingredient that I've only ever seen in the north of the country: the tomato. I appreciate a pork relish sounds a little nutty for the uninitiated, but you just need to look at it as a gutsy version of crudité. I serve it with classic Thai accompaniments of steamed squash or pumpkin, barbecued aubergine, white cabbage leaves (yes it's served with cabbage, not iceberg lettuce) and pork crackling (shop-bought is fine here), and all the vegetables can be grown in the British allotment. I find these cultural exchanges, in that we can now grow Southeast Asian foods in the English country garden, charming. It's an epic thing to put on your table for everyone to dig into. This is exactly the type of food I love to eat.

Pound the paste ingredients to form a coarse relish in a pestle and mortar. This is Northern Thai cuisine, which for me is the most delicious but is also more rustic than Southern Thai cuisine, so you want the pounded texture of a relish here.

Heat the fat or oil in a wok or frying pan over a high heat, add the mince and fry for a couple of minutes until the fat is starting to render but the mince hasn't yet taken on any colour. Add the paste and stir-fry for a few minutes until softened and beginning to become golden, then add the crushed tomatoes and fry for about 5 minutes over a high heat until the tomatoes start breaking down. Add the tamarind, fish sauce, sugar and soy sauce and cook over a high heat for about 20 minutes, stirring, until most of the liquid has evaporated and the mixture has a thick, relish-like consistency.

While the mince mixture is cooking, prepare the vegetables.

The nam prik ong doesn't have to be eaten piping hot – it can be left to cool to room temperature and sometimes it's even left to ferment. I like to serve it warm though, while the fat is still melted, in a bowl and garnish it with shredded spring onions. Arrange the vegetables around it on a platter for dipping.

VEGETABLES: AUTUMN TO WINTER

Szechuan Onion Flower

SERVES 4–6 as a beer snack
Preparation time 15 minutes
Cooking time 15 minutes, plus
15 minutes for the crispy shallots
(if making from scratch)

1 large onion, peeled, 5mm trimmed
    off the top and hairy part of
    root removed
oil, for deep-frying
BBQ sauce or hot sauce, to serve
    (optional)

FOR THE SPICED FLOUR
250g plain flour
1 tsp garlic powder
1 tsp salt
½ tsp onion powder
¼ tsp white pepper
¼ tsp ground Szechuan pepper
pinch of celery salt

FOR THE DREDGE
2 free-range eggs
30ml milk
2 tbsp hot sauce
1 tsp salt

FOR THE SPICED SALT
2 tbsp Crispy Shallots (page 119, or
    use shop-bought)
2 tsp caster sugar
2 tsp fine sea salt
1 large tsp ground Szechuan pepper

This way of cooking onions was made famous by the Outback Steakhouse in America. I've seen it on so many TV shows, but somehow – and I have no idea why – it hasn't made it into the mainstream. Back in the 80s, the Chicago Rib Shack had an onion loaf that was equally as moreish, but there is something altogether more beautiful, ornate, compact and easier about the onion flower. Think of it like something between an onion ring and an onion bhaji. It's crunchy and sweet as it stands, but the Szechuan spicing delivers an extra level of addictiveness which makes it cry out to be shared with mates alongside a few ice-cold lagers.

Cut the onion in half down the middle with a sharp knife, making sure you don't cut through the root so that the onion holds together. Cut across to create quarters, then sixths, eighths, tenths and twelfths, fourteenths, sixteenths… you want to slice it as much as you can, so that it fans out into a chrysanthemum-style flower shape.

Combine the spiced flour ingredients in a bowl, then whisk the eggs with the milk, hot sauce and salt in a second bowl ready for dredging. Dunk the cut onion into the milk and egg mixture so that it is well coated. Let the onion sit in the eggy milk for a couple of minutes as the salt in it will help to start softening the onion. Remove the onion from the eggy milk and dredge it in the flour mix, making sure you get it all into the grooves of the onion so that it is well battered. The best way to do this is to put the onion on a plate and sprinkle the flour into it, getting into all the nooks and crannies. For maximum crunch I recommend a double dip, so repeat this process a second time, dipping it back into the eggy milk then scattering with flour.

Heat the oil in a saucepan or deep-fat fryer to 160°C.

The onion will be quite delicate at this stage, so be gentle with it. Once the oil is up to temperature, lower the onion into the oil so that the root is facing you. You want to fry it for about 15 minutes – as it cooks the onion leaves will open out into a flower shape! Once the onion is crisp and golden, carefully remove it from the oil with a slotted spoon or fryer basket and place onto kitchen paper to drain off any excess oil.

Put the spiced salt ingredients in a pestle and mortar and pound them to a dust. Sprinkle them all over the onion and serve. I think this works really well just as it is with an ice-cold beer, but feel free to dunk it in BBQ or hot sauce if you so wish.

Roasted Cauliflower, Preserved Lemon and Chilli Pasta

SERVES 4
Preparation time 15 minutes
Cooking time 20 minutes

1 medium cauliflower, cut into
    florets, and the inner leaves
100ml olive oil, plus 1 tbsp for
    roasting the cauliflower
40g rye bread, blitzed into
    breadcrumbs
250g ditali pasta, macaroni, mezzi
    rigatoni or orecchiette
6 garlic cloves, finely chopped
1 dried chilli, crushed
3 free-range egg yolks
200g sour cream
80g Parmesan, grated
large handful of flat-leaf parsley,
    leaves finely chopped
2 preserved lemons, pips removed
    and skin thinly sliced
grated zest of 1 lemon
sea salt and freshly ground black
    pepper

Why have I never put cauliflower in any pasta dishes before? It's not like it doesn't make sense to put cauliflower cheese with pasta?! The first time I saw anyone do it in a way that piqued my interest was when cookery writer Rosie Birkett made this lovely roasted cauliflower pasta with preserved lemons. I have messed around with a few different recipes, but there's something in the way the salty, sour and bitter lemons react with the cauliflower and acidulated, silky cheese sauce that give it the adult flare that makes it so special, so well done Rosie for making this a thing! I roast cauliflower leaves for this dish: they are so sweet and delicious, and have a satisfying texture.

Preheat the oven as hot as it can go (about 260°C/240°C fan/gas mark 10).

Spread the cauliflower florets and leaves on a baking tray and drizzle over the tablespoon of olive oil. Season with a teaspoon of salt, mix with your hands so that all the cauliflower is evenly coated in the oil and place in the roasting-hot oven for 15 minutes, until cooked through and nicely browned, even slightly charred.

Once the cauliflower's in the oven, heat half the oil in a small frying pan over a medium heat. Add the breadcrumbs and fry for about 4 minutes until crisp and golden, then transfer to kitchen paper to drain off excess oil and keep them crispy. Set aside.

Cook the pasta in a saucepan of well-salted boiling water for a couple of minutes less than the time stated on the packet (you will finish cooking it with the sauce).

While the pasta's cooking, heat the remaining oil in a separate frying pan with the garlic and chilli and cook gently for 5 minutes, until softened. Set aside.

Drain the pasta, reserving 100ml of the pasta water, and return the pasta to the pan.

Whisk the egg yolks, cream and Parmesan together in a bowl. Place the pasta pan back over a medium heat and stir in the egg mixture, followed by the garlic and chilli oil, parsley, preserved lemon, lemon zest and a generous pinch of black pepper. Mix well over the heat for a couple of minutes until the sauce thickens slightly, check for seasoning and stir through the roasted cauliflower. Serve immediately, with the breadcrumbs sprinkled on top and, if you're like me, an extra grating of Parmesan.

Root Vegetable Bulgar Wheat, 'Cous cous' style, with Merguez Sausages

SERVES 4
Preparation time 20 minutes, plus chickpea soaking time
Cooking time 2 hours

250g dried chickpeas
3 tbsp olive oil, plus extra for frying the sausages
2 large onions, peeled and cut into eighths
4 garlic cloves, finely chopped
2 green chillies, finely chopped (deseeded if you wish)
1 tsp sea salt
½ tsp ground black pepper
½ tsp cayenne
1 tsp ground cumin
1 tsp paprika
2 bay leaves
a few sprigs of thyme
850ml fresh chicken or vegetable stock
2 turnips, peeled and quartered
4 carrots, peeled and cut into thirds lengthways
2 large courgettes, halved lengthways and each cut into thirds lengthways
8 merguez sausages

FOR THE BULGAR WHEAT
250g bulgar wheat
500ml fresh vegetable stock
juice of ½ lemon
2 tbsp olive oil
pinch of salt
large handful of flat-leaf parsley leaves, finely chopped
handful of mint leaves, finely chopped

What many people in the UK know and love as cous cous is not at all how it's served authentically in Morocco. Cous cous is very simply dressed with a little oil and salt, and served alongside a rich but soupy stew (not to be mistaken for the other famous Moroccan dish, tagine). Cous cous is in fact tiny nibs of a pasta-like substance. I love using cous cous, but I also love using bulgar wheat (cracked wheat), which has more texture, bite and a nutty flavour. I like to cook it in stock and serve it very classically, with lots of root vegetables and courgettes, alongside some grilled merguez sausages. This version of a hearty Moroccan dish is a great showcase for how spices used sparingly can still have impact.

First, soak the chickpeas in water for at least 1 hour, or up to 12 hours. Drain, rinse, and put them in a pan of fresh, cold salted water. Cover, bring to the boil and cook for 1 hour 30 minutes.

About 50 minutes into the chickpeas' cooking time get going on the stew. Heat the 3 tablespoons of olive oil in a large heavy-based saucepan. Add the onions and cook for 5 minutes, or until they have softened and started to turn golden. After the onions have been cooking for 4 minutes, add the garlic and chillies and allow to soften for a couple of minutes. Add the salt, spices, bay leaves and thyme sprigs and cook for a further minute, then pour over the stock and add the turnips, carrots and courgettes. Cover and cook at a fast simmer for 25 minutes. Once the chickpeas are cooked through but maintain a firm bite, drain and add them in for the last 10 minutes of cooking.

To cook the bulgar wheat, put it in a saucepan and pour in the stock. Place over a medium heat and cook at a fast simmer for 10 minutes until all the stock has evaporated, then transfer to a large bowl and mix through the lemon juice, olive oil, salt and herbs.

Finally, cook the sausages. Heat a glug of oil in a frying pan and get it really hot. Add your sausages and fry for about 10 minutes, turning them regularly so they are browned evenly on all sides.

To serve, spread the bulgar wheat over a large platter, then spoon the vegetables and chickpeas, along with all the liquid, over the top. Arrange the sausages across it and tuck in!

Roast Carrots with Queso Fresco, Coriander and Jalapeño Oil, and Pumpkin Seeds

SERVES 8 as a large platter
Preparation time 30 minutes
Cooking time 20 minutes, plus
15 minutes for the crispy shallots

50g pumpkin seeds
½ tsp smoked salt
1 fresh jalapeño, very thinly sliced
1 quantity Crispy Shallots (page 119)
½ quantity Jalapeño and Coriander Oil (below)
pinch of chipotle powder

FOR THE CARROTS

bunch of heritage carrots (orange, yellow, purple and white), peeled
1 tbsp oil
2 tsp caster sugar
1 rounded tsp coriander seeds, bashed
¼ tsp salt
¼ tsp ground white pepper

FOR THE JALAPEÑO AND CORIANDER OIL

¼ large bunch of coriander, including stems
1 fresh jalapeño chilli, roughly chopped (seeds in)
¼ tsp salt
150ml pomace oil (this is a combination of sunflower and olive oil)

FOR THE QUESO FRESCO

200g Queso Fresco (page 161), aged for a few days
juice of ½ lemon
2 tbsp sour cream
¼ tsp sea salt

A restaurant called Hartwood, in Tulum on Mexico's Yucatán coast, has been flirting with me for some time. It prides itself on cooking whatever it has harvested or caught each day, meaning there's no menu. It's also based around fire pit and wood cooking. Friends who've gone there when the restaurant has had a bad day's fishing and hunting, and have therefore been served just veggies, recall it being the best meal and experience they've ever had. This dish is inspired by what I've seen of their food. I've written the recipe with conventional oven cooking in mind, but if you are barbecuing, you can roast large multicoloured heritage carrots over the hot coals until they start to char and go black, then move the coals to the side and finish cooking them over a less intense heat. You can wipe off the char easily with a clean, wet cloth. This recipe with creamy Mexican cheese, jalapeño oil and moreish, nutty toasted seeds showcases charred roots so well. The restaurant pop-fries crickets for similar dishes, but here we have a very Gizzi alternative of crispy shallots!

Preheat the oven as hot as it can go (about 260°C/240°C fan/gas mark 10).

Toss the carrots in a large roasting tray with the oil, sugar, coriander seeds, salt and pepper. Cook the purple ones on a separate roasting tray (so their colour doesn't leach). Roast for 15 minutes until soft and caramelised, turning halfway. Set aside.

To make the jalapeño and coriander oil, blanch the coriander in boiling water for a few seconds, then drain and refresh in ice-cold water. Drain again and blitz in a food processor with the jalapeño, salt and oil for at least a minute until finely chopped. Pass through a fine-mesh sieve, pushing as much of the juice through as possible. Season.

Blitz the queso fresco in the cleaned-out food processor with the lemon juice, sour cream and salt until it takes on a smooth, whipped consistency.

Toast the pumpkin seeds in a dry frying pan over a medium-high heat for a few minutes until they start to pop, stirring regularly to prevent them burning. Set aside.

Spread the queso fresco over a large serving platter (or, for individual portions, about 3 tablespoons of the cheese per person). Sprinkle the smoked salt across the cheese, then halve the carrots lengthways and arrange them on top. Sprinkle the jalapeño and crispy shallots across the plate. Drizzle with the half quantity of oil and sprinkle over the toasted pumpkin seeds and a little ground chipotle to bring out a smoky note.

Allotment 'Ital-style' Stew

SERVES 6

Preparation time 30 minutes, plus
chickpea soaking and cooking time
Cooking time 1 hour

4 tbsp oil
1 onion, thinly sliced
1 head of garlic, cloves peeled
5cm piece of fresh ginger, peeled and
   sliced into matchsticks
2 x 400ml tins coconut milk
1 tbsp sea salt flakes
2 Scotch bonnet chillies
2 tbsp rehydrated and strained block
   tamarind
juice of ½ lemon
1 tbsp muscovado sugar

FOR THE WEST INDIAN SPICE MIX
2 tbsp coriander seeds
1 tbsp ground cumin or cumin seeds
2 tsp black peppercorns
6 green cardamom pods
4 cloves or pinch of ground cloves
1 tsp fenugreek seeds
2 tsp ground cinnamon
2 tsp ground ginger
1 tsp ground turmeric
pinch of ground allspice
1 whole nutmeg, grated

FOR THE VEGGIES
1 potato, peeled and roughly chopped
1 peeled carrot, kept whole
250g sweet potato, peeled and cut
   into large chunks
400g deseeded pumpkin or squash,
   cut into 6 slices (skin on)
large bunch of thyme sprigs
1 large courgette, roughly chopped
6 spring onions, cut into 5cm lengths
150g dried chickpeas, soaked and
   cooked until soft but firm (see
   page 80)
300g flat beans, cut into 5cm lengths
handful of coriander leaves, to serve

This is a rich vegetable, pulse and coconut curried stew, derived from Rastafarian culture. 'Ital' represents a way of life that's multilayered and complex, but to put it simply it's about eating from the earth in a natural and spiritual way, and is inherently vegan. It's pretty beautiful and I would recommend reading into it. This recipe was hard to work out, as there are so many different versions out there, so I got on the phone to some West Indian mates, some with Rasta culture in their bones and all having had local allotments in Hackney, and together we came up with a collaborative recipe that I hope does it justice. I also spoke to a good friend, chef Andi Oliver, as I was worried that by following my methodology for approaching stews I would compromise the integrity of the dish – for example, most traditional recipes don't even use onions, let alone sweat them, but I just can't bring myself to not do this, knowing how much sweetness and umami it brings – but we both agreed that it was okay to trust our natural cook's instincts. Serve this with classic Rice and Peas (page 268) and a fruity hot sauce for extra kick.

Heat the oil in a heavy-based casserole dish over a medium heat and throw in the onion. I am a stickler for really cooking down onions in any stew until they are soft and caramelised, as I think this is the best foundation to start building depth of flavour, so be patient and cook them gently for about 20 minutes. Next, add the whole garlic cloves and ginger and fry for 5 minutes.

If you're making your spice mix with whole spices, simply put all of the spices in the bowl of a food processor, pestle and mortar or spice grinder and grind together until as fine as possible. Put all the dry spices into the pan and fry for a couple of minutes before adding the coconut milk, salt, whole Scotch bonnet chillies, tamarind, lemon juice and sugar.

Next to go in is the potato, which you simmer for 5 minutes, before adding the carrot and the sweet potato and simmering for a further 5 minutes. Add the pumpkin and the thyme, cover with a lid, and simmer over a low heat for 30 minutes.

Add the courgette, spring onions, chickpeas and flat beans, re-cover and cook for another 10 minutes so the veg still retain a bit of bite. Finally, turn off the heat and allow the stew to sit for 5 minutes, then pull out the thyme sprigs and serve with a scattering of coriander leaves.

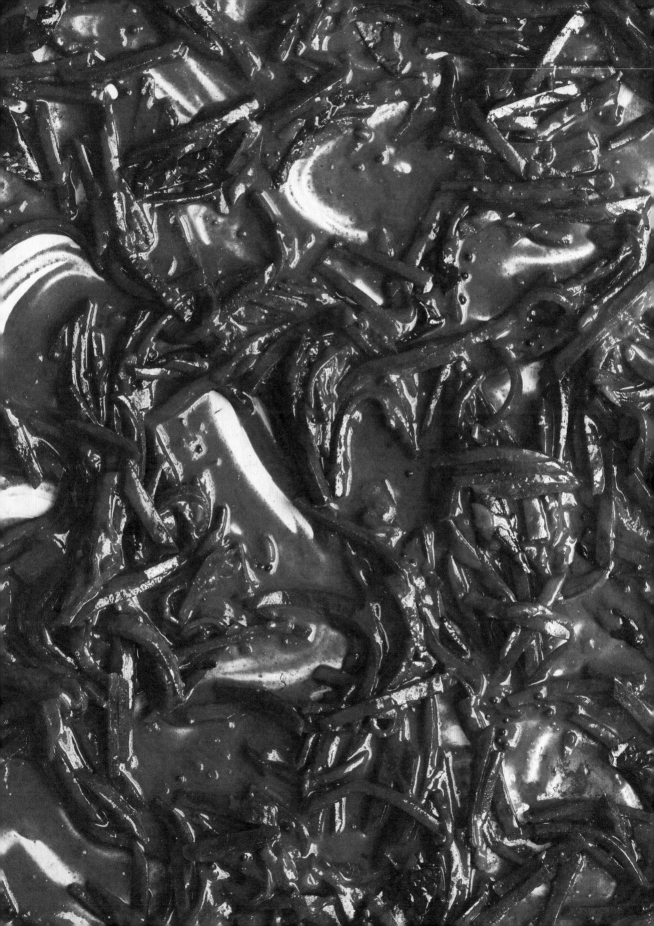

Sri Lankan Beetroot and Coconut Curry

SERVES 4
Preparation time 15 minutes
Cooking time 15 minutes

2 tbsp oil or ghee
½ red onion, thinly sliced
small handful of fresh or dried curry
 leaves
½ tsp black mustard seeds
4 garlic cloves, pounded to a paste
2 tsp ground cumin
1½ tbsp tomato puree
450g beetroot, peeled and cut into
 thin strips
400ml tin coconut milk
2 small whole green chillies
1 tsp salt
juice of 1 lime

I remember seeing beetroot curry for the first time. It was about 2003 in a Stoke Newington restaurant called Rasa. My sister had just moved to the area and everyone was raving about this vegetarian South Indian joint. For some reason the idea of a beetroot curry seemed absurd to me. I couldn't understand why this inherently British ingredient had been made into curry and had already dismissed the idea in my head. That was, until I tried it. While many people don't get off on beetroot's earthiness, there is no denying its sweetness, and mixed with spice and the creaminess of coconut it really turns into something magical. I've raved about this curry for many, many moons and, as it turns out, it does make sense, as the British brought beetroot into both India and Sri Lanka when trade first started hundreds of years ago. Now it grows plentifully in both the warm climate of the hills of south India and the chilly mountains of the north!

This is great eaten alongside my Tarka Dhal and/or Chicken in Weeds on pages 125 and 181, and with rice.

Heat the oil or ghee in a wok, a karahi or large frying pan over a medium-high heat. Add the onion, curry leaves and mustard seeds and fry for 5 minutes.

Once the onion has started to caramelise, add the garlic paste and cumin and cook for 30 seconds before adding the tomato puree. Allow this to cook for 1 minute then add the beetroot strips, coconut milk, chillies, salt and a splash of water.

Simmer over a medium heat for 10 minutes, or until the beetroot is cooked through but still retains some bite. Check for seasoning, squeeze in the lime juice and serve.

Salt-baked Celeriac

SERVES 4
Preparation time 10 minutes
Cooking time 1 hour 10 minutes

3 free-range egg whites
1 celeriac, scrubbed well and dried
500g fine sea salt

I remember coming across celeriac for the first time as a young chef, almost 20 years ago now. While my mother insists I had celeriac's most famous dish, 'remoulade', when I was growing up, it can't have made that much of an impression on me as I have absolutely no memory of it whatsoever. That has since been remedied and I now make Celeriac Remoulade (page 95) a fair bit, but the way I learnt how to prepare celeriac is very different to the French salad. The celeriac is slow-baked in a shell of salt, that keeps its body firm and robust, retains all the juices and perfectly seasons it. Cracking this open at a dinner table and carving it like meat is almost ceremonial, and serving it up alongside a piquant, peppery Greenhouse Romesco Sauce with Chargrilled Spring Onions (page 57) and/or Salsa Verde (page 116) makes for a brilliant centrepiece. You can also serve it Holstein style (page 89), or as the base for my Celeriac Cordon Bleu (page 90).

Preheat the oven to 200°C/180°C fan/gas mark 6 and line a baking tray with oiled baking parchment.

Lightly whisk the egg whites in a bowl for a few minutes to break them up and get some air into them as the base structure of the salt crust. You're not really making a solid salt meringue, as the salt will attack the structure of the egg whites a little, but whisk in the salt and it will become a sticky but smooth paste. Place a scoop of the salt paste in the middle of the oiled sheet of baking parchment as a base for the celeriac to sit upon. Place the celeriac on top, then pat the rest of the paste with your hands all over the celeriac, so it is completely covered. Bake in the oven for 1 hour 10 minutes.

Once cooked, remove from the oven and allow to cool for a few minutes. You can tell if the celeriac is done by sticking a skewer or a sharp knife into the centre, through the crust. It should be soft but still relatively firm. The salt will have formed a rock-hard crust, but this will crack off easily with a few taps of a knife. Remove the crust and allow the celeriac to rest for about 10 minutes, until you can handle it. Carefully slice off the skin with a sharp knife, trim the ends, then slice across the celeriac so that you get 4 round steaks.

Cut each steak into 2.5cm-thick slices and serve with my romesco sauce or salsa verde, serve it Holstein style, or as the base for my Celeriac Cordon Bleu.

Celeriac Holstein

SERVES 4

Preparation time 5 minutes, plus
optional 30 minutes chilling time
Cooking time 5 minutes, plus 1 hour
20 minutes for the salt-baked celeriac

1 × Salt-baked Celeriac (page 86),
  cooled and cut into 4 × 2.5cm-thick
  slices
oil, for frying
100g butter
6 tbsp capers, roughly chopped
4 free-range eggs
8 anchovies
1 lemon, halved, for squeezing
freshly ground black pepper

FOR THE BREADCRUMB COATING

100g plain flour, seasoned with salt
  and black pepper
2 free-range eggs, whisked
300g breadcrumbs (white or panko)

In the same category as the iconic Austrian schnitzel cutlet, a Holstein schnitzel is traditionally veal or pork cutlets, simply dressed with brown butter, anchovies, a fried egg, and – if you're lucky – some sticky veal jus. It's the most superior of all the schnitzels; where the Cordon Bleu could be perceived as the grotty burger of the schnitzels, the Holstein is definitely the roast beef! The magical thing with all of these flavours is that they slide in alongside the salt-baked celeriac very nicely too.

First, you need to breadcrumb (pané) the celeriac. Put the seasoned flour, the whisked eggs and breadcrumbs in three separate bowls. Carefully dip each celeriac slice first into the seasoned flour until well coated, then in plenty of the egg, and lastly the breadcrumbs. You can chill the coated celeriac in the fridge for 30 minutes–1 hour to firm up, but they can be cooked immediately too.

To cook the celeriac cutlets, pour enough oil into a frying pan so that it comes up to 1cm and heat over a medium heat. Once the oil is hot, fry the celeriac slices one at a time (to avoid overcrowding the pan) for about 2 minutes each side, just enough for the breadcrumbs to crisp up and turn a dark golden. Remove from the pan and place on kitchen paper to drain off any excess oil.

Next, melt the butter in a frying pan over a medium-low heat and allow it to gradually get brown. You will know it's reached the right stage when it starts to smell nutty too. Add the chopped capers, stir and heat through. Fry the eggs in a separate frying pan in plenty of oil until they are cooked, with runny yolks.

When you're ready to serve, put the celeriac cutlets on plates, place an egg on top of each cutlet, then divide the caper butter between each plate. Layer on 2 anchovies per person then add a twist of pepper and a good squeeze of lemon juice.

Celeriac Cordon Bleu

SERVES 4
Preparation time 15 minutes, plus minimum 45 minutes cooling time and 1 hour 20 minutes for the salt-baked celeriac
Cooking time 20 minutes

2 free-range eggs, whisked
100g plain flour, seasoned with salt and black pepper
300g breadcrumbs (white or panko)
4 thick slices of good-quality ham
1 × Salt-baked Celeriac (page 86), cooled and cut into 4 × 2.5cm-thick slices
oil, for frying
freshly ground black pepper
lemon wedges, to serve

FOR THE BÉCHAMEL
30g butter
30g plain flour
300ml milk
100g Cheddar, grated
30g Parmesan, grated
generous grating of nutmeg
pinch of cayenne
pinch of white pepper
½ tsp English mustard powder
sea salt flakes

I'm writing this rolling around the floor in hysterics with my assistant, Rose. On trying to remember if I'd ever actually eaten a 'cordon bleu' in a restaurant, I recalled a visit to a famous medical detox clinic in Austria. Being utterly fed up with the vegetable broth and 'chewing trainers' (don't ask), I sneaked off to a local schnitzel restaurant and had Cordon Bleu! Created in the 1940s in Switzerland, it is a cutlet of veal, pork or chicken flattened out, stuffed with ham and cheese (in some cases also a rich cheesy béchamel), folded, then breaded and fried. When I was a girl, my mum, who almost always cooked meals from scratch, would buy it from Marks & Spencer for a treat. In a bid to eat less meat, using salt-baked celeriac as the 'cutlet' base is a great alternative vehicle for oozy béchamel and ham. The flavour combination of celeriac, dairy and ham is superb (think remoulade, which is often served with ham), and this dish also nods towards the Belgian dish of roasted chicory with ham and béchamel. It is a brilliant way to showcase how we can eat a little meat and cheese, without going the whole hog.

To make the béchamel, melt the butter in a saucepan over a medium heat, then add the flour and stir with a wooden spoon to form a smooth paste. Cook for a minute then pour in a quarter of the milk and beat well until smooth. Repeat until you have added all the milk, then cook over a low heat for 2–3 minutes to make a thick white sauce. Stir in both cheeses until melted. Remove from the heat, add the nutmeg, cayenne, white pepper and mustard, and season to taste. Transfer to a heatproof container, cool to room temperature, then chill in the fridge for at least 15 minutes so it firms up.

Put the whisked egg, seasoned flour and breadcrumbs in three separate bowls.

Place one slice of ham on top of each celeriac slice, then spread 2 tablespoons of the cold béchamel on top in a thick, even layer. Repeat with the other three celeriac slices. Carefully dip each celeriac, ham and béchamel slice first into the seasoned flour until well coated, then in plenty of the egg and, lastly, the breadcrumbs. If the breadcrumbs don't easily stick, use a pastry brush to add some more egg and patch up any gaps with some extra breadcrumbs. Place the celeriac slices in the fridge for at least 30 minutes.

Pour enough oil into a frying pan so that it comes up to 1cm and heat over a medium heat. Fry the celeriac slices one at a time (to avoid overcrowding the pan) for about 2 minutes on each side, until the breadcrumbs crisp up and turn dark golden. Remove and drain on kitchen paper. Serve with lemon wedges and a twist of black pepper.

Celeriac Bread Sauce

MAKES 700g

Preparation time 10 minutes, plus
30 minutes minimum infusing
Cooking time 40 minutes

½ celeriac (about 350g once peeled),
  cut into small cubes
500ml whole milk
1 onion, thinly sliced
1 tbsp butter
1 cardamom pod
8 cloves
10 black peppercorns
1 bay leaf
2 small pieces of mace
100ml single cream
50g breadcrumbs
½ tsp sugar (optional)
pinch of ground cloves
good grating of nutmeg
sea salt and freshly ground black
  pepper

Bread sauce is my favourite food. Don't even bother roasting me a chicken or a game bird if it hasn't got bread sauce and a real bone gravy with it. I've written recipes for classic bread sauce, a gingerbread sauce and a rye bread sauce gratin in my previous books so people might think there's nowhere left to go… But let me tell you there is! This incarnation is, I believe, known as a happy accident. I'd made bread sauce and celeriac puree to serve with game. On the plate, they both tasted fantastic and were entirely necessary to complement the dish, but were texturally too similar, so what happened when I mixed them? A bloody sensation, that's what. Bread sauce, with the earthy, sweet body of a silky celeriac puree. Here, I've thrown in some cardamom, because I love cardamom in milky things, as well as cloves, mace and nutmeg, as I'm a mace and nutmeg addict and use them to round off many dishes, but you can keep it classic and just use cloves if you like. I will not make bread sauce for game (such as my Roast Pheasant on page 184) any other way from now on.

This recipe makes quite a lot of sauce, but it freezes brilliantly. And it can be made in advance, too, and reheated before serving.

Put the cubed celeriac in a saucepan of salted water, bring to a simmer over a medium heat and cook for 15–20 minutes until cooked through. Drain and set aside.

Meanwhile, heat the milk in a separate saucepan with the onion, butter, cardamom, cloves, peppercorns, bay leaf and mace. Bring to the boil, then reduce the heat and simmer for 10 minutes. Remove from the heat and steep for at least 30 minutes.

Pick out the bay leaf and spices from the milk, then pour the milk into a food processor and add the single cream, breadcrumbs and celeriac. This is a more refined version of a classic bread sauce in that we want a really smooth, velvety consistency, so blitz it until it is completely smooth.

Return to the saucepan and heat gently, seasoning it liberally with salt and pepper. I like to finish it with a little sugar to round off the flavour (I know this isn't traditional, but it's how I like to season my food), and a pinch of cloves and lots of nutmeg for an extra bit of spice.

If you are making it in advance it will thicken up a bit as it cools, so add a little extra milk to loosen while reheating.

Celeriac Remoulade

SERVES 6 as a side dish
Preparation time 25 minutes, plus
1 hour minimum macerating time

1 small celeriac, peeled and cut into
    matchsticks
2 Granny Smith apples, sliced on a
    mandoline (unpeeled) and cut into
    matchsticks

FOR THE DRESSING
1 free-range egg yolk
1 tsp Dijon mustard
1 tsp wholegrain mustard
1 tbsp cider vinegar
a good squeeze of lemon juice
3 tbsp rapeseed oil
3 tbsp sunflower oil
sea salt and freshly ground black
    pepper

**Celeriac remoulade is something I make all the time and it's mad that despite
having written this recipe yonks ago it has never made it into a book. It is high time
to rectify this! If you haven't had celeriac remoulade before, it's a classic French
accompaniment to cooked meats such as ham; think of it like a French coleslaw.**

Put the celeriac and apple in a bowl and mix to combine.

To make the dressing, put the egg yolk, mustards, cider vinegar and lemon juice in a
bowl and whisk together. Combine the oils in a jug, then pour them into the egg yolk
mixture in a fine, thin stream, whisking continuously, until completely combined and
emulsified. Season liberally and pour the dressing over the celeriac and apple. Toss
gently to coat. I really do think this benefits from being allowed to macerate for an
hour or so before eating.

Rainbow Slaw

SERVES 8 as a side dish
Preparation time 20 minutes

200g white cabbage, thinly shredded
200g peeled celeriac, shredded into
    matchsticks
200g red cabbage, thinly shredded
200g carrots, grated
200g mixed radishes, thinly sliced
200g apples, sliced on a mandoline
    (unpeeled) and cut into matchsticks
sea salt and freshly ground black
    pepper

FOR THE DRESSING
1 quantity Real Salad Cream (page
    54), made with cider vinegar
2 tbsp mayonnaise

The vegetables in this slaw can be swapped for fennel, daikon, watermelon radish, black radish, kohlrabi – whatever's in season and readily available. If you like your slaw crunchy and fresh, eat it straight away, but if you prefer it more like classic coleslaw, leave it to sit for an hour.

Combine the prepared vegetables in a large bowl.

Combine the dressing ingredients in a separate bowl, add to the vegetables and stir through to coat. Season to taste with salt and pepper.

Chrain

SERVES 4–6 as a side dish
Preparation time 5–10 minutes
Cooking time 1 hour (for roasting the
beetroot)

200g beetroot, roasted (see page 116
    for my Roasted Beetroot, Beluga
    Lentil and Watercress Salad)
2 tbsp sour cream
1 large gherkin, finely chopped, plus
    1 tbsp pickle juice from the
    gherkin jar
1 tsp finely grated fresh horseradish
¼ small bunch of dill, fronds finely
    chopped (optional)
sea salt and freshly ground black
    pepper

This classic Jewish beetroot salad is often served with smoked fish or gefilte fish (a dish made of poached, ground white fish). I serve it in all sorts of ways: in one of my restaurants I've served it in an open sandwich with very rare roast beef, straw fries, a beef jus mayonnaise, watercress and smoked salt, which was absolutely delicious, but it would also work with smoked salmon, kippers, smoked trout or smoked eel. Growing up, we had chrain with rollmops (pickled herring).

Roast the beetroot following the method on page 116. Cool and chop very finely.

Simply mix all of the ingredients together in a bowl and season to taste. I think it benefits from sitting out for 30 minutes or so before serving.

Jerusalem Artichoke and Bacon Gratin

SERVES 4 as a side dish
Preparation time 10 minutes
Cooking time 55 minutes

600g Jerusalem artichokes, scrubbed
   clean and sliced extremely thinly
   (use a mandoline if you have one)
400ml whole milk
200ml double cream
¼ nutmeg, grated
1 bay leaf
few sprigs of thyme
200g smoked streaky bacon, cut into
   thin lardons
50g gruyère cheese, grated
sea salt and freshly ground black
   pepper

My love of a gratin knows no bounds, and Jerusalem artichokes are very well suited to this cooking method. I would serve this with a green salad for lunch, or as a decadent accompaniment to a roast.

Preheat the oven to 180°C/160°C fan/gas mark 4.

Put the sliced Jerusalem artichokes in a saucepan, pour over the milk and cream, add the nutmeg and throw in the bay and thyme. Season with salt and a generous grinding of pepper. Bring to the boil then turn down the heat and simmer very gently for 7–10 minutes until the artichokes have softened but still retain a good amount of bite.

While the artichokes are cooking, fry the bacon in a dry frying pan over a medium heat until crisp and caramelised.

Transfer half of the sliced artichokes to a gratin dish (about 2 litre capacity) with a slotted spoon, to form a base layer. Evenly distribute the bacon across the top, then cover with the remaining sliced artichokes. Pour over the residual cream until it reaches the top of the dish. Top with the grated gruyère, cover with foil and bake in the oven for 45 minutes. Remove the foil for the final 10 minutes and whack the oven right up as hot as it can go (about 260°C/240°C fan/gas mark 10) to achieve a crisp, bubbling and golden top.

Remove from the oven and serve.

Parsnip, Miso, Oat and Shallot Boulangère

SERVES 4 as a side dish
Preparation time 15 minutes
Cooking time 45 minutes

2 tbsp oil
4 shallots, very thinly sliced
500g parsnips, cut into very fine
    rounds (ideally using a mandoline
    or a food processor with a thin
    slicing attachment)
500ml fresh chicken or vegetable
    stock
1 tbsp white miso paste
½ tsp salt
250ml oat cream
few sprigs of thyme
freshly ground black pepper

Boulangère is a gratin of potatoes made by cooking potatoes in the juice (stock) and fat of lamb – the unsung hero of the potato dauphinois. Playing around with root vegetables in a gratin is a great way to really understand them. I've replaced the lamb stock and fat with a chicken or vegetable stock pumped up with miso and oat cream, that you can buy or make yourself. The flavour of the oat is what I want here, not the creaminess, and oat and parsnip are dreamy together. This dish is a good way to show how we often overlook the flavours of the modern plant-based movement. This gratin is superb as a main dish for a supper or served as a side dish, and if you make it with vegetable stock, your vegan friends will thank you.

Preheat the oven to 240°C/220°C fan/gas mark 9.

Start by sweating the shallots. Heat the oil in a large frying pan over a medium-low heat, add the shallots and cook gently for about 20 minutes, stirring regularly, until beautifully soft and caramelised.

Add the sliced parsnips (I don't think they need peeling – the peel adds a nice texture) to a separate saucepan, along with the stock, miso paste and salt. Bring to the boil then take off the heat immediately. Drain the parsnips, reserving the stock. Return the stock to the pan and cook over a high heat until the volume has reduced to about 150ml and the stock has a thick, syrupy consistency.

While the stock is reducing, you can start constructing the dish. Once the parsnips are cool enough to handle, take a gratin dish (about 2 litre capacity) and make a layer of parsnips on the bottom, two or three parsnip slices thick. Spoon over a thin layer of the shallots, season with pepper and the leaves from the sprigs of thyme. Repeat this process until you have used everything up.

To finish the sauce, add the oat cream to the stock and allow to reduce further for a couple of minutes until thickened slightly. Pour this over the parsnips and put the dish in the oven to bake for 20 minutes, until the top is crisp and golden. Remove from the oven and leave to sit for a couple of minutes before serving.

FRUIT

A Pistachio Tart for Soft Fruit

SERVES 8–10
Preparation time 20 minutes, plus
1 hour resting time and 20 minutes
cooling for the pastry
Cooking time 1 hour

FOR THE PASTRY
225g plain flour, plus extra for
    dusting
pinch of salt
1 tbsp icing sugar
120g ice-cold butter, cubed
1 free-range egg, whisked

FOR THE PISTACHIO FRANGIPANE
190g unsalted pistachios
200g caster sugar
50g plain flour
pinch of salt
grated zest and juice of 1 lemon
grated zest of 1 orange and juice of ½
200g very soft butter
1 tsp vanilla extract
3 free-range eggs
550g greengages, halved and stones
    removed (or other soft fruit of
    choice)
crème fraîche, to serve (optional)

You will need a 25cm deep, loose-
bottomed tart tin.

When testing this recipe I opted to use greengages, which are a favourite fruit of mine that's often overlooked. It's really important to preserve and promote varieties of fruit and vegetables that are part of our national food heritage, and greengages are the quintessential example of that. The best way to keep them being grown in this country is by eating them! For the uninitiated, greengages are small green plums which are sweet when perfectly ripe. They are easy to find in greengrocers and supermarkets between August and September, when they're at peak season. This tart is the ideal showcase for their distinctive colour, enhanced by the vibrancy of the pistachio frangipane, which is zesty and not cloying in the least. Think of this as a twist on the classic plum and almond tart, without the same detrimental impact on the environment that almonds have. Pistachios have far more sustainable plus-points, requiring less water to grow than almonds do. Also, their waste products, such as the shells and hulls, can be (and are) utilised for fuel and animal feed.

You can, of course, swap the greengages for any other fruit if you can't get hold of them: raspberries or rhubarb would be a particularly good marriage with the pistachios.

To make the pastry, first put a mixing bowl and knife in the fridge. Put the flour in a food processor with the salt and sugar and blitz for a few seconds (this is a great way to avoid having to sift the flour). Add the butter and blitz again for about 20 seconds, or until the mixture resembles breadcrumbs. Turn the mixture out into the fridge-cold mixing bowl (this helps prevent the butter melting) and, with the cold knife, mix in enough of the whisked egg to bind the mixture. Do this gradually until the dough starts to come together – you don't want it to get too wet, so you may not need all of the egg.

Turn the dough out onto a work surface and bring it into a ball with your hands. Kneading will make it tough, so try to handle the pastry as little as possible. Lay the pastry on a baking sheet and roll it out with a rolling pin to flatten it a little (this makes it easier to roll later on). Cover the pastry and sheet with cling film and leave in the fridge to rest for at least 30 minutes, or until you're ready to construct the tart.

Once the pastry has chilled, preheat the oven to 200°C/180°C fan/gas mark 6. Remove the pastry from the fridge and leave it to sit for a minute or two. Dust a work surface and the rolling pin with flour, unwrap the pastry and roll it out to a thickness of 2mm. Keep turning the pastry as you roll it, to ensure you get an even circle, as this will make it much easier to line the tart tin.

Fold one end of the pastry over the rolling pin and quickly transfer it to a 25cm deep, loose-bottomed tart tin. It is not necessary to line the base of the tin with greaseproof paper, as there is so much butter in the pastry it's unlikely to stick, but you can if you wish.

Gently ease the pastry into the sides of the tin, allowing the excess to fall over the edges. I find it easier to trim off the edges once the tart has cooked, to give it a neater finish. Leave in the fridge for 30 minutes: resting helps prevent the pastry from shrinking during baking.

Line the pastry case with a sheet of baking parchment (you can get it into the corners more easily if you crumple the paper first). Fill with ceramic baking beans or dried pulses and blind bake in the oven for 25 minutes, or until the pastry is cooked through but has only a little colour. Remove the beans and parchment and bake for another 5 minutes to guarantee a good snap when the pastry is cut. The edges of the pastry that you folded over the edge of the tin will turn a bit darker than the rest of the pastry, but they will be trimmed off at the end so don't worry.

Remove the pastry from the oven and leave to cool, in the tin, for 20 minutes on a wire rack, then use a knife to gently remove the excess pastry from the edge of the tart tin and neatly level off the edges. The pastry is a bit like Polyfilla at this stage, and more durable than you might think, but still take care while doing this (if the tart breaks or cracks, seal it with some egg wash and pop it back in the oven for a minute or two). Now you're ready to fill the tart.

To make the frangipane, blitz the pistachios in a food processor until finely ground. Add the sugar, flour, salt and citrus zest and mix until well combined. Next, add the wet ingredients, first the butter and vanilla and then the eggs one by one, followed by the orange and lemon juice. Once well combined, pour the mixture into the tart case. Arrange the fruit across the top however you wish, then place the tart in the oven and bake for 35 minutes. It will brown a bit on the top but don't despair, the vibrant green of the inside will endure! Remove from the oven and leave to cool in the tin for as long as your impatience will allow, then cut into slices with a sharp knife. I like to serve this with a dollop of crème fraîche.

Fruit Pie and Crumble – *Fillings*

Sour cherry filling

1.4kg sour cherries (1.1kg pitted weight)
50g caster sugar
juice of 1 lemon
1 tbsp cornflour
50ml water (optional)

Put the cherries, sugar, lemon juice and cornflour in a saucepan over a medium heat, cover and once it starts to boil, take off the lid. Stew the fruit for about 30 minutes. If it starts to look a little dry, add the water to make it saucy.

If you're making this into a pie, it's nice to place strips of pastry in lattice formation on the top instead of a solid lid.

Strawberry and black pepper filling

1.3kg hulled strawberries
50g caster sugar
grated zest and juice of 1 lemon
1 tbsp cornflour
1 vanilla pod, split lengthways
a decent grinding of black pepper

Put the strawberries, sugar, lemon zest and juice, cornflour, vanilla pod and pepper in a saucepan over a gentle heat and cover with a lid. Once it starts to boil, take off the lid. Stew the fruit gently for about 10 minutes until soft but not completely broken down. Remove the pod before using.

Late summer fruit filling

350g plums, halved and stoned
juice of 1½ lemons
1 tsp cornflour
50g caster sugar
200g fresh cherries (pitted weight)
150g blackberries

Put the plums in a saucepan with the lemon juice, cornflour and sugar. Cook over a medium heat for 5 minutes until soft but not totally falling apart. Add the cherries and

blackberries and cook for a further 5 minutes until it bubbles gently and the fruit has softened.

Rhubarb filling

1.1kg rhubarb, cut into 5cm pieces
100g caster sugar
juice of 2 oranges and grated zest of 1
1 tbsp grenadine or Ribena, for colour (optional)

Put the rhubarb, sugar, orange juice and zest in a saucepan over a medium heat and cover. Bring to the boil then take off the lid and let the fruit stew gently for about 20 minutes. Add the grenadine or Ribena (if using). At this stage it is perfect for a crumble, but for a pie let it reduce for a further 5–10 minutes so it's less liquid.

Spiced apple filling
(this makes enough filling for a bigger pie)

1kg Bramley apples, peeled, cored, quartered, then each quarter sliced into 3
60g light brown muscovado sugar
100ml cider vinegar
1 tsp cornflour
pinch of ground cloves
1 tbsp ground cinnamon
decent grating of nutmeg
pinch of ground allspice
decent pinch of finely ground black pepper
1kg dessert apples (ideally Granny Smiths), peeled, cored, quartered, then each quarter sliced into 3

Put the Bramleys in a saucepan with the sugar, vinegar, cornflour and spices over a low heat and cook for 10–15 minutes until they have begun to turn floury, almost souffléd in texture. Slightly soften the dessert apples in a separate pan with a splash of water over a medium-low heat for just a few minutes – you want them to retain bite. Puree the cooked-down Bramleys in a food processor, transfer to a bowl and carefully mix in the dessert apples.

Fruit Pie and Crumble – *Toppings*

Sweet shortcrust pastry for a pie

(Makes enough pastry for one 23cm pie)
Chill your filling first, to avoid a soggy situation!

420g plain flour, plus extra for dusting
250g ice-cold butter, cubed
1 tbsp icing sugar
1 tsp fine salt
about 1 tsp ice-cold water
1 free-range egg, beaten

Briefly blitz the flour, butter, icing sugar and salt in a food processor until the mixture resembles breadcrumbs. Add a little water at a time until the pastry forms a ball (be careful not to make the pastry too wet). Tip the dough onto a floured surface and bring it together, handling it as little as possible. Cut off two thirds of the pastry for the base, leaving one third for the top. Wrap each portion in cling film, flatten a little and chill for 30 minutes, or until needed.

When you're ready to make your pie, unwrap the larger portion of pastry and roll it out to a rough circle shape on a flour-dusted surface to the thickness of a pound coin. Drape the pastry over the flour-dusted rolling pin and roll the pastry off the pin and over the edges of a deep 23cm pie dish. Ease the pastry into the sides of the dish, but do not trim the edges at this stage. Fill the pie with the fridge-cold filling. Glaze the edges of the pastry with beaten egg using a pastry brush. Roll out the smaller portion of pastry to make the lid. Place the lid on top of the pie. Trim off the excess pastry to make a neat edge. Push down the edges with a fork to seal them tight, or crimp them, pinching the pastry to create a scalloped edge. Roll out any excess pastry and make some decorations for the lid of the pie with cutters of choice. Brush with beaten egg and chill for 30 minutes. Preheat the oven to 200°C/180°C fan/gas mark 6.

Glaze the top of the pie again, then bake for 35–40 minutes, or until the pastry is golden brown and cooked through.

Crumble topping

125g ice-cold butter, cubed
180g plain flour
80g golden caster sugar
40g rolled oats
½ tsp fine salt

Preheat the oven to 200°C/180°C fan/gas mark 6. Crumble the butter into the flour with your fingertips until the mixture resembles breadcrumbs (I like a combination of large lumps and finer crumbs), then stir in the sugar, oats and salt. Put the slightly cooled fruit in a 22cm ovenproof pie dish or gratin dish and top the fruit with the crumble mixture. Bake for about 30 minutes, until golden. Serve with custard or double cream.

Slump topping

180g plain flour
70g caster sugar
2 tsp baking powder
½ tsp bicarbonate of soda
¼ tsp fine salt
85ml buttermilk
4 tbsp butter, melted
½ tsp vanilla extract
a little demerara sugar, for sprinkling

Preheat the oven to 220°C/200°C fan/gas mark 7 and put the hot fruit filling in a 22cm deep pie dish.

Whisk the flour, caster sugar, baking powder, bicarbonate of soda and salt in a large bowl. Whisk the buttermilk, melted butter and vanilla in a separate bowl. Add the wet ingredients to the dry and stir until just combined: the more you mix, the tougher the topping will be. Divide the dough into 10 equal pieces and place on the hot filling, leaving a little space between each piece. Sprinkle each mound of dough with a little demerara sugar. Bake for 15–18 minutes until the filling is bubbling and the topping is golden brown, rotating halfway through baking.

Leftover Juicing Cake

SERVES 10
Preparation time 30 minutes
Cooking time 1 hour 10 minutes, plus
2–3 hours cooling time

100g dates, roughly chopped
grated zest and juice of 1 orange
grated zest of 1 lemon
100g walnuts
200g light brown muscovado sugar
250ml olive oil, plus extra for
    greasing
3 medium free-range eggs
280g leftover juicer pulp
1 tsp vanilla bean paste
350g plain flour
2 tsp baking powder
a mixture of 1 tbsp ground
    cinnamon, ¼ tsp ground turmeric
    and a good grinding of black pepper
    (or 1¼ tbsp 'golden blend' powder)
pinch of ground cloves
¼ tsp fine salt

FOR THE ICING
250ml double cream
1 tsp vanilla bean paste
200g icing sugar
540g cream cheese

TO DECORATE
crystallised oranges and lemons
crystallised bay leaves
caramelised walnuts
dates

You will need a 23cm loose-
bottomed cake tin (8cm deep).

In the past I've been stumped about what to do with all the residual pulp and fibre from the fruit and veg that you are left with after making a juice – it always felt a bit counterintuitive to throw it out. I realised it made perfect sense to put it into a cake. This is much the same principle as making a carrot cake, and can work with whatever you've got leftover, as the fibre is still full of flavour and moisture. There's a ton of waste involved in the juice and smoothie industry, so this is a great way to combat it if you have a home juicer. Certain juices work better than others: the pulp from carrot, ginger, turmeric, orange, apple and pear all work really well in this recipe. Beetroot pulp could work well too, perhaps with the addition of cocoa powder.

I've given specified measurements for the individual spices, but there are lots of 'golden' mixes (blends of turmeric, cinnamon and black pepper) available which work well too.

Preheat the oven to 185°C/165°C fan/gas mark 4.

Grease the bottom and sides of a 23cm diameter loose-bottomed cake tin (8cm deep) with oil and line it with greaseproof paper. This will prevent the cake from sticking to the tin and also from burning – this cake takes a relatively long time to cook.

Put the dates in a bowl, add the orange juice, orange zest and lemon zest and set aside.

Put the walnuts on a baking tray and toast in the oven for 10 minutes, being careful not to let them burn.

Whisk the muscovado sugar and olive oil in a bowl for about 2 minutes until the mixture is a pale coffee colour. Crack one egg into the mixture at a time, whisking each egg into the mixture for 1 minute before adding the next. After you've added the third egg, whisk for a further 2 minutes. Whisk in the juicer pulp, followed by the vanilla bean paste, until evenly dispersed. Combine the flour, baking powder, spices and salt then add to the wet mixture and whisk until well combined. Finally, stir in the toasted walnuts, dates, orange juice and zests and mix with a spatula until they are evenly distributed.

CONTINUED ››

Pour the mixture into the cake tin and bake in the oven for 1 hour 10 minutes.

Remove from the oven and allow to cool in the tin for 2–3 hours.

To make the icing, whisk the double cream, vanilla and icing sugar in a bowl until the mixture is thick and retains its shape. Fold the cream cheese into the cream and sugar mixture until smooth and spreadable. Chill it for an hour or two while the cake is cooling.

Remove the cake from the tin. If the top is a little crusty and domed, level it off with a sharp knife, then cut the cake horizontally into 3 even slices. Lay the base slice on a cake plate or stand. Spread over 4–5 tablespoons of the icing, sandwich the next layer on, then repeat. Take half the remaining icing and ice the sides of the cake, levelling it to a smooth, 3mm-thick layer. Pour the remaining icing on top and level it out flat. You may have some icing left over, and it's up to you how thick you want to make it. Personally, I prefer a slightly thinner layer, but I know many of you out there will opt for more!

Decorate the top of the cake however you like. I love to use whole fresh dates, caramelised walnuts and crystallised citrus and bay leaves.

A Glut of Jams

MAKES 2 litres
Preparation time 10 minutes
Cooking time 30 minutes

1kg gooseberries, washed, topped
   and tailed (or any fruit of your
   choice)
500ml water
juice of 2 lemons
1kg jam sugar

You will need enough sterilised
preserving jars for 2 litres of jam.

When testing this recipe I had a load of gooseberries that needed putting to use, and I couldn't resist the temptation of jamming them, simply so I could call it 'Gizberry Jam'. Oh how we laughed. This method obviously works for any variety of soft fruit you have to hand, and is an age-old way of preserving the glut of late summer's fruit harvest for the dreary winter months ahead. You will need to invest in a bit of kit: obviously jars with airtight seals to store it in, also a jam thermometer, which is invaluable to achieve the correct setting point, and a preserving pan, which helps cook the fruit quickly due to its low sides and width (the pan is not essential – a wide stainless-steel pan will work well, but avoid aluminium as it can impart a slightly metallic flavour to the jam).

This method also works brilliantly using frozen fruit, such as sour cherries (sour cherry jam is put to excellent use in my Sourdough Doughnuts with White Chocolate Custard and Sour Cherry Jam on page 148–49), the only difference being that you need to add a splash of water with the fruit to get it going (1kg should be the pitted sour cherry weight). If you want to make jam with less fruit, just ensure that you have an equal ratio of fruit to sugar.

Place the topped and tailed gooseberries (or whatever fruit you have chosen) in a preserving pan with the water and lemon juice. Cook gently for about 20 minutes until the fruit has softened, popped and broken down. Next, add the sugar, stirring it in carefully. Allow it to dissolve for a few minutes, then bring to a rolling boil, reduce the temperature to a slow simmer (it can burn easily) and cook for about 10 minutes. You will notice a foam form on the top as it comes to the boil – skim this off very carefully.

Place your jam thermometer in the pan and keep checking it until it reaches 150°C (setting point). If you don't have a jam thermometer, you can also test if it's ready by dropping a little jam onto a frozen plate and seeing if it sets to jam within about 30 seconds.

Once it's ready, remove from the heat and allow to cool for 10 minutes. Using a funnel, pour the jam into sterilised jars and seal the jars.

The jam will keep, stored in a cool, dark place, for up to 12 months. Store in the fridge once opened.

Summer Fruit Cordial

MAKES 300g
Preparation time 10 minutes
Cooking time 15 minutes

250g strawberries (about 1 punnet),
   hulled (or any other soft fruit)
150g caster sugar
50ml water
juice of 2 lemons

This recipe came about as I had a punnet of strawberries that were quickly getting past their best, and were definitely too squishy to eat. This method would work with any kind of soft fruit and is a brilliant way to extract the essence of the fruit's flavour, and avoiding having to chuck fruit that's on the turn in the bin!

Put everything in a saucepan and place over a high heat for about 15 minutes to dissolve the sugar, break down the strawberries (or other soft fruit) and intensify the flavour, stirring occasionally.

Remove from the heat and allow to cool for a couple of minutes, then transfer to a food processor and blitz until smooth. Pass through a chinois (conical sieve) or fine sieve to get rid of any pips or lumps.

The cordial will keep for ages in a sterilised airtight bottle or jar in the fridge. Simply dilute it with cold water and serve with ice.

PULSES, BEANS & GRAINS

PULSES, BEANS AND GRAINS

Eating pulses, beans or grains is probably one of the truly guilt-free ways to feed ourselves. Pulses and beans are members of the legume family, and legumes are fantastic at fixing nitrogen into the soil and improving its structure, feeding the soil's microbial life and fertility. Not only that, they are amazing at sequestering carbon into the soil which makes them a hero crop, as scientists believe this is one of the best weapons we have in our arsenal to tackle greenhouse gas emissions. They are rich in protein, fibre, antioxidants and folic acid, and when paired with grains such as rice, pulses combine to form what is known as a 'complete protein', full of amino acids and nutrients: there's a reason why the UN calls pulses 'the special forces of the plant world'. Their low glycemic index means they are great at stabilising blood sugar, and they fill you up a treat. Perhaps they have suffered the reputation of being 'boring' in the taste stakes, but they are a brilliant vehicle for big flavours.

As some of the first crops ever to be domesticated by humans, pulses, beans and grains have been farmed for millennia in pretty much every country on Earth. I want to focus on the cultivation of grain in particular, as it has been a central foundation of civilisation. The way we grow and process grain has changed dramatically in the last 150 years. The invention of the steel roller mill revolutionised grain milling in the 1870s, replacing the traditional stone mills. This new system ground the grains through a series of metal rollers, breaking down the kernel progressively at each stage, separating almost all the bran and producing a finer white flour. This white flour signified affluence and sophistication and was hailed as an innovation in modern living, but producing it meant discarding the most nutritious parts of the grain, rich in proteins, lipids, vitamins and minerals. This was the first step in the diminishing of the nutritional quality of wheat. The more dramatic shift occurred in the 1950s and 60s, with the development of high yielding, genetically modified, hybridised grain breeds, propagated by companies like Monsanto and heralded for solving the problem of world hunger. While the intentions of these advancements might have been admirable, this revolution has led to a whole host of unforeseen consequences, detrimental to both the health of our bodies and the planet.

Genetic modification has led to development of mutant wheat strains that are more resistant to pests and drought, and have higher gluten levels in order to produce 'fluffier' bread products. They are grown in synthetically treated soils soaked in chemicals, pulverised to a fine and nutritionally barren dust, then bleached, and this has led to all sorts of chronic inflammatory digestive problems in humans, as well as being a big contributor to global obesity levels. Our stomachs are simply not evolved to digest it. Being 'gluten intolerant' has become a familiar phrase these days, especially among the health conscious, but it's a common misconception. Coeliac disease, a severe form of gluten intolerance, is actually quite rare; most of us are simply suffering from the effects of mutated modern grains battling with our digestive systems. Most gluten-free products that people think are healthy are effectively junk food full of highly refined industrial starches that spike blood sugar just as much as (or even more than) white flour. A traditional wheat grain is hardy and tough to the touch, but when you squeeze a modern wheat grain between your fingers it disintegrates immediately – this mirrors how it breaks down in the body, having an immediate effect on your glycemic index as it turns into

114

sugars far more quickly. This type of wheat effectively attacks the gut. Evidence has shown that people who believe they have gluten intolerances, on switching to eating heritage grains and natural yeasts within sourdough breads, report a disappearance of their symptoms.

This modern wheat bears little resemblance to ancient, heritage grains such as spelt, barley, millet or pseudo cereals such as buckwheat, amaranth and quinoa, which have hardly changed from what our ancestors would have eaten centuries ago, but thankfully we are now seeing the rise of farms growing these heritage crops in the UK. These grains are full of nutrients and far easier to digest, and their diversity is key in terms of what it can bring to our farming systems. As I mention in the Fruit and Vegetable Agriculture essay on pages 38–41, monocultural farming practices are responsible for the decimation of our planet's soil health: modern wheat does nothing to impart nutrients into the soil and requires huge amounts of chemical input. Older varieties tend to have longer, deeper roots, and their diversity is something to aspire to.

One of the great examples of people voting with their wallets is the rise in sourdough, heirloom grain breads and more traditional bakeries and flour mills than ever (don't be fooled by supermarkets claiming their products to be 'sourdough', when in actual fact they are often simply slow-risen doughs made from fake yeasts). The only way you can guarantee you're getting the real deal is by buying from a real bakery or, indeed, making your own!

Roasted Beetroot, Beluga Lentil and Watercress Salad with Goat's Cheese Croute

SERVES 6
Preparation time 30 minutes
Cooking time 1 hour

FOR THE BEETROOT

3 purple beetroot, washed
3 golden beetroot, washed
1 tbsp sherry vinegar
2 tbsp olive oil
½ tsp sea salt
¼ tsp sugar

FOR THE LENTILS

250g beluga lentils, rinsed
1 tbsp lemon juice
2 tbsp extra-virgin olive oil
1 tsp sea salt

FOR THE SALSA VERDE DRESSING

2 garlic cloves, peeled
1 tbsp capers
1 tbsp gherkins
bunch of flat-leaf parsley leaves
1½ tbsp basil leaves
½ tbsp tarragon leaves
1 tbsp Dijon mustard
3 tbsp sherry vinegar
1 tbsp lemon juice
150ml extra-virgin olive oil, plus
    extra for drizzling
½ tsp sea salt
freshly ground black pepper

FOR THE GOAT'S CHEESE CROUTES

6 slices of sourdough baguette
3 tbsp Wild Garlic Butter (page 247)
6 × 1cm-thick slices of goat's cheese
3 tbsp runny honey

TO SERVE

100g watercress, washed and dried
1 candied beetroot (unpeeled), thinly
    sliced on a mandoline, or by hand
    (if slicing in advance, keep crisp in
    ice-cold water)
sea salt

I developed this recipe for the lunch menu at my restaurant, The Nitery. Roasting beetroot couldn't be simpler and it concentrates its flavour and sweetness, and beetroot and goat's cheese are classic bedfellows, but the addition of salsa verde (which is also great alongside grilled fish or meat) really lifts this salad with a zingy vibrancy. I'm always on the lookout for a salad that feels fulfilling but not monotonous to eat, and this is one of those salads, full of contrasting textures. Not only that, but it looks beautiful, especially if you can source golden and candied beetroot. A thick slice of great goat's cheese is key for the croute: I favour Ragstone, a delicious English cheese with a lovely acidity that works brilliantly here. Drizzling it with honey and sticking it under a hot grill achieves a golden brûlée which is pretty irresistible.

Preheat the oven to 180°C/160°C fan/gas mark 4.

Roast the whole beetroots (unpeeled) in a roasting tray in the oven for 1 hour until cooked through but still relatively firm. Remove and set aside to cool.

Cook the lentils in a saucepan of boiling water for about 15 minutes until cooked through but still retaining some bite. Drain and dress with the lemon juice, olive oil and salt while warm. Set aside.

To make the salsa verde dressing, put all of the ingredients in a food processor and pulse until everything is finely chopped but retains some texture. Season with pepper.

Peel the roasted beetroots then, depending on their size, cut them into sixths or eighths. Dress them with the sherry vinegar, oil, salt and sugar. Set aside.

Preheat the grill. Spread half a tablespoon of wild garlic butter on each slice of bread. Heat a dry frying pan over a medium-high heat and toast the bread in the pan, butter side down, for a couple of minutes. Turn and toast the other side for a minute or two. Remove and lay the goat's cheese on top of each croute. Drizzle half a tablespoon of honey on top, then place on a tray under the hot grill for a few minutes, until golden.

Combine the lentils, watercress, sliced candied beetroot and roasted beetroot and any residual dressing in a bowl. Spoon the salsa verde dressing across the base of a large dish or divide it equally among plates. Pile on the lentil mixture and top with the croutes. Drizzle with olive oil, sprinkle with sea salt and serve.

Black Lentil and Beetroot Larb

SERVES 8
Preparation time 10 minutes, plus
30 minutes macerating time
Cooking time 1 hour 20 minutes

4 purple and golden beetroots,
    washed but unpeeled
40g white rice, ideally sticky Thai
    (but anything will do)
3 banana shallots, peeled and very
    thinly sliced into rings
250g cooked beluga or Puy lentils

FOR THE CRISPY SHALLOTS

4 tbsp rapeseed oil
4 banana shallots, peeled and thinly
    sliced into rings

FOR THE DRESSING

4–5 fresh lime leaves, thinly sliced
juice of 3 limes
5 tbsp fish sauce or soy sauce
1 tsp Thai chilli powder, pul biber or
    Korean chilli powder
1½ tbsp sugar
3 tbsp sunflower or groundnut oil

TO SERVE

large handful of coriander leaves
large handful of mint leaves
large handful of Thai basil leaves

My good friend Neil Rankin, who is perhaps known primarily as a meat chef (and also features in each and every one of my books), actually hates that reputation as deep down he is a plant-loving teddy bear. It's always interesting to look at his Instagram for plant-based food ideas – as a meat lover he's always pushing boundaries for how he thinks about cooking with plants, and he is the one who gave me the idea for this. Larb is a Northern Thai dish, normally made with pork, where rice is roasted and ground for a delicious crunch. The most intense version is actually made of pig's blood, so the beetroot provides an irony backbone (not to mention the colour). This is just a very clever, yet simple salad.

Preheat the oven to 200°C/180°C fan/gas mark 6.

Place the beetroots on a baking tray or roasting tray and roast in the oven for 1 hour 20 minutes until softened. Remove from the oven and leave until cool enough to handle. The skins should peel away very easily. Chop each beetroot into small cubes and set aside.

Heat a dry frying pan or wok over a high heat. Once hot, add the rice and toast for a few minutes, until the grains begin to turn vaguely golden. Treat the rice like toasting sesame seeds, and be sure to keep it moving around the pan to prevent it burning. Transfer to a food processor and blitz to a coarse powder.

To make the crispy shallots, heat the oil in a frying pan over a low heat and fry the shallots for 10–15 minutes, or until they start to crisp up and turn a light golden colour. Scoop out the shallots with a slotted spoon and drain on kitchen paper to absorb any excess oil.

To make the dressing, mix together the lime leaves, lime juice, fish sauce or soy sauce, chilli powder, sugar and oil until well combined. Mix the beetroot, sliced fresh shallots, lentils and ground rice in a bowl with the dressing and leave to macerate for about 30 minutes.

Once ready to serve, combine the beetroot and lentil mixture with all of the herbs. Top with the crispy shallots and serve immediately.

Puy Lentils, a Big Red and Roasted Toulouse Sausage

SERVES 6
Preparation time 20 minutes
Cooking time 1 hour

FOR THE LENTILS
3 tbsp olive oil
1 large onion, very finely chopped
2 celery sticks, very finely chopped
2 carrots, very finely chopped
6 garlic cloves, very finely chopped
500g Puy lentils, rinsed
500ml big red wine like claret or
 Rioja
500ml fresh brown chicken or beef
 stock
2 bay leaves
5 sprigs of rosemary
a few sprigs of thyme
1 tbsp butter
200ml Red Wine and Beef Sauce, to
 serve (optional) (page 268)
extra-virgin olive oil, for drizzling
sea salt and freshly ground black
 pepper

FOR THE SAUSAGES
oil, for frying
12 top quality Toulouse sausages,
 with a good dispersal of fat

This dish has become something of a stone-cold classic at my restaurant, The Nitery. My mother, the definitive Francophile, spent a number of her formative years in Paris and counted lentils cooked like this as one of her favourite foods. The French are so good at showcasing an ingredient that isn't meat, and making it almost more valuable to the dish than the meat itself. I serve lentils with sausages here, but they work with everything from roast chicken, hake or salmon to roast beetroots or Salt-baked Celeriac (page 88). The key thing is to not overcook the lentils: they need bite.

At the restaurant we add an extra component to this dish – a few tablespoons of demi-glace, a rich and glossy 50/50 wine-to-stock reduction sauce, that has a delicious meaty flavour. It's not critical but it really elevates the dish. I leave it up to you! Don't swap it for a stock cube though – you don't get the gelatinous stickiness and it will just be a shock of too much salt.

Heat the oil for the lentils in a heavy-based saucepan over a medium heat, add the onion, celery and carrots and sweat for 15–20 minutes, stirring, until they soften and begin to caramelise. Add the garlic and cook for a further couple of minutes to soften.

Preheat the oven as hot as it can go (about 260°C/240°C fan/gas mark 10).

Tip the lentils into the pan and stir them through so that they are nicely coated in oil, then pour in the wine. Allow it to bubble vigorously for 3–4 minutes, then add the stock, bay leaves, rosemary and thyme. Cook, uncovered, at a rolling simmer for 30 minutes, until the lentils are cooked through but still al dente.

About 15 minutes before the lentils are done, cook the sausages. Brown them in a hot ovenproof frying pan with a little oil, then finish them in the hot oven for 8 minutes.

Once the sausages are cooked, remove the herb stalks and bay leaves from the lentils and season the lentils generously with salt and pepper.

Now for the final three flourishes: the addition of butter, sauce and oil. Stir the butter through the lentils – this adds velvety texture and is a quintessentially French way to finish the dish – then spoon 2–3 tablespoons of lentils in an even layer on each plate, and place the sausages on top. If you're using the sauce, pour 2 tablespoons over the sausages and another around the lentils. Drizzle with extra-virgin olive oil and serve.

Ethiopian Lentil Stew

SERVES 6
Preparation time 15 minutes
Cooking time 1 hour 20 minutes

4 tbsp ghee or oil
2 onions, finely chopped
1 head of garlic, cloves peeled and
    finely chopped
50g piece of fresh ginger, peeled and
    finely chopped
2 tbsp Berbere Spice Mix (see below)
550g tomatoes, blitzed to a puree
300g dried black lentils, rinsed
1 litre fresh chicken or vegetable
    stock
juice of 2 lemons
1 tbsp sugar
1 tsp salt

FOR THE BERBERE SPICE MIX
2 tsp dried chilli flakes
1 tsp black peppercorns
1 tsp coriander seeds
1 tsp cumin seeds
5 cardamom pods
1 tsp fenugreek seeds
4 cloves
½ tsp sea salt flakes
1 tsp hot smoked paprika
1 tsp sweet paprika
½ tsp ground ginger
½ tsp ground cinnamon
½ tsp freshly grated nutmeg

TO SERVE
cooked rice
yoghurt
coriander leaves
mint leaves

Ethiopian food has been bubbling under the surface in the UK for years, but is perhaps overshadowed by other more famous African cuisines such as Moroccan, Nigerian or Ghanaian, and I think that's a crying shame. It's just delicious. I would characterise Ethiopian cuisine as consisting of lightly spiced, simply cooked dishes, which are served with lots of different sides, almost like an Indian thali, just a bit more rustic. It is an inherently meat-free cuisine, with brilliant breads; their most famous bread is injera, which is like a cross between a dosa and an idli. I'd serve this stew with a grated carrot salad and some rice.

The recipe makes more spice mix than you'll need for the stew. Keep the leftover spice mix in an airtight container for future use.

To make the spice mix, simply grind all the spices in a small food processor, pestle and mortar or spice grinder until as fine as possible.

Heat the fat of your choice in a casserole dish over a medium heat, add the onions and cook slowly for about 15 minutes until they soften and begin to caramelise. Add the garlic and ginger and cook for a further 10 minutes, then add the 2 tablespoons of spice mix (keeping the rest for another dish) and cook for 2–3 minutes, before adding the blitzed tomatoes. Cook gently for about 20 minutes, to give the stew a real depth of flavour, stirring regularly to avoid the mixture scorching at the bottom, then stir in the lentils and pour in the stock. Bring to a simmer and cook, uncovered, over a low heat for 35–40 minutes, until the lentils are soft and just beginning to break down into the sauce. Add the lemon juice, sugar and salt and cook for a further 5 minutes.

Remove from the heat and serve alongside rice, with a dollop of yoghurt and a generous handful each of coriander and mint leaves scattered across the top.

Carlin Pea and Pumpkin Massaman

SERVES 4

Preparation time 15 minutes, plus
1 hour 20 minutes for the XO Sauce
Cooking time 40 minutes, plus
cooking time for the carlin peas (if
using dried)

½ small-medium pumpkin or squash
    (about 400g), peeled, deseeded and
    cut into thin wedges
2 small onions, peeled and cut into
    eighths
1 tbsp oil
½ tsp salt
100g green beans, topped and tailed,
    and cut in half diagonally
400g dried carlin peas, soaked
    overnight, cooked until al dente
    and drained (or 2 x 400g tins of
    cooked carlin peas, drained)
juice of ½ lemon or lime

FOR THE CURRY SAUCE

150g Vegan XO Sauce (page 23)
2 stalks of lemongrass, outer leaves
    removed, tender stalks roughly
    chopped
400ml tin coconut milk
1 tbsp ground coriander
¼ tsp black peppercorns
½ tsp ground turmeric
2 tbsp ground cumin
½ tsp freshly grated nutmeg
1 tsp ground cinnamon
¼ tsp ground cloves
300ml fresh vegetable stock
2 bay leaves
1 star anise
2 tbsp soy sauce
1 tsp salt
1 tbsp dark muscovado sugar

TO SERVE

coconut cream, for pouring
small bunch of coriander, leaves
    picked
cooked basmati or Thai fragrant rice

In early 2019, I spent a month in Thailand at one of the first sports-focused medical facilities testing the impact of a vegan diet on athletes. It was an eye-opening experience, and it turned everything I knew about plant versus animal proteins, and how they function in the body, on its head. Thai vegan food is great, and the food at the facility was super, particularly a chickpea massaman curry that I knew immediately I would have to feature in this book. Carlin peas, a British heritage pea, are like firm, small, dark chickpeas. Go to town to hunt them down – they are delicious.

The body of this dish comes from XO sauce. Normally made with pork and/or prawns, my recipe on page 23 is a vegan version made with garlic, ginger, chillies, seaweed, Shaoxing wine and miso for umami punch. It's a bit of a bitch to make, but for vegans it adds the kind of depth that something like fish sauce adds. It also lasts for ages. For vegan cooking I would get into the groove of making it.

Massaman is a Muslim Thai dish, a rich, mildly spiced coconut curry that's usually made with lamb or beef. While coconut milk is not conventionally the most sustainable product, eating in a sustainable way is about balance, and if we're cutting back on meat, I hope this seems like a decent swap for a meat curry. For more on the coconut, see page 173.

Preheat the oven as hot as it can go (about 260°C/240°C fan/gas mark 10).

Lay the pumpkin and onions on a baking tray, coat them in the oil and season with the salt. Roast for about 20 minutes, until the pumpkin and onions begin to caramelise and darken around the edges, turning them halfway through.

Blitz the XO sauce in a food processor with the lemongrass, coconut milk and all of the spices (excluding the bay leaves and star anise) until smooth. Transfer to a saucepan and add the vegetable stock, bay leaves, star anise, soy sauce, salt and sugar. Simmer for 20 minutes then add the green beans and cook for a further 3 minutes. Mix in the carlin peas and, finally, gently stir through the roasted pumpkin and onion, trying not to break them up too much. Simmer for a minute or two then finish by gently stirring through the lime or lemon juice.

Remove from the heat and serve with a lick of coconut cream and scattering of coriander leaves, and cooked rice.

Tarka Dhal

SERVES 4
Preparation time 25 minutes, plus
overnight soaking
Cooking time 1 hour 20 minutes

FOR THE DHAL

200g split yellow peas, soaked
  overnight
1 litre water, or vegetable or chicken
  stock
½ tsp sugar
a decent pinch of red chilli powder
  (ideally Kashmiri chilli powder, if
  you can find it)
1½ tsp ground turmeric
¼ tsp black mustard seeds
¼ tsp nigella seeds
1 tbsp tomato puree
1 good-quality cinnamon stick
30g fresh ginger, blitzed or pounded
  into a paste
1 tsp salt
5 fresh coriander roots, pounded (this
  is not the stalk, it's the small root at
  the end of the coriander plant, and
  is optional)

FOR THE TARKA

2 tbsp ghee or oil
2 white onions, thinly sliced
4 garlic cloves, pounded to a paste
½ tsp ground cumin
3 or 4 bay leaves
4 cloves
1 tsp ground black pepper
a decent pinch of garam masala
large handful of coriander leaves

Dhal is the dish that I trust to appease all dietary likes and loathes. It is the dish that comforts, makes you feel like you're doing something good for yourself, but also feels suitably grotty and hits the junk-food spot. So here's where this gets really great. The best dhal in London is from the all-hailed Whitechapel Punjabi/Pakistani restaurant, Tayyabs. Tayyabs is famous for its lamb cutlets, but for me it's all about the dhal. I've managed to hoodwink a lesson in dhal-making from the owner, Wasim Tayyab. Now, he has withheld 'some' secrets from me, but has let me publish this, which frankly is the best god-damn lentil dish (aside from the black dhal makhani I published in my last book, *Slow*). These are two absolutely necessary recipes to have up your sleeve, and the fact that this one is so unbelievably easy makes it more of an everyday recipe to boot. This dhal is a lovely dish on its own, but the addition of the hot, heavily spiced splash of oil at the end (known as the 'tarka') brings the whole thing to life. It pairs beautifully with the Sri Lankan Beetroot and Coconut Curry on page 85 (pictured opposite).

The dhal part of the recipe couldn't be easier: simply put all of the dhal ingredients in a large saucepan, bring to the boil, then turn down the heat to medium. Cook for about 1 hour, until the split peas are cooked through. You want them to be quite soupy, with some lentils breaking up and some still holding their shape a little.

After the dhal has been cooking for about 45 minutes, heat the ghee or oil for the tarka in a frying pan over a high heat. Add the onions and cook them down slowly and gently, allowing them to caramelise, for at least 15–20 minutes. Once they are turning golden, add the garlic, cumin, bay leaves, cloves and pepper. Stir through the spices and cook for a few more minutes (you can even let the onions start to reach a really dark caramel if you are brave). Take the pan off the heat then pour the tarka over the dhal. Be careful when you do this as it will sizzle and spit! Finally, scatter over the garam masala and coriander leaves before serving.

Egyptian Fava Bean Falafels and Sauces

SERVES 5–6
(3–4 falafels per person)
Preparation time 30 minutes, plus
overnight soaking, minimum 2 hours
cabbage pickling, and 30 minutes
cooling time
Cooking time 40 minutes

250g dried fava (broad) beans, soaked
    in water overnight then drained
2 tbsp olive oil
1 medium onion, finely chopped
3–4 garlic cloves, finely grated or
    pureed
1 tsp ground coriander
1 tsp ground cumin
½ tsp chilli powder
small bunch of flat-leaf parsley,
    finely chopped
1–3 tbsp gram (chickpea) flour or
    plain wheat flour
1 tsp salt
a really generous grinding of black
    pepper
sunflower or rapeseed oil, for
    deep-frying
1 tbsp sesame seeds

FOR THE QUICK PICKLED RED CABBAGE
½ red cabbage, very thinly sliced (use
    a mandoline if you have one)
2½ tsp salt
100ml vinegar (anything except
    balsamic vinegar)
50ml water
2 tsp caster sugar

FOR THE TURKISH CHILLI SAUCE
3 red peppers
1 small onion, peeled
2 garlic cloves
2 tomatoes, roughly chopped
2–5 fresh red chillies (depending how
    hot you want it), chopped
large handful of chopped flat-leaf
    parsley
1 tsp salt

When I think of fava beans I can't not think of the horrible Dr. Hannibal Lecter quote from *Silence of the Lambs*, 'I ate his liver with some fava beans and a nice Chianti.' This would always sucker-punch me from the sidelines, because we don't call them fava beans in the UK. To us they are broad beans, delicious broad beans, so whenever I was in the States, out of the blue a broad bean dish would stop me in my tracks, take me back to this point in that film and make me gag. It was the first indication of how a food's PR can completely change how we looked at it.

Anyway... Most people believe that falafels are made from chickpeas, and most are, but the traditional Egyptian method calls for the broad bean, which just happens to be Britain's biggest export (peas and beans are our most commonly exported vegetables). Therefore, this quintessential British ingredient is able to be put to great use with this classic Egyptian recipe and method. There's something great about us being able to utilise British produce in recipes borrowed from other cultures. Whether or not you've made falafels before, I think you'll find this a goody.

Serve the falafels warm or at room temperature with hummus, garlic sauce and/or tahini, Turkish chilli sauce, salad and quick pickled red cabbage in warm pittas.

First, make the pickled cabbage. Put the cabbage in a bowl, add ½ teaspoon of the salt and massage it into the cabbage thoroughly – this will begin to break down the cabbage ready for pickling. Put the vinegar in a small saucepan with the water, sugar and the rest of the salt. Bring to the boil and simmer until the sugar and salt have dissolved, remove from the heat, allow to cool a little, then pour over the cabbage. Leave at room temperature for a minimum of 2 hours, stirring every so often to help the cabbage take on the pickle. (You can leave it for up to 2–3 days, but the longer you leave it, the softer it will be.)

To make the Turkish chilli sauce, blacken the red peppers directly on the flame of your hob (or on hot coals for extra smokiness) for 10–15 minutes until the skins are nice and charred. Alternatively, roast them in an oven turned up to full whack until the skins are blackened. Once the peppers are cool enough to handle, peel off the skins (you don't have to be too uptight about this – a bit of the blackened skin in the mix adds a lovely charred flavour), remove the stalks and seeds and roughly chop. Blitz the onion with the garlic in a food processor, add the chopped peppers, tomatoes, red chillies, parsley, salt and sugar. Blitz at full speed until everything is

1 tsp sugar
juice of 1 lemon

FOR THE GARLIC SAUCE

2 tbsp natural yoghurt
3–4 garlic cloves, finely grated
juice of 1½ lemons
1 tsp salt
500ml sunflower oil, frozen in a
    freezerproof jug for 30 minutes

TO SERVE

warm pitta breads
shredded iceberg lettuce
thinly sliced onions sprinkled with
    sumac
thinly sliced cucumber
thinly sliced tomato
grated carrot
pickled whole chillies

well combined: it doesn't have to be super smooth, just the consistency of a finely chopped, thick salsa. Transfer to a bowl and stir in the lemon juice.

Give the soaked beans a good rinse and transfer to a clean saucepan of cold water. Bring to the boil and cook for 20–25 minutes or until they are cooked through but still have some bite. It's a bit of a game of Russian roulette, as the beans can go from having bite to mush in a matter of minutes. If they are overcooked, they will be sludgy when you blend them, but too firm and they'll be sandy and won't bind. You're looking for the point where you can just break them up with your fingers. Drain, then leave to dry on a tray lined with kitchen paper for 30–40 minutes until fully cooled. During this process they will steam a bit and became more evenly cooked, so you're better off draining the beans when they're on the firm side than the mushy side.

While the beans are cooling, heat the oil in a frying pan over a medium heat, add the onion and fry for 15–20 minutes until soft and a little golden. Remove from the heat, leave to cool, then mix with the cooked beans in a bowl. Add the garlic, spices, parsley, flour and seasoning. How much flour you need will depend on how wet the mix is – you need to be able to shape the mixture into small golf ball-sized rounds without them falling apart. I put 3 tablespoons in my mixture, but when I retested it, I only used 2. Some don't use any. It's really down to intuition and feel.

To make the garlic sauce, mix the yoghurt in a bowl with the grated garlic, lemon juice and salt. Pour a fine stream of the ice-cold oil very slowly into the yoghurt, whisking as you go, until the oil is completely emulsified into the yoghurt and you have a thick garlicky sauce.

Heat the oil in a wok or deep-fryer to 160°C (a high-quality cooking thermometer or jam thermometer is good for testing, if you're using a wok), and while it's heating up shape the mixture into 20–22 balls and line a plate with kitchen paper. Deep-fry the falafel in three or four batches for 4–5 minutes per batch until nicely crisp and golden. Remove with a spider utensil or slotted metal spoon and drain on the lined plate.

To build the kebab, take a warm pitta bread and open up the pocket. Put iceberg lettuce in the bottom, followed by a good helping of the pickled cabbage, onions sprinkled with sumac, cucumber, tomato and grated carrot. Place as many falafels as you can fit on top, followed by a generous amount of garlic sauce, chilli sauce and a pickled chilli or two. Then attempt to get it all into your mouth!

Cheese Semolina Grits

SERVES 8 as a side dish
Preparation time 5 minutes
Cooking time 30 minutes

2 litres fresh chicken or vegetable
  stock
250g semolina
1 sprig of thyme
1 tsp sea salt, plus more to taste
120g Cheddar, grated
30g Parmesan, grated
30g butter
pinch of cayenne
pinch of ground white pepper
truffle oil (optional)

Many people have been traumatised by memories of semolina from the grey slop served at school (although, perversely, I actually loved the stuff), but this is an entirely different proposition. Think of this more along the lines of classic cheesy polenta, but instead of polenta I'm using semolina which is a wheat-based flour that grows in abundance in the UK, and is excellent value. When we were testing this recipe, we happened to have some truffle Cheddar which was actually a very welcome addition, as is a lick of truffle oil, but it works just as well with plain Cheddar.

This is the perfect accompaniment to my Braised Beef Shin with Barbecue Sauce on page 199, or the Antipasto on pages 43–44.

Stir the chicken stock, semolina, thyme and salt together in a medium saucepan and bring to the boil. Reduce the heat to very low and simmer for 30 minutes. Initially it will just look like murky yellow water, but have patience: it will come together pretty quickly as the water is absorbed by the semolina grains.

Keep whisking it regularly, to avoid the semolina scorching at the bottom of the pan. Once it has a nice, thick gloopy consistency similar almost to a wet mash, mix in the cheeses, butter, cayenne and pepper. Season with salt to taste.

Remove from the heat and leave the grits to stand for a minute or two before serving, so it firms up slightly (but don't let it develop a skin). If using truffle oil, stir in a little drizzle now, before serving.

Three Ways with Mexican Braised Pinto Beans

SERVES 4–6
Preparation time 10 minutes, plus overnight soaking
Cooking time 3 hours 30 minutes

2 tbsp olive oil
3 onions, finely chopped
1 head of garlic, halved widthways
1 tbsp ground coriander
1 tbsp ground cumin
500g dried pinto beans, soaked in water overnight
1 dried ñoras secas pepper
2 dried guindilla peppers
3 vine-ripened tomatoes, quartered
2 bay leaves
a few sprigs of thyme
2 sprigs of rosemary
2 litres water
sea salt flakes
cooked rice, to serve

This is a base recipe that can be turned into various things. In the same way I would make a roast with a huge roasting joint then use the leftovers in other meals, I can make these braised beans and the leftovers can become a few different dishes. Classically, I love them with rice or in fresh hot tortillas (I won't pretend that I don't love them with a slow-cooked pork or heavily-spiced grilled prawns and some fried green plantain, but they are a plant-based dish). The next day, you can fry them up as refried beans, which I like to eat hot on tortilla chips with melted cheese, guacamole, salsa, sour cream and jalapeño pickles, or you can make it into a bean 'sopas' which is a smooth and brothy bean soup dotted with sour cream, Fairtrade avocado, smoked chillies and coriander. It's the dish that keeps on giving.

I have used dried Mexican chilli peppers, which you can buy online and in specialist food shops, and even grow yourself, but a couple of dried red chillies would also be super.

Heat the oil in a heavy-based casserole dish over a medium-low heat, add the onions and sweat them gently for 30 minutes until they become soft, sticky and golden. Add the garlic bulb halves for the last few minutes, cut side down, and fry until they begin to caramelise. Add the ground coriander and cumin and fry for a minute or two, stirring, then drain the beans and add them to the dish along with the dried peppers, tomatoes, bay leaves, thyme and rosemary. Pour over the water, cover with a lid and cook gently over a low heat for 2–3 hours, until the sauce has reduced to a thick, soupy consistency. The peppers will break down into the sauce as they cook. Remove the herb sprigs and bay leaves and check for seasoning, before serving with rice.

Sopas Tarasca: Simply add 200ml of hot chicken or vegetable stock to 500g of the braised beans and blend until very smooth.

Refried beans: Heat 1–2 tablespoons of oil or lard in a frying pan. Add 500g of the braised beans, mash with a potato masher and fry over a medium-high heat while moving them around the pan constantly. You want the beans to be drying out a little and, as when making a bubble and squeak, to allow some crispy caramelisation to occur.

Marmite, Onion and Roast Root Vegetable Stew with Cheesy Scones

SERVES 6
Preparation time 25 minutes
Cooking time 1 hour 45 minutes

2–3 tbsp oil
5 onions, thinly sliced
5 garlic cloves, finely chopped
40g dried porcini mushrooms
1 parsnip, peeled and cut in half
   lengthways
2 carrots, peeled
1 tsp tomato puree
1 tsp English mustard
1 tbsp plain flour
250ml red or white wine
250ml dark ale
1 tsp Marmite
1 tbsp red wine vinegar
1 tbsp brown sauce
2 bay leaves
1–2 sprigs of rosemary
400g tin carlin peas
sea salt and freshly ground black
   pepper

FOR THE CHEESY SCONES
(MAKES 8–10 SCONES)
350g self-raising flour
1 tsp English mustard powder
¼ tsp cayenne
1 tsp salt
200g cold butter, cut into cubes
100g whatever cheese you have to
   hand (hard and blue cheeses are
   ideal), cut into small cubes
1 tbsp Marmite
200ml buttermilk
40g Parmesan, grated
plain flour, for dusting
1 free-range egg, whisked

Carlin peas are a heritage British pea. They are very similar to the chickpea, but a little bit smaller and in my opinion more delicious, with a much better bite. Think of this stew as a deeply concentrated onion soup studded with these peas and some roasted root vegetables, giving it the full body of a meat stew. I have deliberately not done a vegetable stew until now, as I've never quite achieved that combination of umami, depth and richness, but while developing a vegetarian French onion soup for my restaurant, The Nitery, I rediscovered how valuable the onion is in getting intense savoury flavour into a sauce base. The stew is delicious on its own but, my god, it's something else topped like a cobbler with these cheesy scones. If you want to leave out the scones, it's also great with mash.

The scones can be veganised with high-quality vegan butter and cheese, and non-dairy yoghurt in place of the buttermilk. They are delicious on their own, as well as baked on the stew – bake them as they are on a lined baking tray in an oven preheated to 220°C/200°C fan/gas mark 7 for 13 minutes, until risen and golden.

First, you want to get your onions on for the stew. Heat 2 tablespoons of the oil in a heavy-based ovenproof casserole dish over a medium heat and throw in the onions. Cook them right down, very slowly, for 40 minutes–1 hour, so they develop that deep sweetness, richness and body, as well as the kind of umami you can only achieve through long cooking. Stir them regularly to prevent any scorching, and add the garlic about 20 minutes into cooking.

Place the dried mushrooms in a bowl and cover with warm water to rehydrate. Set aside. Meanwhile, preheat the oven as hot as it can go (about 260°C/240°C fan/ gas mark 10).

Spread the parsnip and carrots on a baking tray, rub with the remaining oil and a sprinkling of salt. Roast in the oven for 20 minutes, turning them halfway through cooking. Remove from the oven when the time is up, set aside and turn the oven down to 200°C/180°C fan/gas mark 6.

About 35 minutes into the cooking of the onions, stir in the tomato puree and mustard. Cook for a minute or two, then add the flour. Stir thoroughly for a further

CONTINUED ››

minute before pouring in the wine and ale. Stir in the Marmite, vinegar and brown sauce. Strain the mushrooms, reserving the soaking liquor, dry them on kitchen paper then shred them into fine strips like the onions. Add both the mushrooms and the liquor to the stew (leaving the last bit of liquor at the bottom in case there is any grit), along with the bay and rosemary. Drain the peas and add them to the casserole dish.

Place the stew in the oven, uncovered, for 35 minutes. While it's bubbling away, slice the roasted roots into nice chunks (I like to cut them diagonally across the middle). Add them to the stew after it's been cooking for 35 minutes, return to the oven and cook for a further 15 minutes. After the cooking time has elapsed, stir in a teaspoon of salt and a good grinding of black pepper.

While the stew is in the oven, make the scone dough. Put the flour, mustard powder, cayenne and salt in a food processor and blitz briefly to remove any lumps. Add the butter and blitz again until it has a sandy texture.

In a small bowl, mix the cubes of cheese with the Marmite so that they are well coated (this is a bit messy, but it works best to use your hands).

Put the flour and butter mixture in a mixing bowl. With a knife, mix in the buttermilk, half the grated Parmesan, and the Marmitey cheese until well distributed. Turn out this mixture onto a flat, floured surface and bring it together briefly with your hands into a smooth dough. Roll out the dough with a floured rolling pin until it is 4cm thick. Cut out 8–10 scones with a 7cm round cutter. Brush the tops with whisked egg to glaze and sprinkle over the rest of the Parmesan.

Place the cut rounds of dough on top of the stew, turn the oven up to 220°C/ 200°C fan/gas mark 7 and cook for 13 minutes, until the scones are risen and golden.

Remove from the oven and serve.

Mushy Peas

SERVES 4 as a side dish
Soaking time minimum of 2 hours,
maximum overnight
Cooking time 20 minutes (or 1 hour
for marrowfat peas), plus 30 minutes
standing time

250g organic split green peas
1 tsp baking powder, plus a pinch
500ml water, or vegetable or chicken
    stock, for split peas (or 1 litre for
    marrowfat peas)
½ tsp celery salt (optional)
pinch of sea salt

It's well known that one of Britain's most famous dishes is fish and chips. The middle classes have brought mashed garden peas into the equation, but I prefer the traditional mushy pea. It's a totally different thing, and for me you can't beat that texture or mellow flavour which you only get with proper mushy peas. Traditionally we use marrowfat peas, but I find it really easy to work with split peas (which also grow in the UK) and, dare I say it, they end up sweeter and tastier. Of course you can use marrowfat peas, just be aware that they take about an hour longer to cook, and you will need double the amount of liquid – I have given you amounts for both, so it's up to you. I can't resist reaching for stock to cook them in, but they work well just cooked in water too.

Put the peas in a bowl with enough cold water to cover and leave to soak for a minimum of 2 hours, maximum overnight, with the teaspoon of baking powder. This helps begin the process of breaking down the structure of the pea, to get that classic mushy pea texture. Once soaked, drain and rinse the peas under cold running water. Transfer to a saucepan and add the stock or water. Add the extra pinch of baking powder and bring to the boil. The baking powder foams up and looks initially as if it needs to be skimmed off, but don't fear – it is just there to help break down the peas.

Lower the temperature and simmer the split peas for 20 minutes (or 1 hour if using marrowfat peas). For the final 5 minutes of cooking add the celery salt and sea salt. The celery salt helps to give the peas a slightly rounder umami flavour, but if you don't have it just substitute it with regular sea salt.

After the cooking time has elapsed, remove from the heat and leave it to stand for 30 minutes so that the peas absorb any excess liquid. They will really thicken up during this time, and traditionally mushy peas are served warm rather than piping hot. Check for seasoning and serve.

Barley and Mushroom Risotto with Pan-roasted King Oyster

SERVES 4
Preparation time 15 minutes
Cooking time 40 minutes

30g dried porcini mushrooms
300ml warm water
5–6 tbsp oil
1 onion, finely chopped
6 garlic cloves, finely chopped
a few sprigs of thyme, leaves picked
2 sprigs of rosemary, leaves finely
  chopped
220g pearl barley
350ml white wine
500ml fresh chicken or vegetable
  stock
250g chestnut mushrooms, thinly
  sliced
250ml oat cream
grated zest of 1 lemon
4 king oyster mushrooms, halved
  lengthways, the cut faces scored in
  cross-hatch pattern
1 tbsp nutritional yeast or grated
  Parmesan
handful of flat-leaf parsley, leaves
  finely chopped
white truffle oil (optional) or olive oil
sea salt and freshly ground black
  pepper

We are great at growing barley in this country, driven in a large part by our deep love of beer. We're well acquainted with the classic rice risotto, but barley has a nuttiness that is a brilliant foundation for the earthiness of mushrooms. King oyster mushrooms are a treat and, as cultivated mushrooms such as these are cultured, they are available all year round. Porcinis are full of savouriness and have a meaty texture too, and the umami nature of this dish is heightened all the more by white truffle oil (if you have any). I've got into oat cream lately (see page 172), and it makes perfect sense to pair it with barley, as they are both British cereal crops. To make this dish vegan, use nutritional yeast instead of Parmesan and vegetable stock instead of chicken.

Soak the dried mushrooms in a bowl with the warm water for at least 20 minutes.

Heat 2 tablespoons of the oil in a large saucepan over a medium heat, add the onion and sweat for 5 minutes, then add the garlic, thyme and rosemary. Cook for 5–10 minutes, then add the barley. Stir for a couple of minutes to coat it in the oil, add the wine and let it bubble for a minute or two to cook off some of the alcohol, then add the stock and the mushroom soaking water (leave the last bit in the bowl as it can be gritty). Roughly chop the porcini then add them to the pan and bring to a low simmer.

Meanwhile, heat another 2 tablespoons of oil in a separate frying pan over a high heat, add half the sliced chestnut mushrooms and fry until they start to caramelise and release some of their juices. Add the mushrooms to the risotto then fry the remaining chestnut mushrooms, but keep these aside for serving at the end.

Simmer the risotto, stirring regularly. Barley takes longer to cook than risotto rice, so be patient. About 15 minutes after adding the mushrooms, stir in the oat cream and lemon zest. Cook for a further 10 minutes, until the barley is cooked through but still retains a little bite.

When the barley is almost done, heat the frying pan again with another 1–2 tablespoons of oil over a high heat. Add the oyster mushrooms, cut side down and fry for 5–6 minutes, turning halfway through and allowing them to develop golden caramelisation.

To finish the risotto, remove from the heat, stir through the yeast or Parmesan, the remaining chestnut mushrooms, parsley, and a good grind of pepper. Season and serve with two pieces of oyster mushroom per person, and a drizzle of truffle or olive oil.

Bibimbap

SERVES 2
Preparation time 45 minutes
Cooking time 15 minutes

200g sushi rice
400ml water
1 tbsp sesame oil
2 tbsp sunflower oil
150g spinach
1 courgette, thinly sliced
1 large carrot, finely julienned
100g beansprouts
6 spring onions, shredded
100g shiitake mushrooms, thinly
   sliced
1 corn on the cob
2 free-range egg yolks
300g rump steak, finely chopped
sea salt and freshly ground black
   pepper
1 tbsp black or white toasted sesame
   seeds, to serve

FOR THE SAUCE

6 tbsp gochujang
2 tbsp Korean or Japanese soy sauce
1 tbsp rice wine vinegar
2 tbsp sesame oil
1½ tbsp caster sugar

One of my breakthroughs was bringing attention to Korean food in the UK back in about 2007. While working as a chef in NYC, I'd hit Koreatown in my downtime with my mates, drink ice-cold beers and eat Korean fried chicken. Koreatown was open late, and you could go from restaurant to karaoke bar eating and drinking yourself into a stupor. I fell in love with Korean food there, and fell in love with the culture 5 years later when I first visited Korea, later moving there to film my TV show *Seoul Food*. I'm certain that the popular 'buddha bowl' has Korean culinary heritage, as it's similar to a dish called 'bibimbap'. In a bibimbap bowl, rice is topped with vegetables, meat (optional), egg yolk and a spicy sauce. It is quite refined – you can't say that about a lot of Korean food – and is cooked in a searing hot cast-iron pot which is oiled before adding the rice; the vegetables and egg (and meat, if using) are swiftly put on top. By the time the rice gets to the table it has a fantastic caramelised crust that you peel away from the pot and you stir-fry everything at the table. It's real theatre. Fear not if you don't have cast-iron pots – you can eat it like Hawaiian poke, in a bowl with hot rice. Bibimbap is delicious, healthy and a great way to tackle a fridge forage. I've used traditional toppings, but do play around with seafood, tofu and different veg: the only mainstays are the rice, egg yolk and sauce.

Put the rice and water in a large saucepan with a good pinch of salt. Cover, bring to a simmer and cook for 12 minutes. Take off the heat and steam (lid on) for 10 minutes.

Gently heat the sauce ingredients in a small saucepan until emulsified. Set aside.

Mix together the sesame and sunflower oils. Heat a large wok or frying pan over a high heat, add 1 tablespoon of the oil mix and add half the spinach with a pinch of salt. Cook briefly until wilted, then remove and drain on kitchen paper, squeezing out any liquid. Repeat with the remaining spinach. Add another splash of oil and briefly fry the courgette until golden. Remove and set aside. Repeat this process with the carrot, beansprouts, spring onions and shiitake mushrooms. Rub the sweetcorn cob with oil, salt and pepper, then brown in the pan until the kernels start to char.

Heat two stone bibimbap dishes or a wok on the hob until smoking hot. Place the stone dishes on a heatproof surface (if using). Brush the insides of the dishes (or hot wok) with the remaining oil and add the rice. Group vegetables around the edge, put the raw meat in the middle, then the egg yolks and 2 tablespoons of the sauce for each serving. Top with sesame seeds. Mix the sauce into the rice at the table with a spoon.

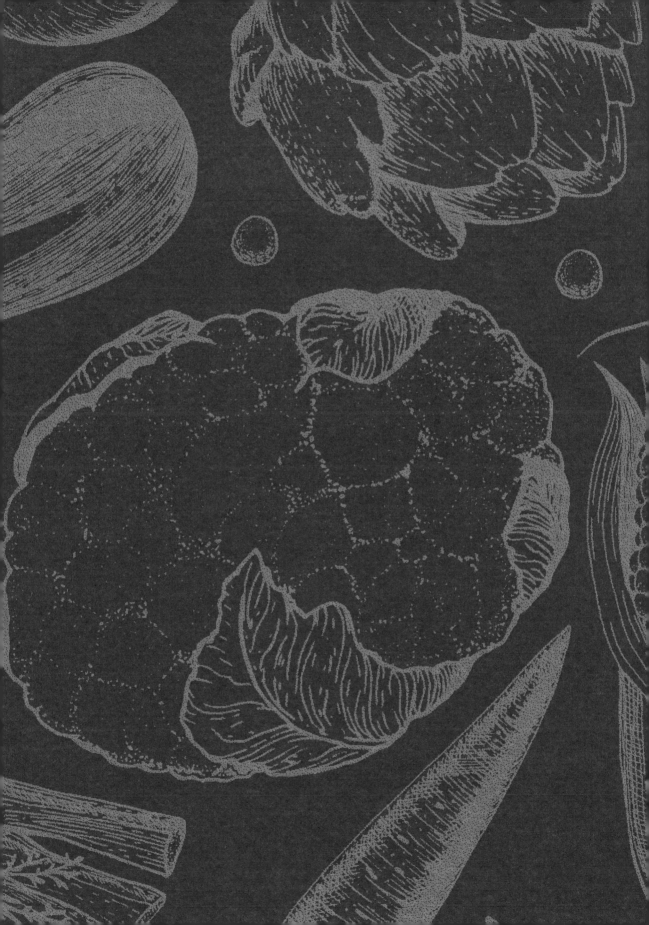

SUGAR, FLOUR, FAT, EGGS & MILK

FATS AND OILS

Fat, particularly lard, butter and dripping, have been wrongly perceived to be unhealthy and 'fattening' since the early 20th century. The origin of this belief is one of the biggest cons in food history, and it all began in North America in the 1900s. Cotton production was booming, and one of the by-products of this industry was cotton seed. At first it was used as fertiliser, then it was used as animal feed, then a process was invented to extract oil from the seed and then to stabilise it by hydrogenating it (meaning it would keep for long periods of time). Vegetable oil was born and a huge money-spinner was on the horizon. Due to one of the first truly modern, psychologically propagandist advertising campaigns ever seen, this oil would eventually become the dominant fat, eclipsing lard and butter. More money was spent on the marketing of this food product than any other up until this point in history, and a large part of the campaign was promoting and instilling a huge myth into the minds of the general populace: that this cheap oil was healthier than 'artery clogging' fats such as butter, lard and beef dripping. Thus, the world turned its back on animal fat. It was a perfect example of big business putting profit before the truth and, more importantly, before the health of the consumer.

Nothing could be further from the reality. Modern diseases in the western world such as diabetes and heart disease have skyrocketed since the mainstream introduction of factory fats like these vegetable oils, and margarines, into our diets. What's more, the fields of genetically modified, pesticide-drowned synthetically fertilised monocultures of corn, palm and soybeans (among others) required to produce these oils is hardly something to aspire to.

It's important to make informed choices when choosing which fat to buy and cook with. As with so many food products, no product is 'squeaky clean' on both the environment and health stakes, so it's a case of weighing up the information and choosing where to make the smallest compromises possible. It's complicated, but this is the world we live in.

Ghee

I've been using ghee (clarified butter) more and more in my cooking, as it is one of the healthier fats, full of vitamins and omegas 3 and 9. The clarification process removes the milk solids so it can be heated to a higher temperature, and it is so easy to make at home: simply melt butter in a pan and you will start to see froth appear on the surface. Skim this off. The butter fat will have separated and there will be a clear yellow liquid and a more milky white layer below it. Carefully pour off the top yellow layer of fat and there you have your ghee. Discard the milky residue or use it in whey recipes. Ghee from grass-fed cows is increasingly widely available.

Frying oils

I find it frustrating how rife homogenised and refined cooking oils are in the oil market, and particularly in professional kitchens. Most chefs don't realise that the 'light' (refined) rapeseed oil they use has e-numbers in it for consistency, 'anti foaming' or to maintain the 'flash point' (how hot it can get before burning). These are things that we lived happily without for years.

The best fish and chip shops use beef dripping, which is a pure and a brilliantly sustainable option, giving beefy flavour to chips and the batter: potatoes, animal fats and salt are magic food unions. However, this is problematic for a plant-based diet, so what is the best alternative fat?

Let's take a look at sunflower and rapeseed oil, which are both nutritionally dense. Opting for cold pressed oils is better than refined homogenised oils as they are made from the first press, the oils are more dense and thick, and they still contain all the naturally occurring vitamins and antioxidants.

Rapeseed oil has become really popular in recent years. It has the lowest level of saturated fat compared to other widely used oils and has a high 'flash point', so you can fry with it, but I tend to use it in the same way as I use olive oil, in salads and as a base everyday cooking oil, as the yellow pressed rapeseed oil is too heavy for frying most food. Despite it being grown in large swathes as a monoculture crop, its lurid yellow flowers are full of pollen and are a brilliant source of food for bees. A recent ban on an insecticide that was previously used on this crop makes it better environmentally, and another plus point is that it's grown in the UK, so has minimal food miles and by buying it we're supporting our farmers. Crop surpluses are currently being sold to Germany to be turned into bio diesel, so it's pretty good in the sustainability stakes.

I'm not giving up fried foods (eaten in moderation) any time soon, so it's worth knowing which ones are the good guys and how to choose a light oil that has almost definitely been purified to release the dominant plant colours, flavours and odours. Pure sunflower oil, just as with pure rapeseed, is too heavy and too strongly flavoured for frying: I prefer to deep-fry with 'pure light organic' sunflower or refined rapeseed oils over anything else. Oil for deep-frying needs to be a little refined, but that's not always a bad thing (again, in moderation).

Olive oil

I use olive oil for Mediterranean food and dressings. Olives are still grown in the traditional method – and there are so many good growers out there – but many of the ancient olive groves are dying because of lack of water and a deadly olive tree disease driven by a horrible pathogen being passed on by 'spittlebugs' that started in Italy and is now spreading through Spain, Greece and France. The olive farmers need our support, and one way we can do this is by buying good olive oil. We must hope that the solution doesn't end up being that genetically modified olive trees become the norm, but it's looking bleak.

Coconut oil

I've written about my feelings on coconut oil on page 173, and in general it is something I choose to avoid unless the recipe absolutely demanded it, from a sustainability point of view as well as a chef's one. Even the flavourless coconut oils reek of coconut flavour and I only find them of value in Asian or middle or South American coconutty recipes, or in place of butter in baking. Use it in moderation.

Rendering fat from meat

Lard, an amazing source of vitamin D, with high levels of monounsaturated fat, is one of the healthier fats. It was used for centuries, when each pig that was killed would be completely utilised, and it is time to reclaim its joys. In the spirit of making the most of the occasions when we do eat meat, it is only right that we learn to value every potential opportunity to avoid waste, and that goes for the fat, too!

There are two methods of rendering lard, wet rendering and dry rendering. With wet rendering, the fat is simply melted down with a little water. This lard has a more neutral flavour and paler colour than dry rendering, which follows the same process but with the water omitted, and tends to result in a slightly browner fat with a more porky flavour. When buying lard in the supermarket, watch out for anything that has been bleached, mixed with hydrogenated oil or generally messed about with. The best way to ensure excellent lard (and dripping too) is to make it yourself. Any good butcher will be more than happy to unload excess pig fat to you for a minimal price (often giving it to you for free). Lard is the best fat to use in both savoury and sweet pastry, resulting in an unexpectedly light and crisp texture, but still with a special richness you can't get any other way.

Beef dripping might be one of my favourite things in life. It helps you absorb nutrients from your food, and is rich in vitamins A, D, E, K and B1, and CLA (nature's best metabolic stabiliser and anti-inflammatory). Any decent cook knows that good flavour in meat comes from good fat content, and the higher quality the meat, the higher quality the fat. Older generations among us will recall beef dripping being a household staple, and I think it is starting to make a comeback, especially since science has started to uncover the truth about fat not being the enemy that the 20th century purported it to be. Everyone knows it makes the best chips or roast potatoes, providing an unrivalled depth of flavour. At my restaurant, The Nitery, we make our own dripping from the roast beef on Sundays, render it down, mix it with Marmite and spread it over brioche to provide the most delicious foundation for steak tartare. It couldn't be simpler to make lard: just heat beef

fat gently in a saucepan or the oven (being careful to avoid roasting it), until it has melted away from any connective tissue and become a clear liquid, then strain. Like lard, it will keep for over a month and can be used two or three times. Once it gets darkish brown, throw it away.

Rendering fat from meat (you can do the same with chicken) is the ultimate in cost effectiveness, and for me this process completely encapsulates a large part of the ethos of this book; to value every part of the animal and avoid waste wherever possible, harnessing a few forgotten skills from the past in the process.

Palm oil

Palm oil has become a dirty word for anyone vaguely environmentally conscious. The growth of massive commercial palm oil operations in Indonesia and Malaysia has seen the deforestation of vast tracts of rainforest and caused the decimation of populations of some of the world's most endangered animals, including tigers and orangutans. It's impossible to ignore that it's been deforestation for expanding palm plantations that has pushed farm land into the jungle; the movement of these animals into human areas has been deemed responsible by the WWF for causing pandemics such as COVID-19 and this will continue in the future.

Palm oil can be found in an almost limitless number of products. According to the WWF, nearly half of all pre-packaged products, from bread to shampoo, contain palm oil. It is everywhere, and demand is only growing.

Sadly, replacing palm plantations with other similar vegetable oil crops such as rapeseed or soy would require even more land than palm, so this does not fix the problem, and an out-and-out ban is simply unrealistic. The demand is not going to go away, and boycotting it would most likely shift production to other parts of the world where it could be even more unregulated.

Attempts have been made to manage this situation. In 2004, the RSPO (Roundtable on Sustainable Palm Oil) was formed with the mission to enforce rules and regulations in an attempt to reduce the environmental impact of palm plantations. The aim is to create wildlife zones on farms, not clear any primary forest, ensure transparent supply chains, protect workers' rights and monitor carbon emissions. This body has certainly not escaped criticism (especially from wildlife charities, which don't believe the measures go far enough), but in 2016, 75 per cent of palm oil imported into the UK fell within these sustainable guidelines so we're moving in the right direction.

In the majority of the recipes in this book I leave it up to you which oil or fat you use, but here's a list of fats and oils I opt for, and for what purposes:

General cooking
olive oil
rapeseed oil
ghee
rendered animal fats

Deep-frying
light pure sunflower oil (organic if possible)
light pure rapeseed oil (organic if possible)
beef dripping

Baking
butter
lard
coconut oil

Sourdough Doughnuts with White Chocolate Custard and Sour Cherry Jam

MAKES 20 doughnuts
Preparation time 30 minutes, plus 24 hours rising and 48 hours proving
Cooking time 20 minutes (for all 20 doughnuts)

FOR THE DOUGH

650g strong white flour
60g caster sugar
7g sachet of dried yeast
35g Sourdough Starter (pages 270–71)
150ml tepid water
4 free-range eggs, whisked
125g butter, melted

FOR COOKING

about 2 litres sunflower or rapeseed oil, for deep-frying, plus extra for greasing
caster sugar, for tossing

FOR THE WHITE CHOCOLATE AND VANILLA PÂTISSIÈRE CUSTARD

250ml whole milk
1 vanilla pod, split lengthways and seeds scraped out
10g plain flour
10g cornflour
50g caster sugar
4 free-range egg yolks
200g white chocolate, broken into pieces
200ml whipping cream

400g Sour Cherry Jam (see A Glut of Jams on page 110), blitzed to a puree

You will need a stand mixer and 2 piping bags.

I feel like I'm cheating by calling this a sourdough doughnut, but I guess it will leave you as cheated as I felt when I learnt that you were allowed to call an activated dried yeast that had spent 48 hours proving in the fridge a 'sour dough' (hang your heads in shame, all you pizzerias and supermarkets with your 'sourdoughs'). If you use a proper sourdough dough for doughnuts, they can be mighty heavy. The British-style ones often have other raising agents in them like baking powder, to make them lighter, and sourdough maestros could perhaps show you a fully fledged sourdough number, but my confidence is not there yet and there is a lot to be said for the slow fermenting of dried yeast with a bit of sourdough starter, where the yeast activates in the starter's hydration stage. A doughnut dough is considered an enriched dough because of the amount of butter and egg yolks (fats) it contains. The addition of sourdough starter with the dried yeast gives the dough a better chance of a super rise, and encourages the aggressive yeastiness of the dried yeast to dissipate into the air as the dough rises. The longer you prove it, the sourer it tastes and the less abrasive the flavour – think of a sour beer, rather than a heavy, yeasty taste.

This doughnut dough takes two days to make, but it's bloody nice, especially when the doughnuts are filled with white chocolate and vanilla pâtissière custard and sour cherry jam (or rhubarb or raspberry jam). The dough freezes well.

First, make your dough. Put all of the dough ingredients, except the butter and the eggs, in the bowl of a stand mixer fitted with a dough hook and mix well. With your mixer at medium speed, add the eggs and allow them to become incorporated before pouring in the warm melted butter. Beat for about 8 minutes, until the dough starts to come away from the sides of the bowl and forms a ball. Transfer to a larger oiled bowl, cover with oiled cling film (to prevent sticking) and leave in a warm place, like an airing cupboard or a sunny windowsill, until doubled in size. As this is a very enriched dough, and it contains sourdough starter, it will need a slow rise, so be patient! Leave it for a full day (9–12 hours) and then overnight. The next day, take huge pleasure in knocking all the air out of the dough, then give it a little knead to ensure any extra air is squeezed out. Return the dough to the cleaned and re-oiled bowl, cover with oiled cling film and leave in the fridge for another 2 days for a very, very slow prove.

If you are organised, you can make the crème pâtissière the day before portioning the dough and frying the doughnuts – it benefits from being chilled overnight (or, make it while the proved and portioned pieces of dough are rising).

For the crème pâtissière, heat the milk in a saucepan with the vanilla seeds over a medium heat, but don't let it boil. Mix the flours and sugar in a large bowl and whisk in the egg yolks to form a smooth paste, then once the milk is warm, slowly pour it into the egg mixture, whisking as you go. It will quickly thicken. Once all the milk is added, you can pass it through a sieve for a really smooth, silky crème. Leave to cool.

Gently melt the chocolate in a heatproof bowl over a pan of simmering water. In a separate bowl, whisk the cream until relatively stiff but not over-whipped. Fold the cream and melted chocolate thoroughly but gently into the cooled custard, until well combined and smooth. Chill, if made ahead, or set aside while you fry the doughnuts.

After two days' proving, take the dough out of the fridge, knock it back once more and cut it into 20 × 50g pieces. (You can freeze the dough portions at this stage, separated in an airtight container for up to 6 months, or chill to cook the next day.) Using oiled hands, roll the pieces into smooth, taut, round buns and place them on a baking tray lined with greaseproof paper, leaving plenty of space between them. Cover with oiled cling film and prove in a warm place for 3–4 hours, until doubled in size. (If proving from frozen, leave them to prove for 6–10 hours.)

Once the dough has risen for the second time you are ready to fry your doughnuts! Pour the oil into a large, heavy-based saucepan so that it comes to just under the halfway point of the pan (or use a deep-fat fryer), heat it to 170°C and line a tray with kitchen paper. Carefully remove the doughnut dough pieces from the baking tray with a spatula, making sure you don't deflate them, then drop them into the oil. Fry 4 or 5 at a time (so the oil temperature doesn't drop) for about 4 minutes on each side until they puff up and bob to the surface, turning them over carefully with a metal spoon until evenly golden all over. These doughnuts benefit from a slower fry than you might expect. Transfer the cooked doughnuts to the lined tray to drain any excess oil and cool a little. Tip some caster sugar onto a plate and, while they are still warm, roll the doughnuts to cover them in sugar.

Now you are ready to fill your doughnuts. Fill two piping bags fitted with round nozzles with some of the custard and sour cherry jam respectively. Make an incision into the centre of each doughnut with a sharp knife, being careful not to pierce it all the way through. Insert the piping bag deep into the doughnut and squeeze the bag firmly to ensure a healthy amount of filling goes in. Be generous. I cannot abide a meanly filled doughnut! Finally, try not to eat the whole lot in one go.

Garbage Pail Cookies – a homage to Momofuku Milk Bar

MAKES about 28 cookies
Preparation time 10 minutes, plus 30 minutes minimum chilling time
Cooking time 7–8 minutes

250g light muscovado sugar
120g golden granulated sugar
250g butter, at room temperature, cut into cubes
1 free-range egg
1 tsp vanilla extract
300g plain flour
1 tsp baking powder
½ tsp salt

500g combination of any of the following, including at least 150g chocolatey things:
    porridge oats
    mixed chocolate or caramels
    marshmallows/dried fruit
    rice crispies/cornflakes/any cereal/ pretzels/ready-salted crisps
    nuts, such as peanuts or hazelnuts

This is a great way to use up not only Easter eggs, chocolate drops or forgotten chocolate at the back of the cupboard, but also other miscellaneous snacks – anything from pretzels and ready-salted crisps, cereal and oats to Turkish delight and marshmallows. You can pretty much put whatever you want in these. I can't take glory for the recipe: a Momofuku pastry chef called Christina Tosi had this brilliantly useful and witty idea years and years ago, and this is my variation on it. I wanted to share the concept with you all.

Cream together both the sugars with the butter using an electric handheld whisk, or a food processor fitted with the whisk attachment. Once it has become pale and creamy, add the egg and the vanilla extract and continue mixing for about 5 minutes. Combine the flour, baking powder and salt then add to the butter and sugar mixture and continue to mix until well combined. Now add the ingredients of your choice, making sure that whatever you decide to use, the final weight comes to 500g: you can use any combination of flavours and textures you like and have to hand. It's best to mix them into the dough with your hands so as not to break the dough up too much. When everything is well distributed, wrap the dough in cling film or greaseproof paper and put in the fridge to chill for a minimum of 30 minutes.

Preheat the oven to 200°C/180°C fan/gas mark 6 and line two baking trays with baking parchment.

Unwrap the dough and mould it into about 28 × 50g balls. Put a few dough balls, well spaced out, on the lined baking trays (the cookies do spread quite a lot while cooking, so you may need to bake them in batches). Bake in the oven for 7–8 minutes, until they have begun to turn slightly golden but are still quite soft.

Remove from the oven and allow the cookies to cool briefly before eating (they are irresistible warm, with a glass of cold milk). They keep well in an airtight container for a few days.

Burnt Basque Country Cheesecake with Gooseberries in Green Wine

SERVES 8–10
Preparation time 20 minutes
Cooking time 30 minutes

oil or butter, for greasing
350g cream cheese
180g sour or single cream
20g plain flour
160g caster sugar
1 tsp vanilla extract (I love the seedy
    one) or the seeds scraped from
    1 vanilla pod
grated zest of 1 lemon
pinch of salt
3 free-range eggs plus 1 extra
    egg yolk

**FOR THE GOOSEBERRIES IN
GREEN WINE**

300g gooseberries, topped and tailed
70g caster sugar
100ml dry green or white wine,
    preferably Vino Verde or Alvarinho

You will need a 21cm springform
cake tin (9cm deep).

Going to San Sebastián for the first time was one of my most eye-opening food trips. Nowhere else can I think of has so many great restaurants and tapas bars in such a small vicinity. San Sebastián is right by the Basque country and if you ever visit, I would bid you to go to Asador Etxebarri in the hills: the restaurant is about excellent produce cooked over wood and going there changed my life. The area is famous for its outstanding cheesecake that's cooked in a very hot oven, puffs up like a soufflé, scorches a little, and has a gooey middle when cool. I love the one at Brat Restaurant in Shoreditch so much that I harangued chef and owner Tomas Parry for the recipe. I'm a 'more is more' girl so I've given it a Gizzi spin, adding vanilla and lemon zest. Served with seasonal fruits, it's a showstopper of a pudding. As the cheesecake derives from the Basque country, it makes sense to use a wine from the same region, and the sharpness of gooseberries is an excellent pairing with the floral dryness of green wine.

Preheat the oven to 260°C/240°C fan/gas mark 10 and double-line a 21cm springform cake tin (9cm deep) with baking parchment, letting the parchment come a few centimetres above the top of the tin – this protects the cheesecake and makes it easier to remove – and grease the inner and outer layers thoroughly with oil or butter.

Put all the ingredients for the gooseberries in a large shallow pan and boil over a medium heat for 5 minutes until the wine and sugar have reduced to a light syrup. The gooseberries should hold their shape. Remove and allow to cool.

Whisk the cream cheese, sour or single cream, flour, sugar, vanilla, lemon zest and salt in a bowl until smooth. Using a clean whisk and a separate bowl, whisk the eggs and yolk for 5 minutes until aerated and pale yellow, with the consistency of a loose mousse. Using a large metal spoon, fold 2 spoonfuls of eggs into the cream cheese mixture, followed by the remaining eggs (this loosens the mixture and makes it easier to fold in the rest of the eggs without beating out too much air, much like making a soufflé).

Once well combined, swiftly pour the mixture into the lined tin. Bake for 15 minutes, until the cheesecake has an almost burnt crust. Turn the oven down to 200°C/180°C fan/gas mark 6 and bake for a further 10 minutes to cook through. When the cheesecake is ready, the sides will curl in and the centre will dramatically sink – don't be alarmed; unlike other cheesecakes, this is pouffy round the sides and creamy in the middle. Remove from the oven and cool to room temperature. Serve slices of cheesecake with spoonfuls of gooseberries.

Banana Cream Pie

SERVES 8–10
Preparation time 20 minutes, plus
1 hour (or 15 minutes) chilling
Cooking time 25 minutes, plus
chilling overnight

FOR THE CRUST
300g mixed old biscuits, oats,
    crackers, cereal and ready-salted
    crisps
100g demerara sugar
140g butter, melted, plus extra for
    greasing

FOR THE FILLING
2 gelatine leaves
300g overripe bananas, peeled
80ml double cream
80ml whole milk
60g caster sugar
½ tsp salt
1 free-range egg plus 2 egg yolks
25g cornflour
a few drops of yellow food colouring
    (optional)
2 firmer bananas, sliced

FOR THE TOPPING
400ml double cream
2 tbsp icing sugar
milk or dark chocolate, for grating

You will need a 23cm pie dish.

As I write this, we are into week 8 of lockdown due to the COVID-19 pandemic. When I started writing this book I planned to include a banana bread recipe, but honestly I think we are all sick to the back teeth of Instagram pictures of homemade banana breads, so I just couldn't bring myself to do it. However, the problem of what to do with overripe bananas hasn't gone away, so may I present an even better way to use them! An extra advantage is that the base of this pie is a highly satisfying way of using up old biscuits, crackers, cereal or even crisps you might have lurking at the back of the cupboard (it might sound odd, and I wouldn't suggest any strong flavours like cheese and onion, but a bit of salty crisp is a welcome addition to the party).

To make the crust, blitz your mix of biscuits, crackers, cereal, crisps and sugar in a food processor until they resemble breadcrumbs. Pour in the melted butter and pulse briefly to combine. Grease a 23cm pie dish with a little butter and tip the crust into the dish. Compress the mixture in the base of the dish and up the sides with your hands to create an even, solid crust. Put in the fridge to firm up for about an hour (or 15 minutes in the freezer) and preheat the oven to 200°C/180°C fan/gas mark 6.

Line the chilled crust with a layer of baking parchment and fill with baking beans. Bake in the oven for 15 minutes, then remove from the oven. At this point, if you're a neat freak like me, you can trim the edges of the crust with a sharp knife. Remove the baking beans and baking parchment and set aside to cool.

Now make the filling. Soften the gelatine leaves in a bowl of cold water for 10 minutes. While they are softening, blitz the bananas in the food processor with the cream, milk, sugar, salt, egg, egg yolks and cornflour for a minute or two until completely smooth. Transfer to a saucepan and warm very slowly over a gentle heat, stirring constantly, for about 10 minutes as it gradually starts to thicken. When it has reached a smooth custard-like consistency, take it off the heat to cool slightly. Squeeze the water from the gelatine leaves then stir them into the custard until dissolved. (There is something very pleasing about a Day-Glow yellow filling, so if that takes your fancy, add a few drops of yellow food colouring to the custard.) Line the base of the pie crust with sliced bananas, pour over the custard in an even layer and chill overnight.

Whisk the double cream with the icing sugar in a bowl until it forms stiff peaks. It goes against my instincts to whip cream stiffly but here it does need to be stiff and not too sloppy. Dollop it onto the pie and finish with a generous grating of chocolate.

EGGS

Eggs are a highly nutritious and, these days, cheap food. The UK consumes over 30 million eggs a day, but 68 per cent of those are produced through intensive farming, which keeps prices down. We've all seen footage of rows upon rows of stacked cages, crammed full of distressed-looking hens being forced to lay eggs all year round, and hatcheries where chicks on conveyor belts are sucked into 'vacuums', sexed, then the males 'dispatched' (a term used in intensive farming for incineration). This is the unforgiving truth about egg farming – it's no wonder vegans and many others are so outraged.

I wish I could cite progress. The battery-cage system was banned in the UK in 2012 and has been replaced with an 'enriched cage system' which implements the use of larger cages with perches, scratch areas and nest boxes, an intensive system touted as being far more humane compared to the old battery cage system, but to me it still feels like the fundamentally wrong way to treat a living creature: the hens have no access to fresh air or daylight, there are frequent reports of severe health problems, and beak trimming and cramped conditions are still prevalent.

The whole system has an inherent disregard for the value of life and the planet's resources. Factory farmed hens are considered 'spent' when their productivity begins to drop after around one year of life, and are simply slaughtered, discarded and replaced with new hens, and the commercial grain feed used to feed factory-farmed hens is largely made up of soybeans, one of the primary crops that are having a decimating environmental impact on Earth (hens reared in free-range or organic egg-production systems can roam outside, which means their diets are supplemented with insects and vegetation). Another major issue with large-scale chicken rearing in both the egg and poultry industry is the amount of manure they produce, which at massive volumes goes from being a fertiliser for the soil into a poison and pollutant, killing plant life and increasing parasite levels in the soil. If a free-range egg or poultry farm is well managed and is not overloading the land with too many birds per acre, these issues can be avoided, and hens can have a better quality of life.

As with anything, buying better-quality food, produced with higher welfare standards, is one of the best things we can do as consumers to send a message to the market and encourage investment in these practices for the future. Growth in the free-range eggs market proves that shoppers are willing to pay a higher price for higher welfare, but the question of whether raising welfare standards diminishes the industry's environmental impact is complex: some studies suggest free-range eggs in fact have a bigger carbon footprint than intensively farmed eggs.

The conditions eggs are produced in has a direct effect on how they store nutrients. Eggs are brilliant, affordable sources of protein, and studies have proven that free-range eggs have been found to have significantly higher levels of vitamin A, E and omega 3, with lower levels of fat, cholesterol and omega 6 fatty acids compared to eggs from indoor grain-fed hens reared in an intensive system.

Throughout this book I aimed to go light on using eggs (and dairy) as – just like my attitude to meat – I think the only way we can justify eating these animal products is by doing so sparingly and with an awareness of how they were produced, from both an animal welfare and environmental perspective.

Vanilla School Cake and Custard

MAKES 9 squares, but recipe makes enough custard for 6 (you'll be hard-pressed to eat all the cake in one go)

Preparation time 10 minutes

Cooking time 30 minutes, plus cooling time

FOR THE CAKE

200g caster sugar

200g butter, at room temperature, plus extra for greasing

4 free-range eggs

200g plain flour (or swap for self-raising flour and omit the baking powder)

½ tsp baking powder

pinch of salt

2 tbsp milk

1 tbsp vanilla extract

FOR THE ICING

150g icing sugar

½ tsp vanilla extract

1 tbsp cold water

multicoloured sugar sprinkles

FOR THE VANILLA CUSTARD

30g caster sugar

35g Bird's custard powder

1 tsp vanilla extract

600ml whole milk

You will need a 23cm brownie tin.

I've been making school cake and custard for quite a while, and every time I post it on Instagram, my Instagram goes berserk, which can only be an indication of the deep-rooted love of this nostalgic British school pudding. And here it is – your classic vanilla sponge with vanilla custard. I have no shame in using Bird's custard powder, which I was surprised to learn is in fact egg free. It was developed in the 1830s and became a household name during the Second World War, as a frugal substitute for eggy custard. What I'm trying to do in this book is be economical with ingredients and resources, and with good-quality eggs being expensive, both for the wallet and the planet, it felt appropriate to put it to use here, and frankly it's a great product! I've included this cake because, when times are tight, it's good to have a store-cupboard bake that you can make with what you more than likely always have in stock.

Preheat the oven to 190°C/170°C fan/gas mark 5. Grease a 23cm brownie tin and line the base and sides with baking parchment.

Using a stand mixer fitted with the whisk attachment or a bowl and an electric handheld whisk, cream the sugar and butter for about 3 minutes until pale and creamy. This stage is really important as it's the first opportunity to get plenty of air into the mixture (you can do this stage by hand, but this method is far less efficient at breaking down the sugar crystals). Add the eggs one by one, whisking continuously (don't worry if the egg splits the mixture a little). Once all the eggs are combined, sift in the flour, baking powder (or self-raising flour) and salt and quickly mix together. Loosen the mixture with the milk and the vanilla extract.

Spoon the mixture into the lined tin, level it out and bake in the oven for 25 minutes, or until golden and cooked through. Slide a skewer into the middle of the cake, and if it comes away clean, the cake is done. Remove from the oven and set aside to cool in the tin for 15–20 minutes.

To make the icing, simply whisk the icing sugar and vanilla extract in a bowl with the water until it has a smooth pouring consistency but is not too thin. Remove the cooled cake from the tin, pour over the icing and smooth it with the back of a spatula so there is an even layer across the top. Cover generously with sprinkles and allow to set.

CONTINUED ››

Now for the custard. Mix the sugar, custard powder and vanilla extract in a heatproof bowl. Heat the milk in a saucepan until almost boiling, then add 2 tablespoons of the milk to the sugar and custard powder, mixing together to make a smooth paste. Pour in the remaining milk, mixing well, then return the whole lot to the saucepan and gently bring to the boil, stirring continuously, until it thickens.

This may be the most important part: the cake needs to be at room temperature, and the custard properly hot. Cut the cake into squares and serve it with a good helping of hot custard.

Chocolate School Cake with Chocolate Custard

Simply add 60g cocoa powder to the flour when you sift it into the creamed butter, sugar and egg mixture, followed by 1 extra tablespoon of milk.

To make chocolate icing, mix together 170g icing sugar with 50g cocoa powder, a pinch of salt and 5 tablespoons of cold water, until smooth and shiny.

To make chocolate custard, add 30g cocoa powder to the caster sugar and custard powder. The vanilla extract is optional.

Jam and Coconut Sponge

FOR THE ICING
200g smooth raspberry or strawberry jam
100g desiccated coconut

Follow the vanilla sponge recipe on page 159, but ice it with a smooth layer of jam instead (you may find it easier to spread if it's warmed up a little), then sprinkle the desiccated coconut evenly across the top.

Queso Fresco

MAKES 1.25kg
Preparation time 5 minutes
Cooking time 10–15 minutes

1.25 litres whole milk (preferably raw milk)
1 tbsp salt
juice of 1 lemon

The process utilised here is one harnessed all over the world in all kinds of simple cheesemaking, and works on the simple foundation of separating milk's curds from the whey. I think many people are scared of it because a lot of cheeses are made using rennet (a liquid made with the acid of the stomach of an animal, most commonly sheep), but vegetarian rennet is now available. Rennet is the best product for true separation and the firming up of the curds, but for making a fresh cheese like queso fresco, ricotta, cottage cheese, quark and fetas, the process is very easy and no rennet is required. I use this queso fresco in the Roast Carrots recipes on page 81, and for that the queso fresco requires a few days of ageing. Once aged, you can pop it in olive oil flavoured, perhaps, with rosemary, lemon peel and garlic. Making fresh cheese is a really fun process to get into and an insightful way of looking at early-stage cheesemaking.

Put the milk in a heavy-based saucepan with the salt. Bring to the boil and, as soon as it starts boiling, turn the heat down to the lowest flame. Stir in the lemon juice, which will begin to separate the milk into curds and whey. Keep stirring for 5–10 minutes until the milk has fully separated and you have thick, creamy lumps of curd.

Line a sieve or colander with a double layer of cheesecloth or muslin and pour the mixture through it to strain out the whey and collect the curds. At this stage you can use these curds for salads.

To go further and make a more compressed, firm cheese, gather up the sides of the cloth and give it a gentle squeeze to push out more liquid. You should be left with a single solid mass of curd. You can eat it straight away or allow it to become a bit firmer in the fridge, wrapped in the cloth, placed in a sieve with a bowl underneath, and weighted down with a couple of tins (or something similar) for a minimum of 2 hours (out of the fridge) or up to 24 hours (in the fridge).

It will keep nicely for up to 2 weeks in the fridge, in an airtight container or submerged in olive oil, and develops more of a tangy flavour as it matures.

Gözleme

SERVES 4
Preparation time 10 minutes, plus
1–2 hours for the dough to rest
Cooking time 25 minutes

FOR THE DOUGH
270g white bread flour, plus extra for
   dusting
2 tbsp oil, plus extra for greasing
7g sachet of dried yeast
pinch of sugar
3 tbsp Greek yoghurt
150ml lukewarm water

FOR THE FILLING
1 tbsp oil, plus extra for frying
½ red onion, thinly sliced
150g chard, leaves roughly chopped,
   stems more thinly chopped
150g feta cheese
15g Parmesan, grated
3 tbsp Greek yoghurt
good grating of nutmeg
pinch of cayenne
sea salt and freshly ground black
   pepper

You will need a stand mixer.

The area I live in in Hackney is home to a massive Turkish community, and you can find this quintessential Turkish fast food, known as gözleme, everywhere. Gözleme is a stuffed pastry and women can be seen in Turkish restaurants rolling out dough and cooking them on special heated griddles called 'sacs' at lightning speed: it's an art form in itself. They are filled with all sorts of things, from meat and potato to a wide array of vegetables, but the chard and cheese filling is the classic for me.

This is a bit unorthodox, but I like to finish them in a warm oven for a few minutes, as it ensures the dough is properly cooked through and the cheese has melted nicely.

Put the flour, oil, yeast, sugar, yoghurt and water in the bowl of a stand mixer fitted with a dough hook (the sugar helps activate the yeast – it won't make the dough sweet). Mix at slow speed, then once the dough begins to come together turn it up to full speed and mix for about 5 minutes. Transfer the dough to an oiled bowl, cover with cling film, and rest for 1–2 hours in a warm place until doubled in size. Knock back the dough by scraping it out of the bowl and kneading it briefly until smooth and elastic. Return to the bowl and re-cover with cling film while you make the filling.

Heat the tablespoon of oil for the filling in a large frying pan over a medium heat, add the onion and cook for about 5 minutes, then add the chard leaves and stems. Cook for a couple of minutes until the chard has wilted, then set aside. Crumble the feta into a bowl and mix in the Parmesan, yoghurt, nutmeg, cayenne, a good pinch of salt and a generous grind of pepper.

Preheat the oven to 140°C/120°C fan/gas mark 1.

When you're ready to make the gözleme, roll out a quarter of the dough on a floured surface with a flour-dusted rolling pin as thinly as you can, into a big square about 18 × 18cm. It should be stretchy, so if there's a hole just patch it back together. Spread a quarter of the cheese mixture on the dough into a 1cm-thick 10 × 15cm rectangle. Put a thin, even layer of chard on top. Fold the sides of the dough into the middle, then the top and bottom edges, to make a little parcel. Repeat with the remaining dough. Heat a frying pan or crêpe pan over a medium heat with a brush of oil. Gently fry the gözleme for about 3 minutes on each side, until golden, with a little crispness. Put them on a baking tray in the oven for 10 minutes to finish cooking. Cut into 8–10 pieces, allow to cool for a couple of minutes, and serve (or serve at room temperature).

Flatbreads

We're mid COVID-19 lockdown and I've got my sourdough starter on the go, which I share with my neighbour (the starter is called Cedric and sharing responsibility happened because he was eating more flour than I was using by making anything). I've tried making sourdough bread several times in the past and I'm going to say it: for me, it's not as much fun as Instagram lets on. I find bread-making in general a bit of a pain, but I've learnt that blending sourdoughs with a little fast-acting yeast and giving them a slow rise is more easy to get right and gives lighter results. So, if like me you love to cook, but the investment in real baking stresses you out, here are some bread recipes for the commitment-phobes.

Sourdough Flatbreads

These are terrific puffy flatbreads. You could put them in the Middle Eastern category or even consider them a little like naans – as all-rounders, they're good with grills and curries or braises, and you can also play with them to make lahmachun or even cheats' pizzas. I am lucky and I have a tiny Roccbox wood-fired outdoor pizza oven in my garden, but you can get good results from a frying pan and a really hot grill instead. You can also exchange the butter for leftover animal fat which is delicious.

MAKES 8 flatbreads
Preparation time 15 minutes, plus 2–3 hours rising time and 30 minutes resting time
Cooking time 6–8 minutes

semolina flour, for dusting
100g butter, melted

FOR THE DOUGH

250g strong white bread flour
250g Sourdough Starter (pages 270–71)
7g sachet of dried yeast
100ml milk, heated gently to blood temperature (so when you stick your finger in you can't feel it)
10g fine sea salt
1 tbsp oil, plus extra for greasing
1 tbsp caster sugar

You will need a stand mixer.

First, make the dough. Put all of the dough ingredients in a stand mixer fitted with a dough hook. Start mixing at slow speed, then gradually speed it up and mix at full power for 5–10 minutes until you have a smooth elastic dough. Transfer the dough to an oiled bowl, cover with cling film or a tea towel and leave in a warm place to rise for 2–3 hours, until it has doubled in size and you can see bubbles starting to form.

Once the dough has proved sufficiently, divide it into 8 × 90g pieces. With oiled hands, make them into balls by pulling and stretching the dough, then folding the outer edges in to create a smooth, taut surface. Leave the balls to rest, covered with cling film or a tea towel, on a semolina-floured tray or surface for about 30 minutes.

Dust a clean, flat surface with semolina flour (it isn't traditional to use semolina flour, but it burns a lot slower than normal flour, so is ideal here, where we're using a hot grill). Roll each ball out into a really thin (1–2mm) circle with a floured rolling pin, but don't be too fastidious – it doesn't have to be perfect.

Preheat the grill as hot as it will go. Sprinkle a little more semolina flour in a frying pan and get it really hot on the hob. Place a flatbread in the pan and cook for 2–3 minutes until it bubbles up and starts to look like its rising. Place the pan under the grill to cook the top (a little bit of char on the surface is a welcome thing). Finally, brush some melted butter on top. Continue this process until you've used up all of the dough, setting each one aside, covered with a tea towel to keep warm, as you go.

Rye Tortillas

We make tacos a lot, but that means using corn tortillas, so I wanted to play around with the more wholesome flavour of rye flour, a grain we grow plenty of in the UK. The nuttiness of the flour is a welcome foundation for the smokiness of lots of Mexican food, such as my Pumpkin Seed and Cocoa Mole Sauce (page 52–3). I make the small taco-sized tortillas, which are about 10cm in diameter when cooked, but you can make them full-sized (about 25cm) if you wish. They freeze well both pre and post cooking, rolled out or as dough balls. To defrost the dough, simply remove from the freezer and allow to soften at room temperature before rolling out or cooking. Make use of a tortilla press here, if you have one.

MAKES 25 taco-sized tortillas (or about 10 full-size tortillas)
Preparation time 10 minutes, plus at least 1 hour rising time
Cooking time 4 minutes each

7g sachet of dried yeast
300ml warm water
pinch of sugar
500g rye flour, plus extra for dusting
½ tsp salt
1 tbsp sesame seeds, plus extra for sprinkling (optional)
2 tsp oil

First, you need to activate the yeast. Put it in the warm water with the sugar (which will help speed up the activation process), set aside and leave for 10–15 minutes until bubbles form on the surface. Add it to the rye flour, salt, sesame seeds (if using) and oil in a bowl or in a stand mixer fitted with a dough hook and knead for 4 minutes until you have a smooth dough. Place the dough in an oiled bowl, cover with a tea towel and leave in a warm place for at least an hour to rise.

Once the dough has risen, divide it into 25 equal pieces. Roll these into smooth balls between your hands, then roll out each ball on a floured surface into a rough circle, about 12cm in diameter and the thickness of a coin (use a tortilla press if you have one). Sprinkle a few sesame seeds on top (if using) and push them down with your hands so they stick to the tortilla.

Heat a dry frying pan over a high heat. Cook the tortillas one at a time, for a couple of minutes on each side until beginning to brown, layering them on a plate and covering them with a tea towel as you go, until you have used up all the dough.

Cheese Ends Soufflé Omelette

SERVES 2
Preparation time 10 minutes
Cooking time 2–3 minutes

2 free-range eggs plus 2 egg whites
¼ tsp cornflour
pinch of ground white pepper
pinch of cayenne
pinch of freshly grated nutmeg
pinch of celery salt
pinch of sea salt
40g Cheddar, grated
15g Parmesan, grated
a decent knob of butter, for frying

Cheese soufflé couldn't be more out of fashion right now, which is a crying shame as it's one of my favourite things to make with eggs. The irony of this recipe is that an omelette is actually my least favourite incarnation of eggs, the reason being that even on their best delivery, they end up dry and rubbery more often than not, but this technique transforms an omelette into something special. The word 'soufflé' strikes fear into the hearts of many, but they really aren't as difficult as you might think. In fact, if you can make a basic cake there's no reason why you can't master a soufflé. All it requires you to do is make a base from the fatty parts and flavouring – the egg yolks, cheese and spices – which then have aerated egg whites folded into them. The rise comes from the air in the eggs expanding, and the cheese and cornflour stabilise the structure. The hardest part is when you have to flip one half over the other.

This recipe is how I'd have it for breakfast, but for supper, simply warm together 200ml single cream with 50ml whole milk and 40g grated Parmesan, with the same spicing as the soufflé omelette, sprinkle with a few snipped chives and serve with a bitter leaf salad. This is a great way to use up any old ends of hard cheese you may have lurking in the back of the fridge.

Separate the two whole eggs, adding the new whites to the existing two. Using a stand mixer fitted with the whisk attachment, or an electric handheld whisk, whisk the egg yolks for a couple of minutes until pale. Add the cornflour, pepper, cayenne, nutmeg, celery salt, sea salt and Cheddar and Parmesan cheeses and whisk for a further 30 seconds.

Next, with a clean whisk and bowl, whisk the egg whites for 3–4 minutes until they have medium to stiff peaks. Take 1 tablespoon of the egg white and beat it into the egg yolk and cheese mixture to loosen it. Fold in the rest of the egg white with a metal spoon, being careful not to beat the air out of it, as this will result in a sad, deflated soufflé and no one wants that!

Heat the butter in a medium frying pan (that has a lid) over a high heat, and when it starts to sizzle, pour in the egg mixture. Cover with a lid to keep the heat in. Cook for 1 minute, then reduce the heat to medium and cook for another minute. You should have a lovely puffed-up omelette, so now, using a palette knife, gently fold over one half on top of the other to reveal a caramelised sheet of cheesy egg. Slide out of the pan and cut in half. Eat immediately.

MILKS

Dairy milk and milk alternatives have been under the spotlight in recent years, and there has been a huge boom in the non-dairy milk market. It is often touted as the answer to counteracting the perceived negative environmental impacts of the traditional dairy industry, however it's crucial to understand the realities of what goes into producing these non-dairy alternatives and challenge the notion that all non-dairy milks are automatically better for the environment, and that they are the healthier option. I strongly believe in the potential of well-managed dairy farms to be a force for good rather than evil, but I also agree that cutting back on our dairy intake in general is something that we have to get on board with.

The milk market is flooded with myriad options, so how do you make the right choices? I've broken down the facts to help demystify the whole thing. Out of all the non-dairy milks, blended milks give the best flavour profile, and Rebel Kitchen's Mylk is my number one choice (as a company, they also have brilliant sustainability practices).

Dairy milk

• Rich in proteins, fat, calcium, potassium and vitamin D.
• There has been so much press over the past few years about the negative impact dairy farming is having globally, especially since the UN's report, 'Livestock's Long Shadow: Environmental Issues and Options', was released in 2006, claiming livestock was responsible for 18 per cent of the world's greenhouse gas emissions. Globally, dairy farming requires huge amounts of land and energy, fertiliser and food for the cows that produce the milk.
• Cows produce vast amounts of methane, which is more environmentally harmful than carbon dioxide.
• The carbon footprint of dairy milk varies largely depending on where it comes from. 'The UK's carbon footprint of milk production has been placed at 1.25kg per litre, making the UK amongst the world's best in sustainable milk production,' says Dairy UK CEO Dr Judith Bryans. Dairy cattle are almost exclusively grass fed here in the UK, which isn't the case in many hotter, drier countries.
• Many of the dairy industry's critics cite mega indoor dairies in countries like America, where cows are fed on soya and grain, as the basis for much of their criticism, but it is important to differentiate between the types of dairies. For example, smaller farms raising grass-fed animals like those in the UK have really positive environmental impacts, and make great societal contributions.
• Grass pasture offers many environmental benefits: it has a huge role to play in supporting biodiversity, and is a vital aid to sequestering (or 'locking up') of carbon in the soil (see page 193 for more about regenerative farming).
• We need to support our agricultural industry by using what our native lands and climate enable us to produce, and in this country milk is one those things.

Soy milk

• High in protein, fats and carbohydrates, second only to cow's milk in terms of all-round nutritional composition.
• Soy production has a devastating impact on the environment, decimating huge swathes of Amazon rainforest – the world's largest carbon sink (see pages 146).
• Traditionally, soy milk was made using the whole bean, minimising waste, but modern production methods discard the husk, thereby wasting much of the crop.
• The UK imports around 50 per cent of its soybeans from Brazil and 25 per cent from the US. This airfreighting results in a big carbon footprint.

Oat milk

• Contains protein and fibre, and beta-glucans (which help protect against high cholesterol).

• Scores well on sustainable production points, with low levels of water use (it requires six times less water to produce than almond milk), land use and emissions.

• The only non-dairy milk produced in the UK, which makes it a more sustainable choice as it's not imported.

• Oats grow in more temperate climates, which means they are less commonly associated with loss of biodiversity, soil erosion and wildfires.

• The UK has gone mad for oat milk, but for me it's the least delicious of all the non-dairy milks.

Rice milk

• Low nutritional benefits.

• Requires huge amounts of water – 1kg of rice needs 3,000 litres of water to grow – which contributes to an extremely large water footprint, much like almond milk.

• Recently, research has been conducted to develop a rice variety that requires less water to grow, but these are genetically modified (opening a whole other can of worms).

Coconut milk

• Low nutritional benefits and high in saturated fat.

• Every element of the fruit can be used, so there is the potential for minimal waste.

• As coconuts are grown in tropical climates such as Indonesia and the Philippines, their associated products such as coconut milk have to be airfreighted to the UK, which contributes to greenhouse gas emissions.

• From a culinary point of view, it's a brilliant emulsifier, and the high fat content makes it a closer equivalent to dairy milk than most other non-dairy milks, but I'm not a huge fan from an environmental and ethical perspective (see Coconut essay on page 173). However, a little coconut milk within a nut milk blend is still better for the planet than intensively farmed dairy milk.

Almonds

Almonds have become the popular choice of the health conscious and dairy intolerant in the last decade, overtaking soy milk as a dairy alternative, and it's easy to see why: they are high in monosaturated fat and antioxidants, and a great source of fibre, protein, vitamin E, selenium, calcium, magnesium and B vitamins, especially folate and vitamin B7. Many opt for almond milk thinking it has a smaller carbon footprint than dairy milk, however there are many environmental issues relating to almond production:

• Almonds require an enormous amount of water to grow: it takes an alarming 42 gallons of water (192 litres) to produce just 16 almonds (which makes just a single glass of milk). Given droughts and rising temperatures, water usage in all forms is rightfully coming under scrutiny.

• 23,000 acres of natural lands in California (California grows more than 80 per cent of the world's almonds) have been converted to almond farms.

• 16,000 acres of that land was previously classified as wetlands, and the production of almonds is seriously depleting groundwater levels. In turn, the new irrigation systems farmers are having to install to water their almond crops are interfering with the natural water table.

• The increasing demand for almond milk has exacerbated the industry's reliance on single-crop monoculture farming, which – as we know (see page 39) – is detrimental to biodiversity and soil health.

HOW TO MAKE YOUR OWN NON-DAIRY CREAM AND MILK

Nut creams and nut milks are widely available, but you don't always know what's gone into them, so here are a few you can make at home.

Sour Cashew Cream

I learnt how to make this when I was in Thailand. The fat content and texture of cashews makes for an excellent cream which works really well in curries and pasta dishes.

MAKES 350ml
Preparation time 10 minutes, plus 30 minutes soaking time
150g cashews
juice of ½ lemon
1 tsp salt

Put the cashews in a heatproof bowl and cover with boiling water so that it comes 5mm above the nuts. Leave to soak for 30 minutes.

Blitz the cashews and soaking water in a food processor with the lemon juice and salt until you have a smooth paste. The cream will keep in the fridge for up to 5 days.

Oat Cream

This is a good dairy alternative for cream as it utilises British produce and has a lovely mellow flavour and consistency, and is really easy to make at home.

MAKES 250ml
Preparation time 10 minutes, plus 3 hours soaking time

150g rolled oats
1 litre boiling water
2 tbsp flavourless oil, such as almond oil or grape seed oil
¼ tsp salt

Put the oats in a large heatproof bowl and pour the hot water over them. Leave to soak at room temperature for about 3 hours, until the water has been totally absorbed.

Rinse the oats in a sieve under cold running water to remove any sliminess (which comes from the release of starch from the oats into the water). Put the rinsed oats in a food processor and pour in 200ml fresh cold water. Add the oil and salt and blitz on full power for 3 minutes.

Strain for a really smooth, emulsified, creamy texture. The oat cream will keep in the fridge for up to 2–3 days.

Nut Milk

You can make this with a combination of whichever nuts you choose. I like to use a blend of different nuts and rice.

MAKES 1.2 litres
Preparation time 5 minutes, plus minimum 6 hours soaking time (or overnight)

500g nuts (I like 400g cashews and 100g skinless almonds)
100g brown rice
pinch of salt
1.5 litres tepid water
date syrup, maple syrup or honey, for sweetening to taste (optional)

Put all the ingredients except the syrup or honey in a bowl and soak at room temperature for a minimum of 6 hours (or overnight). Drain, transfer to a food processor and add a fresh 1.5 litres of water and another pinch of salt. Blitz until smooth.

Place a sieve lined with muslin over a bowl and strain the milk through it to get a lovely smooth consistency. Sweeten it with a little date syrup, maple syrup or honey if you wish.

COCONUT

We have witnessed a coconut craze this past decade. The 'wonder fruit' is pretty omnipresent, appearing in health food shops and supermarkets in a myriad of forms, from coconut milk, coconut yoghurt and coconut oil to coconut sugar and coconut flour. Coconuts are big business. And they're not just used for eating. Coconut oil is doing a roaring trade in the beauty industry, and the husks are used to make everything from rope to mattresses and flooring, and a less refined version of the oil is sometimes used in eco-detergents. It certainly wins some sustainability points as there is the potential for so little waste.

When it comes to coconut's health benefits, things are less clear. Wild claims are made regarding coconut's magical properties, e.g. oh-so-trendy coconut water, which is allegedly more hydrating than water due to its high levels of potassium: on further inspection, this fact is irrelevant as it doesn't contain the other essential electrolyte, sodium, that enables our bodies to optimally hydrate.

And then there's coconut oil. The internet is rife with coconut enthusiasts evangelising about how coconut oil can burn fat, combat ageing, prevent Alzheimer's, shrink tumours, boost your immune system or simply make your hair softer. Coconut oil has more saturated fat than beef dripping or lard, but it is also very high in MCTs (medium-chain triglycerides), a form of fat molecule with a shorter chain of fatty acid than most others. Trials suggesting that a diet high in MCTs could aid weight loss has been siezed by the health food industry, but there is actually no evidence that coconut oil (which contains only 15 per cent MCTs), is anywhere near as effective as pure MCT oil to aid weight loss or energy release. So, there is little proof it is less fattening than other oils. As research into 'good

fats' and 'bad fats' evolves, I would suggest using coconut oil in moderation. A healthy dose of cynicism regarding its supposed health benefits seems like the wisest approach.

So what about the impact of the coconut industry on the environment? The Philippines, Indonesia and India are the world's largest exporters of coconut. As with any imported products from far flung climes, airfreighting is a big problem. Flying food for thousands of miles means huge greenhouse gas emissions, which makes goods like these score high on the carbon footprint scale. Just as with other crops I mention in this book, high demand for coconuts has led to increasing levels of monoculture. This is terrible for soil quality and diversity of local ecosystems and wildlife, as biodiverse native plants are eradicated. As coconut trees age they become less productive, which leads to more coconut trees needing to be planted to meet demand. In turn, high demand fuels the need for high yields, so many farmers are more likely to opt for chemical fertilisers and pesticides (some governments give farmers subsidies for using them in a bid to bolster their weak economies). Unsurprisingly, much of the profit fails to filter down to the growers themselves: 'Around 40–60% of the 3.5 million coconut farmers in the Philippines are living in poverty, on less than a dollar a day,' says Angie Crone, manager of Fair Trade USA's coconut programme. Buying Fairtrade is one way to ensure you are not part of an entirely exploitative system.

I used to use coconut a lot, particularly the milk and cream, which form the basis of many curries. As a girl who cut her teeth with Thai cookery I'm finding it hard to omit it entirely, but I have pulled back and now regard it as a treat instead of an everyday staple.

POULTRY & GAME

POULTRY AND GAME

Poultry

Globally, the way in which we eat, and therefore rear poultry, has changed dramatically since the 1950s. Up to that point, chicken was considered a rare treat in most households, as opposed to the daily staple it has become today. Developments in antibiotics, animal housing design and breeding programmes – spearheaded by the US in the 1950s – to breed chickens specifically for speedy weight gain and high breast meat yield, has led to an estimated 85 per cent of the UK's poultry meat being produced through intensive farming methods. A direct impact of this type of farming is that far more waste is produced than can be effectively managed by land disposal, resulting in all kinds of environmental problems. Mass poultry slaughtering and processing requires huge amounts of water, resulting in gallons of wastewater containing chemicals, fats and pathogens (and many other nasty substances) which contaminate water systems and then inevitably end up damaging the soil.

Intensively farmed chickens are given tons of antibiotics, simply to ensure they don't die while gaining weight so quickly. These antibiotics have serious consequences for the natural environment when they leach into the water systems. In America, some intensive farms even use arsenic to control intestinal parasites, and chlorine to bleach the chickens as a chemical 'washing' process: the purpose of this 'washing' is purportedly to remove any 'harmful bacteria' once they've been slaughtered and gutted, but the real reason they do this is because the animals are living in such cramped conditions that they end up breaking limbs, living in their own faeces, and are sometimes even surrounded by dead and rotting birds. The idea that you can simply 'wash' this away

indicates that the whole system is yet another symptom of our complete disconnection with the food we eat, and the impact that has on the animals themselves, let alone the world around us. What's more, humans absorb all of the effects of these processes and it's making our bodies weaker; our microbiomes are struggling and our bodies are becoming immune to antibiotic treatment. The truth is, we need some bacteria from the meat we eat – from animals that consume seeds, grass, biodiverse soils and have oxygenated blood (from being free to range) – to keep our own gut flora healthy. You are what you eat!

The carbon footprint of poultry rearing comes out lower than other meat production such as lamb or beef, however debate continues to rage around intensive versus extensive farming (farming on larger plots) in terms of which system has the lower emissions. There is even controversy about how to measure and rate gas emissions and which emissions are the most harmful. Without conclusive evidence, it becomes a case of deciding what your priorities are. For me, rearing animals with the highest possible welfare standards and nutritional value, and the lowest levels of chemicals and antibiotics, must surely be something to strive for.

Within the intensive farming system, chickens are killed at 4–6 weeks, compared to slow-grown, free-range or organic birds which are slaughtered at double that age (about 12 weeks) and are naturally bigger, with a heavier dry meat weight and stronger bones (think about how brittle the bones in fast-food fried chicken are) and the meat-to-bone ratio is exponentially bigger on the higher welfare bird and the eating all round is better. Stock made with a slow-grown bird will give you lots of bone marrow and make a far more 'jellied' stock than one made with a fast-grown bird. A good-quality bird will also contain its offal, which is brilliant in so many dishes, but for the squeamish just finely chopping it and adding it to stuffing mixtures or pasta sauces is a great way to use it.

Another very grim side of the poultry industry is the injection of saline solution into the birds, to make them appear bigger and weigh more. Cook a fast-grown bird that weighs the same as a slow-grown bird and you'll find that post cooking it will have lost a whole heap more water, and it will lack flavour and nutrition density to boot. It's a false economy.

Poultry production is a multi-billion-pound industry that's considered a necessary part of our modern socio-political structure – intensive farming creates a cheap solution to feeding the nation. While it's critical that there's food for everyone, regardless of their economic status, that doesn't mean that we shouldn't hold these producers to account, and that we have to accept rock-bottom standards. Having just turned 40, I can see how this food system has exploded in my time. My mother would feed us chicken on a Sunday and make three meals from the leftovers. Chicken was a luxury – all meat was – but we are now being sold it as part of our daily diet, with some people eating meat three times a day, at every meal. Many argue that this is an oppressive way of eating as opposed to an inclusive one, because the poor quality of this meat is actually undermining (and in many cases, it is actually detrimental to) consumers' health.

At the time of writing, the UK is 65 per cent self-sufficient when it comes to chicken production, which means 35 per cent is imported. As it stands, we don't import chicken from America, as the production standards are so low that they are banned by the EU, but the implications of Brexit and departure from the EU means this could change.

So, what can we do? We can protest through how we buy our food, and source meat directly from high-welfare producers or from reputable local butchers, but if you have to buy from the supermarkets, you need to check the labelling. I personally have issues with the Red Tractor accreditation: it's very low on the food standards list. I prefer the ethics of the RSPCA-assured standards. A Woodland Trust label on poultry is also worth looking out for, because the Woodland Trust works with farms who rear chickens in a free-to-roam woodland habitat. We can also learn a few traditional skills, so we do not fear the chicken in its whole form. Knowing how to butcher a chicken is one of the best life skills one can learn. Once you have this skill you will see how much money can be saved from using every last scrap. Western cultures have been led to believe otherwise (thanks to misleading protein portioning, where it becomes the main focus on our plate), but one breast will easily feed two people.

How to make the most of a bird

A whole bird can be used for roasting or poaching. When the backbone is removed and the bird is spatchcocked it is great grilled over coals, on a griddle or under a grill. Once the bird is broken down into sections, two breasts will serve four, or you can use one breast split into two lengthways (I would coat this with egg and breadcrumbs and fry as an escalope) and slice the other for a stir-fry for two.

I like to portion the thighs and drumsticks and use them for a braise or curry. Any bones you have left are made into stock (pages 262–63).

What you'll need to break down any bird into pieces for casseroles and frying:
• sharp kitchen scissors
• a cleaver or cook's knife
• a chopping board
• a wet cloth, placed under the chopping board

See opposite for step-by-step instructions.

Game

Game typically falls into two categories: truly wild and managed.

Truly wild game, such as rabbit, pigeon, wild venison and squirrel (yes, I know this last one might be a bit of a challenge for some readers) is more ethical as there is no farming involved, therefore the animals live a natural life and there is minimal impact on the environment. They are culled as part of land management to keep species numbers balanced. I've become a real fan of wild rabbit in particular recently, and while testing the recipe for my Rabbit à la Moutarde (page 188) not only butchered my first rabbit but also discovered how delicate and delicious rabbit liver and kidneys are, just flash fried in a little butter and seasoned with salt.

Things get a little murkier from an ethical perspective when it comes to farmed game such as pheasant and grouse. This is big business for rural areas. Pheasant, grouse and guinea fowl shooting has risen in popularity hugely over recent years, with landowners being able to charge large sums for the privilege to come and shoot birds reared exclusively for this purpose. The downside of this is that there is oversupply, with hundreds of shot birds being dumped as there currently just isn't the consumer demand. We have grown so accustomed to the relatively neutral flavour of chicken that the uniquely richer flavours of pheasant, grouse or partridge can be challenging to our taste buds. It feels like such a waste of life to recklessly throw away these beautiful, not to mention delicious birds, birds that get to live a relatively long, natural life, eating a largely foraged diet, resulting in high-quality, delicious meat: all this is a far cry from factory-farmed chickens.

The rising popularity of venison over the last decade illustrates how market demand can work in tandem with animals being reared for the shooting industry, to reach a point of equilibrium, where there is almost zero waste, there's a low impact on the environment, and animals are allowed to live an almost entirely natural life. I accept it is far from a perfect system, but game shoots have become a lifeline for many rural communities and are part of our national cooking heritage.

Another thing that puts people off game is that they assume it's difficult to cook, but this really isn't the case. All the recipes in this chapter are adaptable for whichever bird you decide to use, be it duck or quail or the old classic chicken. I urge you to think a bit more broadly when choosing your bird, as these game birds are incredible meats, and when in season and abundant can do everything from jazzing up your roast to adding interest to your everyday meals.

STEP 1 Place the chicken on a chopping board, held steady by being placed on a wet cloth. With the scissors, cut out the backbone by just snipping along each side of the bird's spine.

STEP 2 Pop the chicken on its bottom then, with your cook's knife, slice along its breastbone, cutting through the carcass to cleave the bird in half.

STEP 3 Carve through the skin between the leg and the breast. With your fingers, feel for the leg joint then carve through it to separate the two pieces.

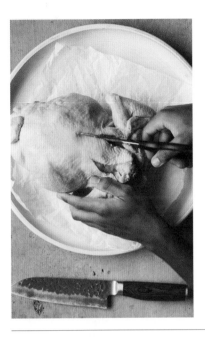

STEP 4 Feel along the chicken leg – you will find a joint that separates the drumstick from the thigh. With your cook's knife, chop through this to divide them.

STEP 5 Turn your attention to the breast. There will be a couple of centimetres of ribcage exposed that you can trim off with your scissors. Remove the tip of the wing. I cut the breasts crossways into three pieces, but cut them into four if they are particularly large.

STEP 6 You will now have 12 portions ready to cook with.

Chicken in Weeds 2020

SERVES 6–8
Preparation time 20 minutes
Cooking time 1 hour 20 minutes

4 tbsp vegetable oil
6 thigh, leg and wing pieces
  (1 chicken – see page 179), skinned
1 onion, roughly chopped
1 head of garlic, cloves peeled and
  roughly chopped
5cm piece of fresh ginger, peeled and
  roughly chopped
2 tsp ground cumin
1 tbsp ground coriander
2 green cardamom pods
pinch of ground cloves
½ tsp Kashmiri chilli powder
½ tsp cayenne
½ tsp ground turmeric
500ml fresh chicken stock
1 cinnamon stick
1 green chilli, kept whole
100g coriander, leaves and stalks
100g unsalted cashews
200g spinach leaves, washed
juice of ½ lemon
1 tsp sea salt
cooked basmati rice, to serve

The first incarnation of 'Chicken in Weeds' appeared in my very first book, *Kitchen Magic*, over 10 years ago. It's a curry that my mother adapted from a Madhur Jaffrey recipe from the 90s, a simple, delicately spiced curry, and I renamed it 'Chicken in Weeds' due to the fact that the chicken swam in a pool of coriander. The dish is much loved by you lot, and I still make it regularly at home, though it has developed into what feels like a very different incarnation, superior in its flavour and viscosity. The chicken is more authentically chopped – I use the whole bird, jointed, making for a richer stock, and cook it low and slow so the meat falls off the bone (you can use leg and thigh pieces if you prefer, but I want you to try breaking up a whole chicken) – and I've upped the spicing too, including cardamom, turmeric, cloves and cinnamon. I've also made it greener with added spinach, and cashews for a gentle, creamy roundness. It's completely inauthentic, yet somehow tastes like a curry that should sit among the classics. It makes the most brilliant everyday meal, but also a terrific dish as part of an Indian or Middle Eastern dinner party.

Heat 2 tablespoons of the oil in a casserole dish over a high heat, then brown the chicken pieces in two batches until they are caramelised all over (you may need to add a little more oil to the pan for the second batch of chicken). Remove and set aside.

Add the rest of the oil to the pan, set the heat to medium-low and throw in the onions, garlic and ginger (it will be blitzed to a paste, so don't worry about chopping everything finely). Sweat for at least 20 minutes, until the onions are really soft and golden and have begun to caramelise, then add all of the spices to the dish, except the cinnamon stick and green chilli, and fry for a minute or two before adding the chicken stock. Return the chicken and any residual juices to the dish and add the cinnamon stick and whole green chilli. Cover and cook over a low heat for 40 minutes, until the chicken is starting to come away from the bone.

Remove the chicken from the sauce once more and set aside. Carefully transfer the sauce to a food processor, removing the cardamom pods and cinnamon stick, but including the whole chilli (don't worry about removing the stalk). Add the coriander, cashews and spinach and blitz until smooth – you want everything to be mulched and blended together well. Return this vibrant green sauce to the casserole dish and put the chicken back in. Heat together for 5 minutes but no longer, as you don't want to lose the bright colour of the sauce. Squeeze in the lemon juice and season with the salt. Serve with basmati rice.

Guinea Fowl alla 'Diavolo'

SERVES 4
Preparation time 15 minutes, plus
1 hour 45 minutes for the tomato
sauce
Cooking time 1 hour

500ml fresh chicken stock
1 guinea fowl, cut into 8 pieces (page
    179) (keep the excess bones)
300ml water
8 tbsp good-quality olive oil
1 head of garlic, cloves peeled and
    thinly sliced
2 sprigs of rosemary
6 whole dried chillies
300ml white wine
500g Slow Cooked Tomato Sauce
    (page 264)
½ tsp sugar
sea salt and freshly ground black
    pepper

You couldn't look at a menu in Italian restaurants in the 90s without spotting a 'diavolo' dish – I used to trek down to Finsbury Park to the very first La Porchetta pizzeria in the mid 90s for Pollo alla Diavola and a Quattro Formaggi pizza. The chicken for the Pollo alla Diavola is braised in a seriously garlicky, chilli tomato sauce, then it's removed before the sauce is reduced down to the point of the sauce almost splitting. I'm applying the same ethos to guinea fowl, a superb meat which is generally reared to much better standards. It's mostly farmed in France, although there are some terrific UK producers.

Serve with garlicky, rosemary-roasted new potatoes and a crispy green or bitter leaf salad.

First, enrich the chicken stock with the excess guinea fowl bones you get after portioning it into pieces. Put the excess bones in a saucepan and add the chicken stock, topping it up with the water. Simmer over a low heat while you get on with the rest of the dish. You may need to occasionally skim off scum from the top.

Season the guinea fowl pieces generously with salt. Heat 2 tablespoons of the oil in a frying pan over a high heat and brown the guinea fowl pieces in batches until well caramelised all over. Set aside.

Heat the remaining 6 tablespoons of oil in a shallow casserole dish over a medium heat, add the garlic and the rosemary and allow to soften for about a minute until the garlic becomes translucent and is starting to caramelise. Add the dried chillies and a really good grinding of black pepper, toast in the oil briefly, then pour in the wine. Allow to bubble and reduce for 3 minutes. Add the tomato sauce and transfer the guinea fowl pieces, excluding the breast pieces (as these require less cooking and have a tendency to become tough and dry). Pour in 400ml of the enriched chicken stock (it will have reduced to about this volume by now) and let the guinea fowl braise, uncovered, over a medium heat for 20 minutes. Season with a teaspoon of salt and the sugar.

Add the breast pieces to the dish and cook for a further 15 minutes, then remove all the meat and set aside while you reduce the sauce.

Turn up the heat under the sauce and reduce it by about a third (this will take about 10 minutes). Due to the amount of oil in this dish, the sauce sometimes splits. Personally, I love this and think it adds to the dish. Return the meat to the reduced sauce and serve.

Roast Pheasant

SERVES 4
Preparation time 5 minutes
Cooking time 30 minutes

2 feathered and drawn pheasants, keeping any offal (ask your butcher for it) for either the stuffing or stock
1 quantity Sage and Onion Stuffing (page 186) (optional)
2 tbsp oil
2 tbsp butter
sea salt and freshly ground black pepper
1 quantity A Delicious Port and Blackberry Sauce for Game (page 186)
1 quantity Celeriac Bread Sauce (page 92)
game chips, to serve

Of all the game birds, pheasant is the most accessible and the easiest to cook, but I have also included cooking methods for other game birds. Pheasant should be eaten with breasts medium-pink, other game birds are best eaten medium-rare, but with all game, the legs should be cooked through, so you need to carve game bird breast crowns away from the leg bones in order to cook it absolutely right. If the idea of jointing the bird intimidates you, then cook it all the way through for the full time it takes for both the leg and breast of each bird, but page 179 will show you that the jointing is not as daunting as you might think. The key to success is in the prep: a hot pan, hot oven, sharp knife, and some Dutch courage. I would drink a cold bullshot (like a bloody Mary, but made with beef stock rather than tomato juice) to get myself in the spirit. I serve roast game birds stuffed with sage and onion stuffing, with game chips, blackberry and port sauce and pools of celeriac bread sauce.

Preheat the oven as hot as it will go (about 260°C/240°C fan/gas mark 10): the birds are so small and you want them to cook briefly so they stay tender. If you're stuffing the birds, stuff them now (tightly).

Heat the oil and butter in a frying pan over a high heat. Season the birds heavily, paying particular attention to the legs, then brown one pheasant at a time for 3–4 minutes on the leg sides then 2–3 minutes on the breasts, until well browned all over. Transfer to a roasting tray breast side up and roast for 15–17 minutes, for perfectly cooked pink meat. I prefer a slightly pinker bird so opt for the lower end of the time scale. This cooking time is inclusive of the stuffing, so if you're not stuffing the birds take a minute off the time. If you have a meat thermometer, slide it into the thickest part of the breast and it should read 55°C (once rested it will hit 60°C). Remove from the oven and reduce the heat to 200°C/180°C fan/gas mark 6.

Cut the legs from the birds with a sharp knife and transfer to a separate roasting tray. Roast for a further 10–15 minutes until crisped up (the rest of the bird will rest during this time). Lean the resting crowns on one side for half of the leg roasting time, then turn them over for remaining roasting time so that the juices disperse evenly throughout the bird. Pour any resting juices into your sauce.

To carve, first remove the breasts: starting at the cavity end, cut with a sharp knife as close to the breast bone as possible, slicing one breast off the carcass, then cut above the wing bone to remove it. Repeat on the other side of the bird. Slice both breasts in half diagonally and serve the pheasant and stuffing with accompaniments suggested opposite.

Here are cooking times for some other birds that I have compiled with my good friend Tomos Parry, chef at Brat, my favourite London restaurant. All the accompaniments suggested opposite work brilliantly with these birds, but for the grouse I would skip the stuffing and serve it instead as follows: fry a round slice of bread in duck or goose fat, then briefly fry the bird's offal, seasoned with salt and pepper, in a very hot pan, until caramelised on the outside but pink in the middle. Put the offal on the toast, then the bird on top of the offal.

Mallard duck

Brown the whole bird's breasts and legs in a hot pan (as opposite) then on a roasting tray in the oven for 13–15 minutes or until internal temperature is 50°C. Remove the legs and return to the oven for 10 minutes at a reduced temperature of 200°C/180°C fan/gas mark 6. Rest the crown for 15 minutes or until the internal temperature hits 55°C (for perfect medium-rare doneness). Serve breasts and legs together.

Wood pigeon and grouse

Brown the birds whole, breasts and legs, in a hot pan (as opposite) then on a roasting tray in the hot oven for 10–13 minutes or until internal temperature is 45°C. Remove the legs and put them back in the oven for 10 minutes at a reduced temperature of 200°C/180°C fan/gas mark 6. Rest the crown for 15 minutes or until the internal temperature has hit 50°C (for perfect rare bordering medium-rare doneness). Serve breasts and legs together, as above.

Spatchcocking

Tomos tells me they spatchcock game birds at the restaurant as it allows the skin side to crisp up without overcooking the meat. To do this, preheat the oven to 200°C/180°C fan/gas mark 6, place the bird skin side down in an ovenproof pan or on the bars of a grill or a griddle pan over a medium heat and once you have a nice colour on the skin, place the pan in the oven and cook for 5 minutes, or until the internal temperature has reached 45°C. Remove from the oven and rest for 10 minutes – when it reaches an internal temperature of 52°C (medium-rare doneness), it's ready.

A Delicious Port and Blackberry Sauce for Game

SERVES 4
Preparation time 5 minutes
Cooking time 15 minutes

1 tbsp oil (optional)
1 tsp plain flour
100ml port
250ml white wine
500ml fresh dark brown chicken or
   pheasant stock
3 juniper berries, crushed with the
   back of a knife
1 tbsp butter
125g blackberries
sea salt and freshly ground black
   pepper

There isn't much game that port doesn't enhance, especially when combined with an acidic berry. Be it feathered or furred, all roasted game needs something sweet to cut through it (see pages 184–85 for Roast Pheasant and tips for roasting other game birds).

Place the game roasting tray over a medium heat. Depending on the type of bird you've roasted, you may need to add a tablespoon of oil to the tray – there needs to be about 2 tablespoons of fat in the tray. Add the flour and scrape with a wooden spoon to loosen all the meaty residue from roasting. Add the port and stir to form a paste. Beat in the wine until smooth and bubble for a few minutes to cook off the alcohol, mix in the stock until smooth, add the juniper berries and simmer for about 10 minutes until the sauce has reduced and is glossy and rich. Add the butter and blackberries and season, swilling the pan to emulsify the butter and heat the berries through before serving.

Sage and Onion Stuffing

**MAKES enough stuffing for
2 large game birds (or 4 small)**
Preparation time 10 minutes
Cooking time 25 minutes, plus
roasting time of the bird

1 tbsp oil
2 onions, finely chopped
2 sprigs of thyme, leaves chopped
small bunch of sage, leaves thinly
   sliced
100g breadcrumbs
50ml fresh chicken or vegetable stock
pluck/offal from 2–4 game birds,
   trimmed and finely chopped
1 free-range egg, whisked
sea salt and freshly ground black
   pepper

This simple sage and onion stuffing recipe is made with game offal. I am normally a sausagemeat stuffing kind of person, but when stuffing game birds I think it can be a bit much. Instead, I really finely chop the offal of the bird and stir it through the stuffing mixture. You will absolutely not taste the offal in this – it just adds richness and umami!

Heat the oil in a frying pan over a low heat, add the onions and herbs and cook for about 25 minutes, until soft and golden. Transfer to a large bowl, mix in the breadcrumbs, stock and offal, and season with salt and pepper. Set aside and allow to cool before mixing in the whisked egg.

Divide the stuffing in half and shape both halves into a ball with your hands. Stuff enough mixture into the cavity of the birds so there's a little bit poking out of the gap.

Korma Wings

SERVES 4
Preparation time 10 minutes, plus
2 hours minimum marinating time
(ideally overnight)
Cooking time 15 minutes

750g–1kg chicken wings, cut in half
at the joint

FOR THE MARINADE
5cm piece of fresh ginger, peeled
1 head of garlic, cloves separated
   and peeled
100ml oil
1 tbsp Kashmiri chilli powder or
   ½ tsp hot chilli powder
½ tsp ground coriander
2 tsp garam masala
1 tsp ground fenugreek
1 tbsp salt
2 tsp caster sugar
80g coconut or dairy yoghurt

FOR THE CASHEW SAUCE
120g unsalted cashews
180ml water
½ tsp sea salt
5cm piece of fresh ginger, peeled
1 tsp garam masala
50g butter (preferably ghee) or
   coconut oil
80g coconut yoghurt
juice of ½ lemon
large handful of coriander, leaves
   very finely chopped

This really great recipe mimics the butter chicken wings at Brigadiers restaurant in London. Their wings are absolutely fantastic. Like a curry and classic wing in one, they are charry, spicy and creamy, and unlike any other wing you've ever had. I like to use Kashmiri chilli powder here because it is milder and sweeter than standard chilli powder.

Blitz all the marinade ingredients in a food processor until smooth. Put the chicken wings in a large bowl and pour the marinade all over them. Put in the fridge and leave to marinate, preferably overnight, but for at least 2 hours.

Preheat the oven to 200°C/180°C fan/gas mark 6.

When you're ready to cook the wings, heat the grill to a medium-high heat and place the wings on a rack under the grill. Don't wipe off too much, but give them a little shake to remove excess before grilling; it will char slightly and this adds to the flavour. Grill them for 7–8 minutes then turn the wings over and grill for another 7–8 minutes until cooked through.

While the wings are cooking, start on the sauce. Toast the cashews on a baking tray in the oven for 8 minutes, until they start to develop a light golden colour. Transfer to a food processor, add the water and blitz to a smooth paste. Add the salt, ginger and garam masala and blitz again. Heat the ghee or oil in a saucepan over a low heat, add the cashew mixture and heat through for a few minutes, stirring frequently, to bring it all together and soften the acrid taste of the ginger a little. Taste for seasoning, mix in the yoghurt and add the lemon juice. Finally, stir in most of the chopped coriander, reserving some to garnish at the end.

Once the chicken wings are cooked, transfer them to a large bowl. Toss the cashew sauce over them so they are well coated. Arrange them on a serving platter, sprinkle the remaining coriander on top and eat immediately.

Rabbit à la Moutarde

SERVES 6
Preparation time 10 minutes
Cooking time 1 hour 30 minutes

1 wild rabbit, cut into 6 pieces (ask
  your butcher to do this)
4 tbsp oil
1 onion, thinly sliced
10 garlic cloves, thinly sliced
1 tbsp plain flour
400ml medium-dry white wine, plus
  extra for deglazing
500ml fresh chicken stock
2 bay leaves
a few sprigs of thyme
6 rashers of smoked streaky bacon
100ml double cream
2 tbsp wholegrain mustard
2 tbsp English mustard
sea salt and freshly ground black
  pepper

Rabbit is delicious. We don't eat enough of it in the UK and that's frustrating. Wild rabbit is available all year round and is a huge part of farm management: if we don't cull rabbits, they mate like…er… rabbits, the countryside is overrun with them and they become a pest. It's a sorry tale of agriculture: any kind of growing, particularly of vegetables, becomes problematic with bunnies around. Farmed rabbit is another story. Largely imported from France, the caging is a pretty grim tale (free-range rabbit farming would be almost impossible, due to them burrowing) and by buying farmed rabbit you're supporting an industry that is already fundamentally controversial, but rabbit is still farmed worldwide for its fur – the meat is a by-product, so should we eat it? It's a tricky one. The best option is wild, and it also happens to have more flavour.

This dish was put under my nose by one of my absolute heroes, the majestic cook Henry Harris, once proprietor of the best restaurant in London, Racine, and now owner of many pubs that serve his food: honest, hearty grub made with superb ingredients, classically cooked, with a full understanding of what it takes to make produce shine. Henry grills his rabbit, but I choose to braise it. Serve with creamy mash and greens.

Season the rabbit. Heat 2–3 tablespoons of the oil in a frying pan over a high heat and brown the rabbit in batches, until caramelised, then transfer to a casserole dish.

Heat the remaining oil in the same pan over a medium heat, add the onion and garlic and cook gently for a good 15 minutes, until soft, translucent and beginning to pick up a golden tinge. Stir in the flour, cook for a couple of minutes, then add the wine. Let the wine bubble for a couple of minutes to cook off some of the alcohol, then add the mixture to the rabbit dish. Pour in the stock and add the bay and thyme sprigs.

In a separate pan, fry the bacon, just until it picks up a little colour (don't allow it to get too crisp). Remove and set aside. Deglaze the pan with a splash of wine to loosen the meaty residue, then pour it over the rabbit. Cover and braise over a gentle heat for 1 hour. Towards the end of cooking, preheat the oven to 200°C/180°C fan/gas mark 6.

Remove the rabbit from the sauce and set aside. Strain the sauce into a small pan, stir in the cream and mustards and reduce for a few minutes until thickened. Put the rabbit pieces on a baking tray with a piece of bacon on top of each and heat in the oven for 4–5 minutes, then serve with a few tablespoons of sauce on each plate.

MEAT & OFFAL

ETHICAL MEAT EATING

Throughout my years working as a chef, and more recently as a restaurateur, the provenance of the meat I cook with has always been of the utmost importance to me. I've been on a quest to educate myself and develop a deep understanding of what it means to rear, slaughter and then finally cook meat in a way that is ethical, sustainable and fundamentally respectful to the life that has been sacrificed.

When I was writing my food column for the *Sunday Times* I had the privilege of being able to travel around the country (and the world) to interview and often go on to foster relationships with some of the very best meat farmers, producers and butchers out there; real food heroes who have built their businesses around trying to do things in the best way possible for the animal, and with a total commitment to the land and environment around them. I also got to see the other side of production – the intensive farming systems and abattoirs. The experiences stuck with me to this day and I'm grateful, as it has forced me to have a long, hard look at the reality behind being a meat eater. Eating meat is a choice that I have chosen to make, and I want to share my experiences with you, because the industry is grizzly as hell. Witnessing the savage reality of an animal that's bigger than you on a production line, with life in its eyes and the smell of death in the air, being forced into a chamber where it gets stunned unconscious, then gets hooked up by its ankles and yanked upside down onto a suspended conveyor system where its throat is slit, leaving it bleeding to death, it's hard to believe that any good-intentioned human wouldn't question themselves about the ethics (though it's worth pointing out that there are now also state-of-the-art abattoirs, which have better practices and cause minimal stress for the animal,

which means better-tasting meat, as the animal has far less adrenaline and cortisol in its system). Mindlessly eating meat without educating ourselves and facing the truth behind the demise of these creatures for our own consumption doesn't sit right with me. Knowing what it means for an animal to go to slaughter goes some way to explaining why there is a rift between vegans' empathy and that of meat eaters, who choose to eat meat knowing that killing an animal is never truly ethical.

I've been a fierce advocate for a diet high in plants and low in meat and have been writing about this and researching it for 15 years. I have also spent a lot of time eating a fully plant-based diet and visited plant-based medical facilities around the world in my role as a journalist, in a quest to be more than just a spectator and become an authority on the subject. But all these years of research and some extreme soul searching has led me to still want to eat meat. Why?

Despite humans being conscious creatures that can make choices, for me there is something stronger than this – a calling that I can't ignore. The animalistic side of me is instinctively drawn to a desire to eat meat. I feel healthier when I eat meat. Trust me, I have tried to suppress it, and I respect people who can, but 88 per cent of the population eats meat and this is not down to social programming.

We now know that we don't need animal protein to survive, but it is generally agreed – even by those plant-based medical facilities – that a diet that includes a small amount of CLA (conjugated linoleic acid) is healthier than one that doesn't. In South India there is an area that practises Ayurvedic medicine. One part of the area is entirely vegan, while in the other a small amount of dairy is consumed (in chai teas and ghee). The area where people consume animal protein has better heart health stats, lower cancer rates and therefore those people have longer lifespans. No nutritional scientist can dispute that the evolution of the human brain and development of muscles and bones is down to consumption of high-quality animal proteins and fish oils, and while we now understand that we can get most of these nutrients elsewhere, this is how we can consume these animal proteins and oils in their most unadulterated form.

Vegan science contests that we aren't anatomically designed to eat meat, as we don't have the killer instinct or canines to rip flesh that would qualify us as pure carnivores, but in fact our guts aren't long enough and our teeth aren't quite designed to enable us to be herbivores either. The human gut is the most similar to our closest relatives – monkeys and apes – whose diets are composed largely of nuts, fruit, leaves and insects, with the occasional introduction of flesh, therefore we are most likely meant to be omnivores. I believe this is the approach that we should feel comfortable taking when it comes to our modern diets: eating meat, but in small quantities.

There is another, and for me more pressing, argument as to why eradicating meat from our diets and therefore the world of farming is ultimately detrimental to the future of the planet's health. Let me explain…

Regenerative farming
Regenerative farming is one of the key tenets at the centre of this argument. It is a well-known fact that industrial agriculture has had a catastrophic effect on the environment, especially post World War Two, where the implementation of new technology, vaccines, antibiotics, growth hormones and synthetic fertilisers and pesticides gave rise to the intensive rearing of larger numbers of livestock and bigger crop yields, to feed an ever-expanding population.

Industrial agriculture is a huge contributor to global greenhouse gas emissions, most notably within meat production. It is estimated that British agriculture contributes to 10 per cent of the country's greenhouse gas emissions, through methane produced by cows and sheep, nitrous oxides from fertilisers, and carbon dioxide released from heavy ploughing. As we were taught in biology lessons at school, photosynthesis works on the principle of plants drawing carbon dioxide from the atmosphere, turning it into carbohydrates, transporting it to their roots then depositing it in the soil as carbon (which enriches the soil) and releasing oxygen through respiration back into the air. We all know that planting more trees is one way to tackle the carbon dioxide levels in our atmosphere, but farming practices have the potential to be a major player in redressing the balance too.

There are more micro-organisms in one teaspoon of healthy soil than there are human beings on Earth. However, modern industrial farming practices rely on the heavy tilling of the soil and the spraying of pesticides and chemical fertilisers, which destroys this microbial diversity of the soil, killing life-giving bacteria, protozoa and organisms such as tiny mycorrhizal fungi or earthworms, effectively turning it into lifeless dirt. If there is no microbial life in soil, there are no nutrients for plants to draw through their roots, which of course means they cannot grow. This microbial life also helps maintain porous soil, which means it is more effective at absorbing and retaining water, which is crucial for a future where we are seeing more and more extreme weather events. 'Living' soil continues the cyclical regeneration of plant life and encourages and maintains good soil health. The whole ethos of regenerative farming has a potentially huge positive effect on the carbon cycle and climate change. Its key principles are:

• Putting livestock back on pasture and grazing them in groups. For me, this nuanced approach to the world's farming future is critical. Eating less meat is an imperative we all have to accept, however grasslands rely on animal activity to absorb carbon and regenerate. Holistic, planned grazing works on the principle of rotating herds of livestock which are able to migrate across areas of pasture, allowing grasses and roots to grow back. Grazing, the subsequent excrement which gets trodden into the earth by the herd, and the promotion of deeper root systems, help keep the soil alive and encourage long-term retention of carbon. When pasture is properly managed it also builds up the soil by adding organic matter.
• Feeding the cattle predominantly on pasture so that they are far less dependent on grains – grain farming can have seriously negative impacts on the environment.
• Stopping the use of synthetic fertilisers and pesticides and replacing them with enriching compost and manure (both are natural fertilisers). Reducing the need for these chemicals also reduces the high carbon footprint of producing them in the first place.
• Increasing the biodiversity of crops and animals in and around agricultural systems and practices, and encouraging the integration of trees, hedgerows and wildflowers, which in turn helps the living soil become healthier and more resilient and productive.
• Prioritising perennial crops and trees (plants that grow back year on year) on areas of farmland. These typically grow for longer each season, which in turn results in deeper root systems, which absorb more carbon into the soil.
• Stopping tilling and keeping soil covered and as undisturbed as possible, to maintain the cool, humid conditions needed to protect the ecosystem within the soil, for example by planting clover to reduce soil erosion and increase carbon capture during winter.

Regenerative farming is about being responsible stewards for the natural resources of the land. A future where we are able to rear meat and dairy products in a way that is much more in touch with the environment, and exponentially improve the welfare of animals, is possible. What's more, grass-reared meat is healthier for us: it contains higher quality protein, essential amino acids and micronutrients, iron, zinc and B vitamins, and the fat is an amazing source of conjugated linoleic acid (lauded as being good for our hearts and helping protect against cancer).

I prefer to buy meat from small-scale producers on the whole, but there are some exciting things happening on a larger scale. There is a farm in Suffolk called Dingley Dell, a third-generation regenerative pig farm run by brothers Mark and Paul Hayward. Pork farming is probably one of the most problematic areas of the meat industry, with widespread environmental and ethical issues, especially when it comes to animal welfare. At Dingley Dell Farm they take an inspiring holistic approach to every stage of the rearing process, from farm to plate, with a key focus on supporting the natural environment around the farm and the quality of the lives of the animals. They transformed what was previously an intensive farm into a model that was, in Mark's words, 'animal, people and environment centric', but also – crucially – profitable and operating at a relatively large scale. They passionately believe that farming doesn't just have to be driven by the cheapest way of doing things. The pigs are raised entirely outside and are moved to different land on a rotational cycle so that clover and swathes of diverse wildflowers and plants can be sown, allowing the land to recover, sequester carbon and impart nitrogen into the soil. The planting of 'nectar mixes' around the farm is particularly important. Mark told me that since the 1930s, 76 per cent of bee-forage plants in the UK have disappeared, and 97 per cent of wildflower meadows have vanished since World War Two. These are depressing statistics. As we all know, without bees, this whole show on Earth is pretty much done for, so it makes complete sense that farmers, who are fundamentally the custodians for most of the land, help protect and nurture them. Once you make your land hospitable to bees and insects, you naturally start to fuel an ecosystem for wildlife that can become abundant and work in harmony with the farm itself.

The problem of waste

In 2009, the UN Food and Agriculture Organization warned that the global population will have risen by 34 per cent to 9.1 billion by 2050. In order to feed this exploding population, it predicted that food production would need to increase by a staggering 70 per cent. Critics of farming philosophies like that of regenerative farming, or the re-wilding of farmland, cite a limit to the productivity capacity of land managed in this way.

It's a stark possibility that moving away from industrial farming and all its consequences (including the huge bounties of food being produced) could lead to serious food shortages. The obvious solution to this is to waste less. Years of plenty have made the idea of food shortages inconceivable to most of us, although it is without doubt a deep-rooted human fear (as the ransacking of supermarkets during the COVID-19 crisis revealed). It is estimated that in some parts of the world, over one third of all food produced is wasted. To me, this is criminal and just not a tenable situation. There needs to be a whole sea change in our society's attitude to food, and fast, and I truly believe it is possible to change.

Purchasing power

Supermarkets imposing stringent criteria on the cuts, sizes, colour and fat content of meat, resulting in uniform, pre-packed meat, has cut off society from meat's origins, but it doesn't have to be like this. I'm extremely optimistic that the meat industry can change if the trend for less meat but better meat continues to grow.

Beef production in particular has been under fire for years. We've all heard the horrific statistics: hundreds of thousands of acres of rainforest have been (and are still being) chopped down so the land can be used for grazing cattle, and the huge levels of methane that the cattle release into the atmosphere are contributing significantly to global warming. The market is flooded with cheap beef, with the WWF estimating that 25 per cent of global land use, land-use change, and forestry emissions are driven by beef production. However, there is the possibility of a sustainable future for beef rearing and again, it all comes down to rearing beef on well-managed pasture. So, when you're buying meat, always go for grass fed. It's unlikely you will find this in supermarkets, so head to your local butcher. You'll be doing your bit for the planet and you will also be buying a better product.

Also, think outside the box when it comes down to the cuts of meat you choose, and what breeds. We all love a good steak, but eating meat shouldn't be about only going for the prime cuts. It is a sickening reality that our resistance to taking a broader approach about the cuts of meat we consume means that a lot of the animal, once it has been butchered for the best bits, is discarded. As regular readers will know, I am a huge advocate for lesser-celebrated cuts such as ox cheek, rib, shin or belly and put emphasis on eating offal. The unparalleled gelatinous viscosity from a pig's trotter is what transforms my Tonkotsu Ramen recipe (page 213), and I am a lifelong lover of oxtail, which delivers lip-smacking richness in my 24-hour Beef Tail and Rib Pho (page 216) – it's by utilising as many parts of the animal as possible that I feel I can justify my carnivorous leanings. Many of these cheaper cuts just need a little bit more TLC when it comes to cooking, in order to get the best out of them – low and slow braising is my go-to method to achieve this. Some argue that good-quality meat is expensive, but it is much less expensive when you buy the right amounts, batch cook and opt for lesser-known cuts or mince.

There is a growing trend in the UK for utilising retired dairy cows for meat, inspired by producers in the Basque and Galician regions of Spain who have been doing this for years. Once a dairy cow's milk yield starts to wane at around 15 years old, rather than slaughtering the cow to use their meat in cheap burgers and dog food, the dairy cows are put out to pasture and allowed to fatten up and mature. This results in beautifully marbled meat with buttery yellow fat, which gives it a wonderful pronounced flavour. Eating dairy cows just makes complete sense to me. It's all about using animals in the best possible way, respecting what they provide for us and valuing them instead of flagrantly wasting these amazing resources.

Similarly, I really think we are obliged to eat veal. Veal became a bit of a dirty word in the 80s and 90s, as veal production then involved male calves being reared in cramped, dark barns, and being fed on liquid diets so their muscles couldn't develop properly. Quite rightly, this cruelty was outlawed in the EU in 2007, and things are now very different, especially in the UK. Welfare standards have been greatly improved and British rose veal is a beautiful product that we should be proud of. The reason I think it's important to eat veal is because of the dairy industry. For cows to produce milk they need to be made pregnant, with one calf born a year being the standard for most dairy cows. Any male calves born are obviously unable to produce milk, so most are shot at birth as there's no commercial demand for them. This seems totally unethical to me when there is potential to change our thinking, shopping and eating habits to avoid this senseless waste. If the idea of eating veal makes you feel uncomfortable but you still eat McDonalds, it is worth knowing that McDonalds is now buying up much of the veal that was once exported from this country, making them one of the most sustainable fast-food companies in the UK!

This idea applies to sheep too, and I would love to see hogget and mutton rise in popularity in this country.

Most lamb is slaughtered at 4–12 months old, but hogget is reared more slowly for 1–2 years and mutton is allowed to graze for at least 2 years, meaning they have had time to develop a fuller flavour and a finer grain of meat. Long-haul imports of anaemic-looking lamb from places like New Zealand, fattened up in barns on compound animal feeds, seems ludicrous to me when we have such wonderful produce available here in the UK. Sheep are also the least intensively farmed of any animal, so they have generally had access to pasture for the duration of their lives.

I also urge you to consider goat meat, one of the most sustainable meats out there, and check out Cabrito, who are doing wonderful things, from the rearing of the goats to the distribution of the meat.

It is an unavoidable reality that on a global scale we have to eat far less meat than at the gargantuan rates we do today. I am as horrified as anyone by footage of pigs kept in dark, cramped sheds making them so stressed that they resort to cannibalism, or industrial-scale fattening units keeping up to 3,000 cows at a time in grassless pens (this practice for beef rearing, previously associated as being a predominantly American one, is reported to be growing here in the UK in recent years, with the same going for intensive pig and chicken farming, to meet consumer demand). It is more important than ever to be principled when choosing what meat to buy and how often to buy it. Consumer demand will drive change one way or the other, and I refuse to accept that apocalyptic scenes of the industrial-scale meat industry will be the norm on the farms of the future.

What the labels mean

Make sure that you are aware of the way meat is labelled, especially in the supermarkets. It can be pretty confusing:

• 'Red Tractor' labels are not a good indicator of higher welfare standards, as they only signify the meat coming from the UK and this meat has to comply with only minimal legal standards.
• 'Organic' labels are regulated by EU standards, but a 'Soil Association' (SA) label means that the producer has gone beyond these minimum requirements, for example practising lower antibiotic use and better slaughter practices, so the SA label is a good one to look out for.
• 'Grass Fed' does not necessarily mean the animal has spent most of its life outside, merely that it has been fed on grass products. Look out for 'Pasture Promise' labels, which guarantee that cows have been grazed outside for at least 6 months of the year.
• 'Free Range' is a higher welfare choice as it gives animals access to outdoor space, but there is still an intensive side to this, so be aware that it doesn't mean the animals roam the land as nature intended; buying from small producers is the only way to ensure this.
• 'RSPCA Assured' labels go further to help certify that higher animal welfare has been maintained than the industry standard practices enforce.
• 'Outdoor Bred' can mean animals have only been outside with their mothers for a few weeks, while 'Outdoor Reared' means they can graze outside for most of their lives.

The best way to navigate this minefield is to talk to your butcher and ask questions. Any butcher worth their salt should be able to give you all this information to help you make the best, most well-informed choice.

Greenhouse gas emissions in pastoral farming

The concept of 'carbon footprints' from the meat we eat is an important consideration when it comes to understanding the impact of meat production on the planet. However, it is not a simple black and white value system. Some farming practices which we likely all agree are preferable, such as free range, or smaller, less industrial-scale farms can in fact result in the meat reared producing a higher carbon footprint. Even the phrase 'carbon footprint' is misleading: there is inconclusive evidence regarding the most effective way to measure and rate gas emissions, and which gases are the most harmful. It's all very confusing, so here is a simple breakdown of the key facts.

The key Greenhouse Gas (GHG) emissions from livestock are methane (CH_4) which equates for 44 per cent of all livestock emissions, followed by nitrous oxide (N_2O) at 29 per cent, and carbon dioxide (CO_2) at 27 per cent.

The two main activities that are responsible for these emissions are feed production and processing (45 per cent) and what is known as 'enteric fermentation from ruminants', which is, to put it indelicately, farting (39 per cent). Cows are the biggest culprits when it comes to this. The rest is accounted for through manure storage and the processing and transportation of animal products.

Across all the different livestock species, the consumption of fossil fuels along supply chains accounts for about 20 per cent of the livestock sector's emissions.

Beef, Veal and Dairy Cows

• 2.6 million cattle are slaughtered every year in the UK.
• About 120,000 veal calves are slaughtered for veal meat each year in the UK.
• Cattle, raised for both beef and milk, represent 65 per cent of the livestock sector's GHG emissions.
• Enteric emissions and feed production are the main causes of emissions for cattle.

Pork

• 10 million pigs are slaughtered every year in the UK.
• Pork is responsible for 9 per cent of the livestock sector's GHG emissions.
• The bulk of the emissions are related to feed production and manure processing in pig rearing.
• Unlike cows, sheep and goats, pigs do not help lock carbon into the soil, so do not provide the same potential environmental service. However, pig's manure, if utilised properly and not overused, can help increase soil fertility.

Lamb, Mutton, Hogget and Goat

• 14.5 million sheep and lambs are slaughtered every year in the UK.
• Sheep and goats are responsible for 6 per cent of the livestock sector's GHG emissions.
• The use of natural resources such as land and water and biodiversity loss are the main issues surrounding the rearing of these animals.

Chicken meat and eggs, and other poultry, account for the remaining 20 per cent of the livestock sector's GHG emissions.

Braised Beef Shin with Barbecue Sauce

SERVES 6
Preparation time 15 minutes
Cooking time 4 hours 20 minutes

5 tbsp oil
½ bone-in beef shin (about 3kg) – ask
  your butcher to French-trim it
2 onions, thinly sliced
1 head of garlic, cloves peeled and
  thinly sliced
2 tbsp ground coriander
2 tbsp ground cumin
1 tsp smoked paprika
1 bay leaf
½ tsp dried chipotle flakes or
  chipotle paste
600ml brown ale or medium-bodied
  IPA (American, preferably)
600g tomatoes, blitzed to a puree,
  or passata
500ml fresh beef stock
1 tsp English mustard
3 tbsp Worcestershire sauce
2–3 tbsp liquid smoke (optional)
50g dark brown muscovado sugar
50ml apple cider vinegar
sea salt and freshly ground black
  pepper
Cheese Semolina Grits (page 130),
  to serve

I was once sent the most beautiful shin of an old retired dairy cow, that had been rescued from death after retirement from the dairy industry and sent back out to pasture. People in the UK don't really eat dairy cows because they are prized for their udders and not their meat, and are therefore not widely available. After making milk for us they are slaughtered. It's a grim truth of the food chain. As a meat eater I want to eat meat responsibly. That can mean cutting back on meat and eating more plant-based meals, opting for cheaper cuts and offal instead of prime cuts, and showing some consideration to the animals that have served us in the dairy trade by offering them a longer life, lived in better conditions. The life of an industrial dairy cow is pretty dormant so the muscle tissue is soft and they hold graduated fat well, much like wagyu, but have less forced fat within their feed. I braised the shin in beer and lots of barbecue spices and served it with Cheese Semolina Grits and it is truly exceptional. This recipe would also work well with ox cheek (although you would be foregoing the bone marrow), oxtail or short rib (cooked for the same time).

Preheat the oven to 180°C/160°C fan/gas mark 4.

Heat half the oil in a large frying pan over a high heat, add the shin and brown it well all over for a good 15 minutes, until deeply caramelised. Remove and set aside.

There should be lots of residue left in the pan which is packed with flavour, so you want to utilise it. Add the rest of the oil to the pan with the onions, scrape the base of the pan and soften for 15–20 minutes until they start to caramelise, then add the garlic and soften for a few minutes before adding the ground spices, bay leaf and chipotle. Cook for a few minutes then pour in the beer and let it bubble for a minute or two.

Take a casserole dish large enough to fit the shin. Add the shin, pour over the beery onion mix, add the tomatoes and stock, and stir in the mustard, Worcestershire sauce, liquid smoke (if using), sugar and vinegar. Cover and cook in the oven for 4 hours.

Once the time is up, carefully lift the beef shin out of the sauce and set it aside on a plate. The meat should be beautifully tender. Pull out the bay leaf and transfer the sauce to a food processor. I would normally say you don't have to blitz the sauce, but we want a smooth, glossy BBQ sauce here, so give it a good blitz. Gently return the beef shin to the pan (you don't want it to break up) and pour over the blitzed sauce. Heat through for a few minutes then serve alongside my Cheese Semolina Grits.

Wild Garlic Stuffed Mutton

SERVES 6
Preparation time 20 minutes
Cooking time 35 minutes, plus
25 minutes resting time

50ml extra-virgin olive oil
8 wild garlic leaves (and any flowers),
  very finely chopped, as for a salsa
  verde
½ tsp sea salt
½ tsp freshly ground black pepper
950g boned and butterflied hogget
  leg (about a third of a leg)
glug of oil

FOR THE GRAVY

½ tbsp plain flour
250ml white wine
500ml fresh lamb or chicken stock
2 tbsp small capers (in vinegar)
squeeze of lemon juice
30g butter

I was asked to choose a favourite producer for an appearance on one of Rick and Jack Stein's days of 'live' food demos, mid COVID-19 lockdown. Matt Chatfield of the Cornwall Project is probably my number-one guy when it comes to sustainability within agriculture in the UK. He is also one of the most considerate producers I've ever worked with. He has taken over the production of his mother's sheep farm and transformed it in a very progressive way, adopting sheep at the end of their farm life, such as milk and cheese industry sheep whose udders are not working properly (sheep that would otherwise be culled), and putting them to pasture, then producing beautiful mutton and hogget. He likes to call these rescued sheep Cull Yaw ('Cull' means to be culled, and 'Yaw' is sheep in Cornish). The best chefs in the restaurant industry go mad for his mutton, but diminished demand due to lockdown means that we can all get our mitts on the prized meat. Mutton and wild garlic grow together and this is the perfect easy roast. I ask my butcher to joint a whole leg, butterfly it, then cut it into a neat third that is easy to roll and use the rest of it in my Mutton Nihari curry on page 219.

Preheat the oven to 190°C/170°C fan/gas mark 5.

Mix together the oil, wild garlic and seasoning. Open out the butterflied joint and stuff it with the wild garlic and oil. Roll the meat up and tie it with string, using three or four butcher's knots along the length of the meat (there are lots of YouTube tutorials that show you how to do this).

Get a frying pan really hot on the stove with the glug of oil. Season the meat then sear it all over until fairly darkly caramelised. Remove from the pan (but keep the frying pan with the meaty residue to one side for the sauce) and transfer to a roasting tray. For perfectly pink, medium-rare meat, roast in the oven for 25 minutes. Remove from the oven and rest uncovered for 25 minutes.

To make the gravy, set the pan you sealed the meat in over a medium heat. Add the flour and wine and allow to bubble for a few minutes, scraping the bottom of the pan to retrieve all the meaty goodness. Add the stock and reduce it by about two thirds to achieve an intense flavour – this should take about 20 minutes. Stir in the capers and lemon juice. Finally, whisk in the butter to give the gravy an extra-rich viscosity.

Serve the gravy on the plate, with the lamb and any classic trimmings. I love this with the Flageolet, Anchovy, Rosemary & Confit Garlic Gratin from my last book, *Slow*.

A Really Great Lamb Neck Stew
with lots of flavour but no identity

SERVES 6–8
Preparation time 30 minutes
Cooking time 4 hours

1 whole lamb neck (about 2kg), cut into 6–7 neck chops through the joint
4 tbsp oil
3 onions, peeled and cut into wedges
4 carrots, peeled
2 tsp plain flour
2 bay leaves
3 sprigs of rosemary and a good few sprigs of thyme (or whatever woody herbs you have)
small bunch of flat-leaf parsley, stalks finely chopped and leaves chopped
1.5 litres fresh jellied chicken stock or water
350g waxy potatoes, peeled
400g smallish floury potatoes, peeled and halved
2 tbsp sherry vinegar (or other vinegar, just don't use balsamic)
1 tbsp sugar (any sugar is fine)
½ tsp celery salt
sea salt and freshly ground black pepper

Okay, I should warn you, I'm about to make a simple recipe very complicated. But bear with me and read every word, because, while it's messy, they are all very necessary.

I want to call this an 'Irish stew' but because of one small technique, I can't. We are so protective of the cultural culinary heritage that me browning the meat for a lamb stew makes it have no real identity. You see, in British regional cooking we wouldn't have browned it. And it's not just the British who didn't traditionally brown meat, it's a habit commonplace in much of the world's cookery, from curries to hot pots. I tried to find out how and when browning meat for slow-cooked dishes/stews was introduced and my search was inconclusive. I genuinely couldn't find a (caramelised) sausage, so I procrastinated with my very good friend, food writer and historian for the *Telegraph*, Xanthe Clay, and we came up with something a bit more 'cooked'.

We thought it probably started with people loving the deeper umami that the edge of a cast-iron pan gave meat when cooking a stew over a fire. We know that cooking meat in water came as a secondary skill to cooking it over fire. Barbecuing meat gives it great caramelisation and it's likely that the prime cuts would have been grilled and eaten first and less-admired cuts would be put into a pan to braise in order to prolong keeping times, with the bones boiled to make broths. Attentive cooks would have noticed that the sweet, sticky umami on the browned bits enhanced the meat's flavour and maybe that's when someone clever like Escoffier decided to brown all meat before cooking it. It's not exactly an official answer, but it works for me.

Back to this stew. I make it with lamb neck on the bone, and plead with you to do the same. Slowly cooking meat on the bone enables the gelatin to gently cook out into the sauce and gives a much deeper flavour and a lip-smacking stickiness. Cooking the meat on the bone also prevents shrinkage and there is no better indicator of whether something is cooked enough than it simply 'falling off the bone'!

My disregard for the UK's culinary traditions doesn't just stop at my need to brown the meat. Irish stew purists say no to anything but onions, potatoes and water, so maybe this version leans more towards a Liverpudlian 'Scouse', as I cannot not put carrots in. But we should also nod here to the Welsh cawl that includes leeks and swedes, or Scotch broth with its soupier consistency and the addition of pearl barley… None of the stews above use herbs, but on my watch they do! I add whatever

CONTINUED ››

woody herbs I have available and also do something very French, finishing the stew (as I do many of my braises) with a 'gastrique'. A gastrique is a technique of acidulating caramelised sugar to boost the balance of sweet-umami in a dish. It's traditionally done by making a dry caramel and then pouring vinegar into it and reducing it to a syrup, but I make a shortcut version at home, where I just melt sugar and vinegar together. It's amazing how something so simple can be so dynamic in how it can reinvigorate a dish.

The other law I break is to finish the dish with celery salt. It's such a great flavour enhancer. I use it like MSG (monosodium glutamate), to boost the flavour of stews and soups at the end of cooking.

All this and we haven't even got to the potatoes. I stick to tradition here, using two types, floury and waxy. The floury potatoes need to be well cooked and break up into the stew, while the waxy ones have bite and hold their shape.

At this stage we have broken so many rules that this poor recipe is identity-less, so I'm going to go a step further and suggest serving it with mashed potatoes, greens and buttered white, chewy, crusty bread. I know I will have offended many traditionalists, but I can safely say that it's big in the flavour stakes. Using your gut instinct is almost always the best way to cook. You can use this ethos when making most braises with most meats and take what you like from this recipe. This is how I make a lamb stew.

Season the lamb pieces with salt and pepper.

Heat 2 tablespoons of the oil in a large frying pan over a high heat and brown the meat in two or three batches (to avoid overcrowding the pan) until they take on a rich, dark caramel colour. Avoid moving the pieces while they brown. Deglaze the pan with water between each batch and allow the meaty juices to bubble into a thin syrup, then reserve this as it will have loads of lamby flavour for the stew.

Meanwhile, heat the rest of the oil in a large casserole dish over a medium-low heat, add the onions and carrots and fry gently for about 5 minutes. Normally I'd want to get a lot of sweet umami flavour out of them, but for this stew they just need a quick soften, without taking on too much colour. Add the flour and give the vegetables a quick toss to coat (it's hard with whole carrots, but persevere – I cook the carrots whole so they don't break up in the stew). Next, add the herbs (including the parsley stalks – keep the leaves for the end), then slowly pour over the stock or water and those deglazing pan juices, stirring to create a sauce. There's a lot of liquid at this stage so it will still be very thin, but fear not! With the reduction of the braise, the flour will start to activate as a thickener and the addition of the potatoes later will also help. Lay the lamb pieces into the casserole dish and make sure there is enough liquid to cover.

The next bit is quite a cheffy thing – making a cartouche. It's a way of holding in the condensation while you cook, meaning that the sauce reduces more slowly and evenly. Cut out a piece of greaseproof paper just a bit bigger than the size of the lid of your casserole dish, then wet it and scrunch it up into a ball (this will make it more malleable). Reopen it, flatten it, lay it on top of the stew and push the edges up the wall of the dish. You don't have to do this, but it will help the meat cook evenly and stop the dish drying out during long, slow cooking (this works for all stews). Pop the lid on and bring to the boil. The second it starts to boil, reduce the temperature and simmer slowly for 2 hours 30 minutes. Scrape the bottom of the dish every so often after 2 hours to avoid the stew catching, but do not stir it after that as it will start to break the meat up.

After 2 hours 30 minutes, add the potatoes and push them under the liquid, pop the cartouche and lid back on and cook for 30 minutes, then take off the lid and cartouche and cook for a further 20 minutes or until the lamb is falling off the bone, the sauce has thickened from the potatoes and reduction and the flavour of the lamb is strong.

Now, make the gastrique: heat the vinegar and sugar in a small saucepan until the sugar has dissolved, then bring to the boil. When syrupy, pour into the stew, add the celery salt and lots of salt and pepper and gently mix (so as not to break up the meat).

The stew is ready to eat, but it gets better with age. A few hours is good, one day great, two days and now you're really talking.

Goat Herder's Pie

SERVES 8
Preparation time 30 minutes
Cooking time 4 hours

750g goat mince (minimum 20 per
    cent fat)
3 medium onions, finely chopped
1 large carrot, finely chopped
5 garlic cloves, finely chopped
1 leek, washed, quartered lengthways
    and thinly sliced
1 tsp tomato puree
1 tsp plain flour
175ml white wine
175ml red wine
2 tsp Worcestershire sauce
200ml fresh jellied beef stock
    (chicken or lamb stock would work
    too)
3 sprigs of rosemary, leaves finely
    chopped
10 sprigs of thyme, leaves finely
    chopped
pinch of ground cloves
3 tsp sea salt
½ tbsp freshly ground black pepper

FOR THE MASH
1.25kg floury potatoes, peeled and
    cut into smallish chunks
50g butter
50ml milk or cream
1½ tsp ground white pepper
2 tsp salt
½ nutmeg, grated
20g Parmesan, grated

TO SERVE
peas
brown or Oxford sauce

Goat meat brings new life to lamby classics with its deep and intense flavour, leaner meat and it has a more reliable sustainability trail. It goes without saying that a goat herder's pie will be a hit: it is the ultimate version of a goat or lamb meat pie. When using top-quality meat you must use a good jellified stock that transforms into a glossy and gelatinous sauce. A stock cube isn't just cheating, it would offensively tarnish the dish, so don't let me, the meat, or yourself, down by cheating.

You simply cannot serve shepherd's pie without peas, and that is no different when using goat, and a bit of brown or Oxford sauce is the ideal condiment.

Fry the goat mince, in batches, in a smoking hot frying pan for 6–8 minutes per batch until well browned and caramelised – this will give the dish a properly rich flavour. You don't need to add any oil as there will be enough fat in the mince itself. Drain off excess fat from the pan into a heatproof container as you fry the mince (don't throw it away as you'll need it later). Once the meat is browned, set aside.

Heat 3–4 tablespoons of the goat fat in a large casserole dish over a medium-low heat, add the onions and carrot and sweat for about 25 minutes until well softened, stirring occasionally. Add the garlic and leeks and sweat for a further 10 minutes, then stir in the tomato puree and allow it to caramelise for a couple of minutes before adding the flour. Cook for a further minute then add the browned goat mince. Pour in both wines, Worcestershire sauce and stock, and the chopped herbs and cloves. Braise very gently, covered, for 2 hours 30 minutes then uncover and braise for a further 30 minutes. Add the salt and pepper, transfer the meat to a large ovenproof dish and set aside. Preheat the oven to 200°C/180°C fan/gas mark 6.

To make the mash, put the potatoes in a large saucepan of heavily salted cold water. Bring to the boil and simmer rapidly for 15 minutes until softened and cooked through. Drain and steam dry for about 10 minutes, then return the potatoes to the pan and mash well until smooth (with a masher or potato ricer). Place over a medium heat and add the butter and milk or cream, mashing until the butter melts. Add the white pepper, salt and nutmeg and mix thoroughly until well combined.

Layer the mash onto the meat sauce (I use a piping bag, but you don't have to). Sprinkle over the Parmesan and bake for 40 minutes until the top is golden and crisp. Remove from the oven and serve with peas and sauce of your choice.

Jamaican Goat Curry Patties

MAKES 8 patties
Preparation time 30 minutes, plus chilling time (ideally overnight)
Cooking time 2 hours 30 minutes

FOR THE FILLING

500g goat mince (minimum 20 per cent fat)

1 onion, roughly chopped

12 garlic cloves, peeled

7cm piece of fresh ginger, peeled and roughly chopped

½ small bunch of thyme, leaves picked

1 rounded tsp tomato puree

2 tsp plain flour

500ml fresh beef stock

250ml water

1 tbsp any vinegar (classically, you'd use malt)

1 tbsp brown sauce, plus extra to serve

1 Scotch bonnet chilli

1–2 tbsp West Indian Hot Sauce (page 34), to serve

FOR THE SPICE MIX

1 tbsp coriander seeds

½ tbsp cumin seeds

1 tsp black peppercorns or freshly ground black pepper

3 green cardamom pods

2 whole cloves or a pinch of ground cloves

½ tsp fenugreek seeds

1 tsp ground cinnamon

1 tsp ground ginger

½ tsp ground turmeric

pinch of ground allspice

½ nutmeg, grated

I really want to push mince in this book, mostly because it's the most accessible and affordable way for us to eat sustainable meat, and a little goes a long way, but it's also a way for butchers to make use of all the cuts. Long, slow cooking is a good way to get the best out of the mince too. This Jamaican dish isn't authentic, but it is absolutely delicious. You can make these as hand pies or even put the filling into a big family pie (the patty pastry, minus the spices, works excellently as pie pastry). Always have some coleslaw and West Indian hot sauce to hand.

You can make the filling and the pastry the day before assembling and baking them.

Grind all the spice mix ingredients in a small food processor, pestle and mortar or spice grinder until as fine as possible.

Heat a frying pan over a high heat until smoking hot and brown the goat mince in batches until well browned and caramelised. You don't need to add any oil to the pan, as the fat from the mince will melt in the pan and be enough to fry it in. Drain the fat between batches into a container, but don't throw it away: you need it for the pastry! Once all the mince is browned, remove it from the pan and set aside.

Blitz the onion, garlic, ginger and thyme in a food processor to a puree. Spoon about 2 tablespoons of the goat fat into a casserole dish and place over a medium heat. Add the garlicky puree and fry for 7–8 minutes until softened, stirring regularly. Add the ground spices and fry for a couple of minutes, then stir in the tomato puree and cook for a further minute or two, before adding the flour. Cook for another minute then add the browned goat mince. Pour in the stock, water, vinegar and brown sauce and drop in the Scotch bonnet chilli. Stir and cook over a low heat, covered, for 2 hours.

Once the cooking time is up, remove from the heat and cool to room temperature, then chill it in the fridge (preferably overnight).

To make the pastry, put the flour, salt, baking powder, turmeric, curry powder and sugar in a stand mixer fitted with a dough hook and mix until everything is evenly distributed. Add the suet and goat fat and mix until you achieve a crumb-like texture.

CONTINUED ››

FOR THE PASTRY

350g plain flour, plus extra for
    dusting
¾ tsp fine salt
¼ tsp baking powder
1 tbsp ground turmeric
1 tsp curry powder
1 tbsp caster sugar
170g beef suet
50g goat fat, rendered down from
    the minced curry goat filling
    and cooled
2 free-range eggs, beaten
½ tbsp white vinegar
50ml ice-cold water

In a small bowl, whisk together one of the eggs with the vinegar and water. With the mixer on slow speed, pour in the egg mixture and once the dough starts to come together, turn the mixer to full speed and mix for about 15 seconds. I know this breaks the sacrosanct laws of pastry-making, as you are always told not to overwork a dough, but you need to mix this pastry a little longer to help build up the gluten and create a dough with a more durable, workable consistency.

If you don't have a stand mixer, mix all the dry ingredients together with a whisk then, using a knife, mix in the suet and goat fat until well dispersed and the mixture has a crumb-like texture. Add the egg mixture and use a knife to bind the pastry together before kneading the pastry together for a couple of minutes.

Turn the dough out and bring it together into a ball. Split into 8 equal balls and gently roll them flat to make them easier to manipulate later. Wrap in cling film and chill in the fridge for at least 30 minutes (or overnight).

Preheat the oven to 200°C/180°C fan/gas mark 6.

When you're ready to make the patties, dust your rolling pin on a work surface with a little flour. Take one of the pastry pieces and roll into a circle about 5mm thick and 20cm in diameter (don't roll them too thinly). Place 2–3 tablespoons of the goat curry filling on one half of the circle, with at least a couple of centimetres of pastry clear around the edge. Beat the other egg and brush it around the perimeter of the pastry to help bind the edges together. Fold the other half of the pastry over the top of the mixture to form a half circle. Press the edges tightly together all the way around, then crimp them. Repeat until you have used all the pastry and filling. Glaze the surface of the patties with the egg wash, chill in the fridge for at least 20 minutes, then give them a second, final glaze. Chill in the fridge until you are ready to cook them.

These patties freeze really well and can be cooked from frozen (just add 2 minutes to the cooking time).

When you're ready to eat them, oil a baking tray and line it with baking parchment. Carefully transfer the patties onto the lined baking tray and brush all of the patties with more egg wash. Sprinkle a little sea salt on the top of each. Bake in the oven for 22 minutes, until golden and crisp. Remove from the oven and allow to cool for a couple of minutes before serving with hot sauce or brown sauce (or both, if you're me).

Miso and Apple Pork Rib-eye Steaks

SERVES 4
Preparation time 5 minutes
Cooking time 30 minutes

2 Bramley apples (about 360g total
    weight), peeled, cored and thinly
    sliced
80g caster sugar
2 tbsp rice wine vinegar
100ml water
200g white miso paste
a little oil, for frying
4 x 200g bone-in pork rib-eye
    steaks, roughly 2.5cm thick, at
    room temperature
2 spring onions, very thinly sliced
salt

Pork loin chops, the typical 'steak' cut, are expensive and hard to get right when cooking. Over the last decade it's become more widely recognised that fat and gelatinous collagen are what gives meat flavour and a better cook, and that cooking pork to a pink blush (medium) is actually perfectly safe and gives a much juicier and tastier chop, so I now favour a pork rib-eye, which I get from my butchers, Turner and George. If your butcher isn't at ease with the modern terminology, the cut is in fact from the neck fillet.

A glut of Bramley apples and a need to use up some sad-looking miso inspired this recipe. We all know pork and apple are a good fit, but miso is also used in Japan widely with pork, from udon noodles, and steamy bowls of ramen, to sticky miso glazes for robata-grilled meat. The plan was to treat the meat like Nobu's famous Black Cod and Miso, but while a marinade often maketh the better meal, with this hefty pork chop I wanted the flavour of the meat to come through and only finish it with a glaze. This sauce and technique works well with mackerel too, and in gooseberry season you could make the most outstanding gooseberry miso sauce in the same vein.

Put the apples in a saucepan with the sugar, rice wine vinegar and water, place over a medium-low heat and cook, stirring occasionally, until the apples have completely broken down and have a saucy consistency. Remove from the heat and stir in the miso. I blitz the mixture in a food processor for a few seconds to achieve a really luxurious, smooth consistency, but you could use it as it is, with some texture. Set aside and allow to cool, putting about a third of the sauce in a separate dish to serve at the end.

Once you're ready to cook the meat, heat a griddle or frying pan over a high heat until smoking hot. Drizzle a little oil and sprinkle a pinch of salt on each side of one of the steaks. It's best to cook one steak at a time, as you don't want to overcrowd the pan.

Using a pastry brush or spoon, smother a thin layer of the miso apple sauce all over a steak then lay it in the pan. Fry for 2 minutes, turn the steak over and repeat the process. Remove from the pan and set aside to rest. Fry the remaining steaks, sprinkling with a pinch of salt before cooking. A little residual pinkness is ideal – this delivers the best flavour and juicy texture – but if you prefer, leave the steaks in the pan a minute or two longer, but be really careful not to overcook them as they will become tough and dry. Once the steaks have rested for about 10 minutes, serve them with a big spoonful of extra apple-miso sauce and a sprinkling of very thinly sliced spring onions.

Chashu Pork Belly

SERVES 8
Preparation time 5 minutes
Cooking time 2 hours–2 hours
30 minutes

1.2kg pork belly, rolled and tied (ask
  your butcher to do this)
200ml mirin
750ml Japanese soy sauce
250ml Shaoxing wine or sake
100g caster sugar

This is the classic braised pork served with Tonkotsu Ramen (opposite). It's best made so it's ready at least 2 hours before serving the ramen – if you want to get ahead you can also cook it the day before you serve it. Classically, the braising liquid is simply soy sauce and sugar, but I do think it benefits from the addition of wine and mirin, which gives the pork and liquid a more dynamic final flavour. The braising liquid serves as your 'tare', the base for your tonkotsu, and also as a marinade for boiled eggs.

You can pimp the braising liquid even further with the addition of pieces of ginger, garlic cloves or spring onions if you fancy – it's up to you.

Preheat the oven to 200°C/180°C fan/gas mark 6.

Place the pork in a casserole dish, pour over the mirin, soy sauce, Shaoxing or sake, and add the sugar (and other aromatics, if liked). Cover and put the pork in the oven for 2 hours–2 hours 30 minutes, until the juices run clear when you insert a skewer into the middle of the meat.

Remove from the oven and leave to rest for 30 minutes before slicing, or if you've prepared it earlier it can be kept in the fridge overnight. Cut into 4mm-thick slices and fry in a hot pan for a couple of minutes on each side to reheat and crisp up slightly, or serve it at room temperature.

Tonkotsu Ramen

SERVES 8
Preparation time 15 minutes
Cooking time 12–15 hours

6 pig's trotters, split down the middle
    (ask your butcher to do this)
4 small shallots, skins on
bunch of spring onions, untrimmed,
    cut into 4
4 garlic cloves, unpeeled
2 onions, peeled and quartered
1 tsp black peppercorns
80g fresh ginger, unpeeled and
    thickly sliced

FOR THE BURNT GARLIC OIL (MAYU)
(leftovers will keep for about 2 months
in the fridge)

50g garlic cloves, peeled
200ml vegetable oil

FOR THE MARINATED EGGS

8 free-range eggs
about 400ml Chashu Pork cooking
    liquor (opposite)

TO SERVE (PER PERSON)

80g fresh ramen noodles or 50g dried
    ramen noodles
2 tbsp Chashu Pork cooking liquor
    (opposite)
2–3 thin slices of Chashu Pork
    (opposite)
15g beansprouts
green end of 1 spring onion, very,
    very thinly sliced
drizzle of burnt garlic oil

OTHER TOPPING IDEAS

1 sheet of dried nori seaweed or
    English seaweed
2 tbsp kimchi
2 tbsp tinned bamboo shoots,
    drained and shredded

I think it was Bone Daddies that introduced me to tonkotsu ramen. Before that, most British restaurants didn't really offer an authentic version, and I think sadly most Brits still think that the insipid watery ramen served at restaurants like Wagamama accounts for real ramen broth. There are, in fact, several different types of ramen in Japan. They say it's based around four main styles: shio, a salt-based clear-broth ramen, perhaps the most traditional and popularised style; shoyu, a dark, soy sauce-flavoured ramen (if you've ever had a Tokyo ramen, then this is along those lines, more like chicken broth and a little sweeter than shio ramen); miso ramen, which is richer, full of umami and cloudy, but thinner than my favourite – tonkotsu ramen. The word tonkotsu literally translates as 'pig bone' and the ramen is made with just that – pig bones and skin which are boiled ferociously until the natural collagen and gelatin are knocked out, to create a creamy and cloudy broth. As with all ramens, it is made with a seasoning base called a *tare*. A really good tare usually requires a dashi made of 'katsuobushi' bonito (tuna) flakes. Tuna has sadly become unsustainable, so I had to come up with an alternative and the answer came from what the ramen is served with: braised red pork ('chashu'). The braising pork liquor works as the most delicious tare and flavour booster, which satisfyingly means nothing goes to waste. The broth takes 12–15 hours to cook, but you can split this over two days, or/and make it a few days ahead and chill it. Tonkotsu also has many additions and toppings. As well as the broth, chashu pork and tare, you have the marinated eggs (I make this easy by marinating them in the very same tare) and the burnt garlic oil. You can be playful and add whatever toppings you like. I've not added the traditional toppings of bamboo or black fungus, as we don't grow them here, but use them if you can find them. Some add a dollop of miso mixed with chilli, chilli oil or sriracha and even enrich it (like it needs enriching any more) with a grating of Parmesan.

Rinse the trotters thoroughly in cold water. Add them to a large pan or stockpot and cover with more cold water. Bring to the boil and simmer for 2–3 minutes, skimming off the scum that forms on the surface with a large metal spoon. Drain the trotters and rinse thoroughly to get rid of any residual scum or dirt as this will taint your stock. Clean out the pan too so that you are starting afresh. Return the cleaned trotters to the clean pan and cover with fresh cold water so that it comes a good couple of centimetres above the trotters. Add the shallots, spring onions, garlic, onion, peppercorns and ginger. Bring to the boil then boil gently for 12–15 hours, uncovered.

CONTINUED ››

2 tbsp kikurage (wood ear) mushrooms
2 tbsp shiitake mushrooms, thinly sliced and fried
2 tbsp grilled corn from the cob
1 tbsp roasted sesame seeds
1 tbsp pickled ginger, shredded
½ tsp garlic crisps (you can buy these – they're fried thinly sliced garlic)
1 tbsp grated Parmesan

The broth should be at a constant boil (maybe not quite a rolling boil, but close), as this helps to emulsify the fat from the trotters, resulting in the rich, creamy soup tonkotsu is renowned for. Skim the surface of the stock every so often to maintain a clean taste to the final broth and top up with water if it's reduced too much, so that the trotters are submerged. Stir every so often, so that the trotters don't burn at the bottom.

Meanwhile, make the burnt garlic oil and marinate the eggs. To make the oil, blitz the garlic in a food processor or blender with half the oil to a smooth paste. Transfer to a small saucepan and add the rest of the oil. Cook over a medium-low heat for about 30 minutes, until the garlic very, very slowly becomes black (not technically burnt) – as it cooks it turns almost into a sticky caramel, so scrape the bottom to keep it cooking evenly and prevent it scorching into a solid mass. Leave to cool, then blitz in the food processor or blender for about 1 minute, until emulsified to a smooth black oil.

To marinate the eggs, boil the eggs for 6 minutes only (you want a soft, fudgy centre). Transfer to ice-cold water to cool, then peel carefully and submerge in a bowl of Chashu Pork cooking liquor. Chill for 6 hours, preferably overnight (eat within 24 hours).

Once the 12–15 hours is up, it's time to strain the broth. To achieve that final proper lip-smacking richness, you need to blitz 200g of the trotter meat, skin and fat into the final broth. Pull it out of the gubbins when you strain the broth, discarding any bones, peppercorns, or other aromatic bits. Blitz in a blender until smooth and return to the pan of broth to keep warm while you prepare the garnishes. Have everything laid out in front of you so that you can work quickly and the tonkotsu gets to the table piping hot. You need 2–2.5 litres of broth, so dilute it with a little water if it falls short. The broth is unseasoned, so if you want to get a sense of the final flavour, take a couple of spoonfuls of broth and mix with a little of the tare cooking liquor.

Once you're ready to serve, cook the noodles in a large pan of boiling, heavily salted water according to the packet instructions, then drain.

To construct the ramen, put 2 tablespoons of the Chashu Pork cooking liquor in each bowl. Cover each serving with 300ml of tonkotsu broth and stir. Place a nest of noodles in the centre of each bowl, then top it with your chosen toppings. Arrange the pork slices, egg (halved), beansprouts, spring onion and finally add a good drizzle of burnt garlic oil (this really lifts the dish). Eat while steaming hot.

24-hour Beef Tail and Rib Pho

SERVES 6–8
Preparation time 10 minutes
Cooking time 24 hours

FOR THE STOCK

1kg beef bones, preferably 6cm pieces
    of marrow bones
the whole of the bottom half of the
    end of an oxtail, or 2 large pieces
    from the top end
4 × 6cm pieces of short rib
80g fresh ginger, unpeeled, washed
    and thickly sliced
6 garlic cloves, unpeeled
1 bunch of spring onions, cut
    into 4
2 onions, quartered
1 cinnamon stick
1 star anise
1 tbsp black peppercorns
3–4 tbsp fish sauce
1 tbsp sugar

TO SERVE (per person)

50g dried flat rice noodles
⅙ onion
1 spring onion
a few mint leaves
a few Thai basil leaves
a few coriander leaves
1–2 red bird's-eye chillies
¼ lime
15g beansprouts
sriracha (optional)

For thousands of years, all over the world, and especially in Asia, people have been boiling meat bones to make nutritious stocks and soups. Pho (pronounced 'fer'), one of the cornerstones of Vietnamese cooking, manages to have a satisfying depth in flavour yet also be vibrant and refined. It's a no-brainer as to why: there is so much delicious gelatin and marrow to be drawn from bones over a long, slow cook, and it's surprising how much meat one can retrieve from spent beef ribs and oxtail bones, which are otherwise often thrown away. I swear I managed to pull off about a kilo of tender meat from the quantity of bones in this recipe, which surprised even me. What you end up with is the ultimate in comfort food, a wholly nourishing soup which you know is doing you good with every mouthful. What's more, it's cheap as chips and made from bits that people tend to throw away.

This recipe requires a trip to the butcher, so use the ingredients list as a rough guide, and adjust what you use depending on what the butcher has in. The essential components are at least 2.5kg of beef bones, which should include some meat, tendon and bone marrow. It doesn't really matter, but broths made with plenty of bone marrow will have more toothsome viscosity. It's also worth noting that it doesn't have to be cooking for a constant 24-hour period. You can take it off the heat overnight. It'll take about 6–10 hours to cool so it's fine to keep it out of the fridge. The stock will marinate in the extra time and be really delicious. You can also halve the recipe and cook it really low and slow in a slow cooker.

First, rinse the bones under cold water to get rid of any dirt. Place the cleaned bones in a very large pan or stockpot and cover with fresh cold water so the bones are well submerged. Place over a high heat and bring to the boil, then simmer for a few minutes, skimming off any scum that forms on the top with a large metal spoon. Lower the heat so that the stock is cooking at a gentle simmer, intermittently checking if it needs skimming to remove scum over the subsequent 2 hours or so. Allow to slowly simmer for another 10 hours, so that it has 12 hours cooking for this first phase in total.

Now it's time to add the aromatics. Add the ginger, garlic, spring onions, onions, cinnamon, star anise and peppercorns and simmer for a further 12 hours. This is not like a usual stock, because while we want a clear stock, and classically stirring your

CONTINUED ››

stock risks it getting cloudy, cooking a broth very slowly for 24 hours does risk the ingredients in the pan sticking to the bottom, so it's worth checking the water level, to make sure it is covering the bones, and gently scraping the bottom and stirring occasionally. For the last 3 hours of cooking you don't need to check the water level. It's now time to let it reduce, very slowly but surely. When the time's up the stock should have reduced by about a third.

Strain the stock to remove the bones and aromatics, reserving all that potent broth. Set aside any bones with meat attached, wiping them clean of aromatics. As the broth has not been seasoned and possibly not fully reduced, it will not taste completely ready yet. Wash out the stockpot it's been cooked in, pour the broth back into it and bring it to a rolling boil. It will probably need to reduce by another third, but you're essentially waiting for it to taste really beefy. You won't get the full beef flavour until you add the fish sauce and sugar, so you have to trust your senses. When you're happy, it's time to season the broth with the fish sauce and sugar. Fish sauce is so important as it adds umami, but you may prefer to use salt.

Now it's time to pick the meat off the bones. Make sure you remove the meat and lay it out in its specific parts on a plate or baking tray. I love picking off all the tendon pieces too and pulling out the bone marrow from inside the bones – it's a little gruesome but these are some of the tastiest bits. You can discard the clean bones now.

Prep your garnishes: cook the noodles according the instructions on the packet, very thinly slice your onions, pick the leaves, cut the chillies and lime and lay them out with the beansprouts on a plate.

To serve, fill a pho or ramen bowl with noodles and top with a couple of tablespoons of rib meat, a couple of tablespoons of tail meat and some of the tendon and marrow, add the fresh onions and herbs and then ladle over 400ml of boiling-hot stock. You can add more herbs, the limes, chillies and beansprouts at the table, even some sriracha, and it's time to eat.

Mutton Nihari

SERVES 4
Preparation time 20 minutes
Cooking time 4 hours 30 minutes

1.2kg mutton, cut into large 5–6cm
    pieces
4 tbsp ghee or oil
2 medium onions, thinly sliced
6–8 garlic cloves, peeled
100g fresh ginger, peeled
20g fresh turmeric, peeled, or 1 tsp
    ground turmeric
500ml fresh chicken stock
3 tbsp wine, sherry or cider vinegar
    (don't use balsamic)
1½ tsp sugar
sea salt

FOR THE NIHARI MASALA

1 tbsp cumin seeds
2 tsp coriander seeds
2 tsp fennel seeds
4–5 cloves
5–6 green cardamom pods
2 black cardamom pods
8–10 black peppercorns
1 cinnamon stick
1 bay leaf
1 tbsp Kashmiri chilli powder
¼ tsp grated nutmeg
1 tsp ground ginger

TO SERVE

coriander leaves
cooked rice

East London is famous for its curry houses. Most people go to the Anglo-Indian restaurants along Brick Lane, but if you venture off the beaten track you are more likely to find some great Bangladeshi and Pakistani restaurants, my favourites being Lahore Kebab House, Tayyabs and Needoo Grill. One of the unsung heroes on these menus is a curry that deserves way more attention – the nihari. This is a great way for the uninitiated to use mutton, and I will always jump at the chance to bang the drum for mutton! Consider it a rich lamb stew that happens to be spiced with chilli. It is rich, deep and full of umami, and I can't imagine anyone not liking it – it is that sort of dish.

Start by making the masala. Toast the whole spices (all except the last three ingredients) in a dry frying pan for a few minutes until fragrant. Remove and allow to cool a little, then grind to a fine powder in a small food processor, pestle and mortar or spice grinder with the Kashmiri chilli powder, grated nutmeg and ground ginger.

Season the meat generously. Heat a tablespoon or so of the ghee or oil in a frying pan over a high heat and brown the meat in batches until deeply caramelised all over. You may need to add more fat. Once all the meat is browned, deglaze the pan with a little water and give it a good scrape to loosen all the meaty residue. Set this aside for later.

Heat the remaining ghee or oil in a heavy-based casserole dish over a medium heat. Add the onions and soften and caramelise slowly for 25–30 minutes, stirring regularly.

Blitz the garlic, ginger and turmeric in a small food processor to a smooth paste.

Once the onions are softened and golden, add the ginger-garlic paste and cook for 4–5 minutes, stirring, then add the spice mix and cook for another minute. Pour over the stock and bring to the boil then transfer the mixture to a blender or food processor and blitz for 1–2 minutes until smooth. Return it to the casserole dish and add the mutton to the sauce. Top up with a little water if necessary, so the liquid sits just above the meat. Stir, cover and cook over the lowest heat for a good 4 hours, until the meat is tender. Alternatively, cook it in an oven at 170°C/150°C fan/gas mark 3.

For a final bit of oomph, I like to add a gastrique to really lift the dish (see pages 202–4). Simply simmer the vinegar and sugar in a small saucepan for a few minutes until the sugar has dissolved and the mix has reduced to a syrup. Stir it into the curry, season to taste and serve it with coriander leaves scattered on top, alongside some rice.

Pork and Sage Cannelloni

SERVES 8

SERVES 8
Preparation time 20 minutes, plus overnight chilling time
Cooking time 2 hours 15 minutes

10 lasagne sheets, ideally fresh (see page 260) but dried is fine
Parmesan, for grating (optional)
sea salt and freshly ground black pepper

FOR THE PORK FILLING
2 tbsp oil, plus extra for greasing
600g pork mince
2 onions, finely chopped
1 tsp fennel seeds, crushed
pinch of dried chilli flakes
1 head of garlic, cloves peeled and finely chopped
375ml dry white wine
500ml fresh chicken stock
grated zest and juice of 1 lemon
small bunch of sage, leaves thinly sliced
300ml double cream
¾ tsp salt
a good grinding of black pepper

FOR THE TOMATO SAUCE
3 tbsp olive oil
1 head of garlic, cloves peeled and finely chopped
2kg tomatoes (a mixture of plum, vine and cherry), blitzed to a puree
2 tbsp sherry vinegar, or red or white wine vinegar
large bunch of basil leaves

FOR THE BÉCHAMEL SAUCE
500ml whole milk
1 bay leaf
generous grating of nutmeg
50g butter
50g plain flour
250–300g ball of mozzarella cheese, cut into small cubes

This might read as if it's a heavy dish, but it's actually very dainty. Pasta sheets are stuffed with pork mince lifted with onions, garlic, fennel seeds, chilli, lemon, sage and cream, rolled, then doused in a tomato and basil sauce and covered in a nutmeggy mozzarella béchamel. It may not be a classic cannelloni recipe, but you can't deny its flavours are truly Italian. Cannelloni is not simply an alternative to lasagne, it's something pretty special itself, and it saddens me that it doesn't get the attention it deserves. One of the dishes I grew up making was cannelloni stuffed with spinach, green chillies, lemon, nutmeg and ricotta. Try this if you want a veggie version, but I want to showcase the pork, mostly because it's delicious, but also because it's a good way to eat higher-welfare pork (high-welfare pork mince is really good value). I made this with a double layer of cannelloni in a cast-iron casserole dish, but it would easily make 2 single-layer large(ish) gratins too.

Start making this the day before you plan to eat it, as the pork filling ideally needs to be chilled overnight. The tomato sauce can also be made ahead of time.

Heat the oil for the pork filling in a frying pan over a high heat, add the mince and brown it well. It's important not to overcrowd the pan so brown it in two batches, adding a little extra oil for the second batch if necessary. Once browned, put both batches of mince back in the pan, add the onions, fennel seeds and dried chilli flakes, and cook for 10 minutes until softened, then add the garlic and sweat for a further 10–15 minutes over a low heat or until the meat and onions look homogenised in colour. Add the wine and chicken stock and simmer rapidly for about 30 minutes until the liquid has almost completely evaporated. At this stage, mix in the lemon zest and juice, sliced sage leaves and double cream and cook until the cream has amalgamated into the sauce and the sauce has thickened. Season with the salt and pepper. Remove from the heat, leave to cool, then chill in the fridge for a few hours, preferably overnight, so that the mixture is firm enough to handle and shape to fill the cannelloni.

Next, make the tomato sauce. Heat the oil in a heavy-based casserole dish over a medium-low heat, add the garlic and fry gently for about 10 minutes until softened and beginning to get lightly golden, being careful it doesn't burn. Pour the pureed tomatoes into the dish, season well, add the vinegar and cook very slowly over a

CONTINUED ››

low heat for 1 hour 30 minutes, until the sauce has reduced and developed a deep, concentrated flavour. Remove from the heat. I like to blitz the sauce once more, to ensure it's perfectly smooth, before tearing up the basil leaves and stirring through, but you can leave it as it is if you prefer.

To make the béchamel sauce, warm the milk, bay leaf and nutmeg in a saucepan (be careful not to let it boil). Remove from the heat and allow to infuse for 10 minutes, then discard the bay leaf. Melt the butter in a separate heavy-based saucepan, then whisk in the flour. Allow the flour to cook for a couple of minutes, then slowly add the warm milk bit by bit, whisking as you go to achieve a smooth consistency. Continue until all the milk is combined and the sauce looks glossy. Bring the sauce to the boil slowly to reduce it, making sure you keep scraping the base of the pan with a wooden spoon to avoid the sauce scorching. When it has a good thick viscosity, beat in the mozzarella until completely melted. Season to taste with salt and pepper and a little more nutmeg.

When you're ready to construct the dish, preheat the oven to 200°C/180°C fan/gas mark 6.

Cook 10 dried lasagne sheets in a pan of salted boiling water for 4–6 minutes until they become flexible enough to shape into cannelloni tubes, then refresh in ice-cold water; if you are using fresh pasta – shop-bought or my recipe on page 260 – reduce the boiling time to 1 minute. Cut each sheet of lasagne in half to form 2 × 10cm squares. Roll a small handful of the chilled pork filling into a sausage-shaped cylinder about 10cm long, then wrap it in the pasta to form a tube. Repeat this process until all the pork mince and pasta is used up.

Grease a large, deep ovenproof dish (or 2 gratin dishes) with a little oil to prevent the cannelloni from sticking. Arrange the cannelloni in an even layer across the base. Depending on the size of your dish, you will probably need to do this in two layers, so pour a thin layer of tomato sauce across the bottom layer of cannelloni before arranging the rest on top, then pour the rest of the tomato sauce over, followed by the béchamel. Finish with a grating of Parmesan across the top if you like. (If you prepare it in two separate dishes, you could bake half and freeze half.)

Bake in the oven for 35–40 minutes, until the sauce is bubbling on the sides and the surface is lovely and golden. Remove from the oven and serve.

Roasted Lamb Belly and Ribs *for a multitude of things like Asian-style crispy lamb, tacos and kebabs*

SERVES 6
Preparation time 10 minutes
Cooking time 4 hours–4 hours
30 minutes

1 whole lamb belly with ribs (about
    1.2kg) – it will come in two parts
1 tbsp oil
2 tsp sea salt
½ tsp ground white pepper
a decent grinding of black pepper
80ml water

FOR THE 5-SPICE MIX
¼ tbsp 5-spice powder
1 tbsp caster sugar
1 tbsp salt
¼ tsp powdered MSG (optional)

TO SERVE
6 spring onions, shredded
½ cucumber, deseeded, cut into
    matchsticks
Chinese pancakes (available from
    Chinese supermarkets)
plum hoisin sauce
sriracha

Lamb belly and ribs are so delicious and if you've not tried them yet you must! They have lots of layers of fat, similar to pork belly, that melt away as they cook. You can eat lamb belly in the same way as pork belly, too: a long, slow roast results in soft, yielding meat and ramping up the heat at the end crisps it up. You can also grill them over coals – lamb ribs from an ocakbasi (Turkish grill) are something else. This recipe shows how to prepare it crispy-duck style, with the classic accompaniments, but it suits many other dishes: the meat is great for a lamb version of Mexican carnitas (try my Rye Tortillas on page 167), and leftovers are superb in flatbreads (page 166) as a kebab.

Traditional crispy duck contains MSG (monosodium glutamate). It's often MSG-laced food that fixes my brain, so I've included it, but leave it out if you like.

Preheat the oven to 180°C/160°C fan/gas mark 4.

Rub the lamb belly and ribs with the oil and season with the salt and both peppers (the flavour of this is distinct in its purity, so don't mess about trying to add flavours). Pop the seasoned lamb in a large roasting tray with the water and – this bit is critical – tightly wrap the whole tray in foil so that it's absolutely airtight. Bake in the oven for 3 hours 30 minutes. After this time, have a peek. The meat should be falling off the bone and have shrunk a fair bit, and there may be a little sauce and a fair bit of fat. If it's not ready, then tightly seal again and pop back in the oven for another 30 minutes.

When you've removed it from the oven, take off the foil, turn the oven as hot as it can go (about 260°C/240°C fan/gas mark 10) and, while you wait for the oven to heat up, drain off all the fat (keep it to cook with) and place the shredded spring onions and cucumber matchsticks in a bowl of ice-cold water. Mix together the 5-spice mix ingredients (and MSG, if using) and rub half of this mixture onto the lamb. Roast the meat, uncovered, for 15–25 minutes, or until it is super browned and crispy.

Get all your accompaniments ready. Steam the pancakes, remove the cucumber and spring onions from the water and drain on kitchen paper. Put hoisin and sriracha in bowls and the remaining 5-spice mix in a little bowl. Lay the crispy lamb belly on a serving plate and shred it like duck. I like to put a hot pancake in the palm of my hands and then spread it with hoisin sauce, then pop on some crispy lamb, sprinkle the remaining 5-spice mix on the lamb for extra POW, then top with the shredded greens and a drizzle of sriracha, but you can eat it however you like.

Devilled Kidneys

SERVES 4 as a starter
Preparation time 20 minutes
Cooking time 15 minutes

300g lambs' kidneys
2 tbsp cooking fat (ideally kidney
    suet)
1 large banana shallot, very, very
    finely diced
a few sprigs of thyme, leaves picked
½ –1 tsp Tabasco sauce (depending
    on how spicy you like it)
1 tbsp Worcestershire sauce
½ tsp English mustard
2 tbsp port
2 tbsp madeira, marsala wine or
    sherry
200ml high-quality jellied beef stock
    or Red Wine and Beef Sauce (page
    268)
100ml single cream
handful of flat-leaf parsley, finely
    chopped
salt and freshly ground black pepper

FOR THE TOAST
½ tbsp chicken or beef fat, for frying
4 slices of bread (ideally sourdough)

Kidneys have always been the offal I find most enjoyable to eat, but they get a bad reputation because they do have a faint whiff of wee. There's no getting away from it. This might sound strange, but once you get over it, it just becomes part of the experience and not the dominant bit. To make kidneys taste as delicious as possible, you need a sauce that works with the essence of the kidney's flavour. This umami-rich, gut-busting, heart attack-inducing dish has turned many a naysayer into yaysayer: it can be served for breakfast, a starter or a light supper, but if you want to take it to the next level the kidneys and their sauce would be a pretty amazing modern take on the classic French steak dish Tournedos Rossini (usually served with foie gras). I can't confirm or deny whether I have done this.

First, prep the kidneys by removing any outer membrane: cut them in half and you will find a little white sinewy bit of fat inside which needs to be removed – cut this out with a knife or scissors. Season the prepped kidneys with a little salt.

Heat 1 tablespoon of the fat in a frying pan over a high heat. You want to get a really good caramelisation on the kidneys so allow them to brown in the pan for 2–3 minutes on each side. Remove from the pan, cut each kidney into 3 pieces, then set aside. They will be quite raw inside but don't worry as you will be cooking them further in the sauce – you want them to maintain some nice pinkness. There's nothing worse than an overcooked kidney.

To make the sauce, sweat the shallot with the thyme leaves for a few minutes in the same pan over a medium heat with the second tablespoon of fat, until softened, scraping any residual meatiness from the bottom of the pan.

Whisk the Tabasco, Worcestershire sauce, mustard, port, madeira and stock or red wine and beef sauce in a bowl, then pour it into the pan. Leave it to bubble away for 2–3 minutes until it has reduced to form a silky sauce. Return the kidneys to the pan and cook for a minute, then stir in the cream, a good grind of pepper and the parsley.

For the toast, melt the ½ tablespoon of fat in a separate frying pan and fry the bread for a couple of minutes on each side until crisp and golden.

Put the toast on four plates and divide the kidneys equally between each, making sure each serving gets plenty of sauce. Eat immediately.

Faggots

SERVES 8 (makes 18, and you serve 1 faggot per person, so that leaves you with 10 for the freezer)
Preparation time 30 minutes, plus soaking time
Cooking time 1 hour 30 minutes

300ml madeira or port
2 tbsp beef dripping or lard (oil is fine too)
8 onions, 4 finely chopped, 4 thinly sliced (per half portion, assuming you are freezing half the raw faggots: add 4 more thinly sliced onions if cooking them all)
4 garlic cloves, finely chopped
1 sheep, mutton or hogget pluck – 1 heart, 1 liver, 2 kidneys and 2 lungs – cleaned, trimmed and coarsely minced, or chopped by hand
1kg lamb, mutton or hogget mince (ask for at least 20 per cent fat content if possible)
150g suet (I got kidney suet from the butcher, but you can use shop-bought beef suet)
250g white breadcrumbs
½ bunch of thyme, leaves chopped
large handful of flat-leaf parsley, leaves chopped
small handful of sage, leaves chopped, and/or 5 stalks of rosemary, leaves finely chopped
½ nutmeg, grated
1–1.2kg caul fat, soaked for 2 hours in cold water
oil, for frying the faggots
2 litres high-quality fresh brown chicken stock (scale up to 4 litres if you're cooking them all)
1 tsp cornflour or arrowroot (optional)
sea salt flakes and freshly ground black pepper

This recipe is adapted from Fergus Henderson's modern classic version in *The Book of St John*. No one understands offal better than Fergus, so it would be totally remiss of me to not consult the master. His recipe for faggots uses pork belly and pig's offal, but when testing this recipe I had been sent a big box of Cull Yaw hogget and offal from the lovely Matt Chatfield, creator of the Cornwall Project, so it seemed silly not to put it to good use. It's up to you which meat mince you use – sheep or pig will work well – the mince just needs to have good fat content. You can use packaged suet if needs be, but a good butcher should be able to give you some cheaply. I've tweaked Fergus's recipe slightly by adding nutmeg, as I think I'm addicted to it, and I didn't have any sage (the traditional herb used in faggot recipes) to hand when I tested this so I substituted it with rosemary, but either herb works.

For the faint-hearted out there, it might be worth asking your butcher to mince the offal, as it's a pretty grizzly business. Alternatively do it yourself by hand, it's just a slightly laborious and rather unpleasant bit of chopping (I'm a tough customer but even the lungs threw me for a loop!). You don't want it too fine as it's important the faggots have some good texture.

This recipe makes a lot of mix, and the volume might initially seem slightly alarming, but it's important that we serve the whole animal by using up all of its organs. The recipe makes 18 faggots, and unless you're having a party it's unlikely you'll be eating them in one go, so fortunately they freeze really well (raw). The recipe below is based on cooking half the quantity and freezing the rest.

I serve them with a carrot puree, but any root veg puree or mash would work.

First, simmer the madeira or port in a small saucepan until it has reduced down to a thick syrup (about 2 tablespoons) and set aside.

Heat the fat in a frying pan over a medium-low heat, add the chopped onions and sweat for about 30 minutes until they are really, really soft. You don't need to get too much colour on them, just a golden tinge. Add the garlic for the final couple of minutes to soften, then combine with the reduced alcohol and set aside to cool.

Once you have prepared all of the offal, mix it thoroughly with the mince, onion and booze mixture, suet, breadcrumbs, herbs and a generous amount of grated nutmeg and seasoning until well combined. Fry a little spoonful of the mixture in a pan (I always do this when making stuffing mixtures) and check if you need to tweak the seasoning before making the faggots.

It's now time to weigh out the faggots. Line your weighing scales with baking parchment. The faggot mix will weigh around 2.7kg. Measure out 18 balls each at about 150g, or take the weight of the whole mix and divide it by 18 to see what weight each ball should be. With oiled hands, shape each piece of mixture into a neat ball.

Lay the caul fat out on a surface and cut the pieces into eighteen 18 × 12cm squares (I say squares, but you don't need to be precious about this). Wrap the pieces of faggot mixture in the caul fat, but not too tightly as it'll shrink-wrap the faggots as it cooks.

Heat some oil in a frying pan over a medium heat and brown the faggots all over. Fry 8 or 9 if you're cooking half and freezing half, or all of them if you are going in for the kill. Preheat the oven to 200°C/180°C fan/gas mark 6.

Put the sliced onions in a large casserole dish (I used my largest Le Creuset) over a medium heat and quickly top with the browned faggots. Cover with the stock. Bring the stock to the boil then transfer (with no lid) to the oven and cook for 1 hour. In the last 20 minutes very gently flip the faggots upside down, with two dessertspoons, so they caramelise evenly.

After 1 hour, the stock will have reduced a fair bit and the faggots will have shrunk and be a really deep brown. Remove from the oven and rest for 10 minutes. If you think there's too much fat on the surface, carefully remove the faggots and set aside. Pour the onion gravy (which will be super rich, full of flavour and a little sweet) into a narrow, deep jug and allow the fat to rise to the top, then skim it off with a ladle.

If the sauce needs to be thickened, mix the cornflour or arrowroot with 2 tablespoons of the liquid from the onion gravy and whisk until smooth. Add it back to the pan and bring to the boil until thickened. Put the faggots back in the pan to warm up and they are ready to serve.

Goat Ragu, with its Offal

MAKES 15–20 starter-sized portions
Preparation time 20 minutes
Cooking time 6 hours

about 1.5kg pluck of goat offal
 (the liver, 2 kidneys and 1 heart),
 trimmed of excess fat and sinew
80ml oil, plus 2 tbsp for frying the
 mince
5 onions, finely chopped
4 carrots, finely chopped
3 celery sticks, finely chopped
1 large leek, washed and finely
 chopped
2kg goat mince (double-minced with
 a minimum of 20 per cent fat – ask
 your butcher to do this)
2 heads of garlic, cloves separated,
 peeled and finely chopped
10 sprigs of thyme, leaves finely
 chopped
6 sprigs of sage, leaves finely chopped
6 sprigs of rosemary, leaves finely
 chopped
1 bottle of red wine
1 bottle of white wine
2.5kg mixed fresh tomatoes, blitzed
 to a puree
1½ tbsp freshly ground black pepper
1 tbsp ground white pepper
1 tbsp celery salt
1–1½ tbsp sea salt
½ nutmeg, grated

TO SERVE
cooked pasta
extra-virgin olive oil, for drizzling
Parmesan, for grating

I was recently asked to contribute a recipe to an event hosted by one of my favourite producers, James Whetlor of Cabrito Goat Meat Ltd. I am a huge fan of goat meat. It's officially the most sustainable of all meat, because it's so easy to rear, has to be grass fed and requires little water. It's madness that although we used to eat it more than any meat it's now the least popular. At the event I wanted to show how versatile goat was in a simple ragu, and how easy it is to combine goat offal in a ragu to bring viscosity, make it richer, and more full bodied (with none of the bitterness sometimes associated with offal). In my research for ragus I came across historical recipes that include everything from livers to lungs (in fact, it's still common in Italian ragus to include livers). I've used goat offal here, and any good butcher will sell you both the meat and the pluck of offal (offal is cheap as chips). This ragu makes 15–20 portions and costs about £20 – that's mostly because of the wine! I appreciate this is a lot of ragu but you need to utilise the whole pluck to make this dish sustainable. It freezes brilliantly, and is batch cooking at its best. Serve with tagliolini or pappardelle.

Separately blitz each piece of offal in a food processor briefly to a rough puree. This will look gruesome, but when you brown it, it transforms into a mince-like texture.

Heat the 80ml oil in a very large casserole dish over a medium heat, add the onions, carrot, celery and leek and cook for at least 20 minutes, stirring often, until everything is mulched down and really well softened (this is your sofrito).

Meanwhile, heat the 2 tablespoons of oil in a frying pan over a high heat and brown the goat mince thoroughly, in several batches, really mashing away at it to break it down into finer pieces. Do the same with the offal (also in batches). It's magic how this unsavoury-looking offal puree quickly turns into 'mince'. Once browned, set aside.

Add the garlic to the sofrito and cook for a further 5–10 minutes, then add the herbs. Add the mince, offal and wine and cook for about 20 minutes. Add the blitzed tomatoes, both peppers and celery salt, bring the ragu to a slow simmer, cover and cook over the lowest flame for 6 hours, stirring occasionally and scraping the base of the pan. You are aiming for a really rich, intense ragu with serious depth of flavour.

Add the salt, check the seasoning and add the nutmeg. Mix through pasta, add a decent lick of olive oil and plenty of grated Parmesan. The ragu will keep in the fridge for up to 3 days. As always with a ragu, it's even better the following day.

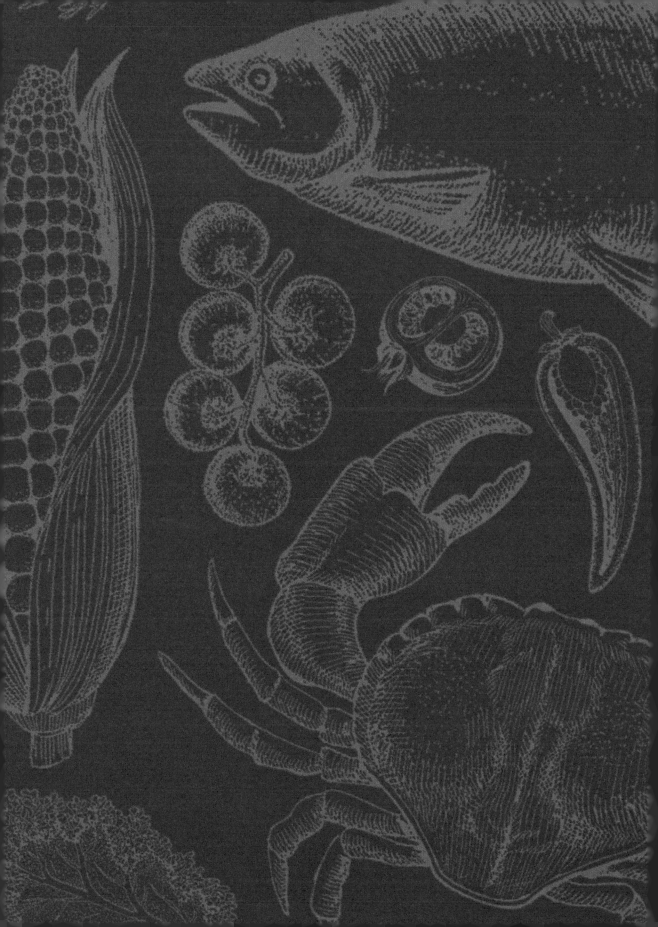

FISH

FISH AND SHELLFISH

The day I wrote this, I had a very special delivery from one of the best fish suppliers in the UK, Wild Harbour from Cornwall, and I broke down a whole hake, cleaned and prepped two of the biggest monkfish I'd ever seen, two John Dory, a gurnard, a bream and two monster live lobsters. This is every chef's dream, but is it a sustainable one? If I'd been writing this book even 2 years ago I would have thought the hake, monkfish and John Dory were on the critical list, but I trust Wild Harbour. They fish with the highest of ethics, by line and only off the Cornish coast, and send pamphlets indicating which fish are in season and highlighting that this will change regularly. This makes them the sustainable chef's choice.

Many people don't really understand fish seasons, or how the seas can replenish if given time to thrive. The single biggest threat to the sea is overfishing. When I first started working as a chef, about 15 years ago, it was announced that cod reserves had been depleted to a critical point. Cod thrives in the North Atlantic and between cod, haddock and salmon, it's the fish us Brits like to eat most, so the news that it is now on the MSC (Marine Stewardship Council) list of sustainable species is a brilliant indication of how, working together, we can replenish stocks.

The United Kingdom consists of several islands and several climates. As the climate changes, so do fish migration patterns. The Gulf Stream currents are directly associated with the climate and thermohaline circulation, which indicates the density of the heat and salt in the water. Warm water has a much higher density of salt (due to evaporation) and this means things rise, while in cold water things sink. The Gulf Stream is sometimes known as the global super-highway as it acts like an ocean conveyor belt where fish will 'latch' onto it to catch a speedy ride around the globe for when they migrate. As the Gulf Stream swoops up from the south coast of the UK it starts to push some of its deep-sea fish out in different directions. There will be fish like sardines, mackerel, bass and breams whooshing along the south coast towards the Mediterranean Sea and then cod, haddock, plaice, monkfish and soles fly up to the North Atlantic past the west coast of the UK.

Climate change is shaking things up a bit here, however. Fisherman friends and fish chef friends Rick and Jack Stein and Mitch Tonks have told me the volume of full-size bluefin tunas appearing in (and being fished from) waters as close as six miles to the south coast is on the rise, and sharks (big sharks such blue and mako sharks), are being spotted along this coast too, with rumoured sightings of the odd Great White.

The population of the UK coast's shellfish is thriving. Our brown crabs, lobsters and oysters are prized internationally, and we have an abundance of mussels, cockles and clams when in season. Until relatively recently all bivalve shellfish (like oysters and mussels) had seasonal availability (any month that had a 'R' in it was good), as they breed and go into bloom in the warmer months, but you can now buy from farms all through the year and this is a good thing.

Fish farming has a really bad rep – the assumption is that welfare standards are low, there are reports of lice and parasites and of some practices being ecologically unsound – but we must change our outlook on this as it's one of the ways we can guarantee that we source fish responsibly. Trout and salmon are a perfect example of this: if I saw wild salmon at the fishmonger I would think it was a more ethical choice, but Mitch told me that he hadn't seen a wild salmon for over 5 years and believes that they will be our first fish to be extinct. The same goes for sea trout. While general sea trout populations aren't in such imminent danger, wild sea trout are on the decline (sea trout is now back in vogue, especially in the smoked fish department – smoked trout is more superior than smoked salmon in my opinion).

There is no doubt that the world's seas are in a precarious state. Overfishing, pollution and rising sea temperatures, and increasing levels of acid in our seas, have led to many fish stocks going into serious decline over the past two decades. As consumers, it is our responsibility to engage with where our fish comes from. Fish sustainability is a complex issue. The sea is an impossible beast to fully understand. It moves so fast and we don't see half of what's going on in there, but we can monitor sea life by its seasonality and its general migration and it's not looking that great. We cannot think in the short term about these issues any more, when the UN Food and Agriculture Organization estimates that 70 per cent of the world's fish population is fished to capacity or overfished or in serious crisis.

The main culprits for overfishing are the Spanish, Italians, Chinese and Japanese. They are huge fish-eating nations and most of the fish and shellfish that we fish on our coasts get sold to these countries. The biggest problem is how these fish are caught. Trawler fishing in particular does untold damage to the sea bed, with gargantuan nets scooping up everything in their paths indiscriminately, stripping the delicate ecosystem and leaving desolate wasteland in their wake. The 2009 documentary *The End of the Line* was one of the first films to sound the alarm for how bad a state the fishing industry is in. Tuna fishing – in particular bluefin tuna fishing – was a central focus of the film, and it's infuriating that very little has changed since then. We have been made more aware of our consumption and MSC certification is now more prevalent in our fishmongers and supermarkets (I really do rate the MSC), and there have been laws put in place by the WTO (World Trade Organization) for bluefin tuna, whales, dolphins and sharks to encourage member countries to put them on their endangered species' lists, but big trawler fishing still exists and millions of fish die worthlessly every day as a result.

One of the exciting new discoveries scientists have made in recent years is what is known as a 'trophic cascade', an ecological process that starts at the top of the food chain and impacts all the way to the bottom. A big example of this is illustrated by the acknowledgement of what an integral role whales play in sustaining the entire living system of the ocean. It was once believed that fish, krill and plankton would thrive if there were fewer whales in the sea predating them, which in theory means more food for humans (an idea promoted by certain Japanese politicians, for example, who were looking for ways to justify the continuation of whale hunting) but it is now known that the opposite is true. Fewer whales in the sea counterintuitively means less fish. Whales feed at deep, dark depths, then rise to lighter parts of the sea where photosynthesis can occur (the photic zone). They then release faecal plumes rich in nutrients such as iron and nitrogen which fertilise the plant plankton in the surface waters, and their constant diving up and down from the depths kicks the plankton and life around, giving it more time to reproduce in the surface waters. Of course, more plant plankton means more animal plankton and therefore food for larger animals as part of the food chain. The great decline in whale populations has had a huge effect on the vertical mixing of waters, which has in turn had a huge impact on the fertility of the world's seas. What's more, plant plankton in the sea is also a crucial aid in absorbing carbon from the atmosphere, and eventually locking it for thousands of years in the depths of the ocean. To put it simply, more whales means more plankton, which in turn means more carbon is sequestered from the atmosphere. It is believed that before great numbers of whales were killed by humans, they may have been responsible for storing tens of millions of tons of carbon every year. Whales change the climate. Allowing great whales to return to our seas could undo decades of destruction and harm to the seas and atmosphere caused by human activity.

The other thing that has been catapulted into our vision over the last few years is how polluted the seas are. Images of turtles with straws up their noses and stories of mercury poisoning in oily fish and microplastics in the bodies of fish are rife, and the fact that there are 'islands' of plastics the size of small countries floating around the world's seas is a devastating reality. The thing about microplastics is that we are all consuming them, and while I have one bonkers theory that we will all evolve into Transformers with gills, it's more likely that these plastics are going to devastate the sea. Humans are killing the planet with their consumption of everything, not just food, and this will have a massive effect on how we get to produce our food, the one main thing we cannot live without. So, think of that next time you are restocking your make-up or beauty products. Many charities have opened up over the last few years and there are new laws about plastics coming into play, but there's a long way to go before things have an ability to reverse.

So how do we know if our fish is British, sustainably sourced and fresh? Sustainability is an impossible word in the world of fishing because it's incredibly hard to measure, so I prefer 'Responsibly Sourced' (a term I was taught by Tonks). The best way to ensure you know where your fish has come from is to establish a good relationship with your local fishmonger, who should be able to give you information on the provenance of the fish you are buying. More often than not, you will find your fishmonger will tell you that a lot of the best fish gets exported. We need to wise up to what we have on our doorstep and try to buy what's in season wherever possible.

Here is a list of the fish that we catch on our coasts and the times of the year in which is best to buy them:

• Black sea bream: June – March
• Brill: May – September
• Brown crab: April – September
• Cornish sardines: All year
• Cuttlefish: January – March and May – September
• Dover sole: April – June and September – November
• Haddock: February – April and September – November
• Hake: All year
• John Dory: All year
• Mackerel: October – May

- Megrim sole: May – November
- Monkfish: April – September
- Native lobster: All year
- Native scallop: April – December
- Plaice: May – August
- Pollack: March – May and November – December
- Red gurnard: March – September
- Red mullet: July – September
- Rock oyster: All year
- Rope-grown mussels: All year
- Spider crab: April – June
- Squid: October – March
- Turbot: May – July

When buying seafood, look out for:
- The Marine Stewardship Council (MSC) logo. It is a good indicator of fish certified to come from sustainably managed stocks.
- The Aquaculture Stewardship Council (ASC) logo. This is applied to fish that is farmed responsibly.
- Organically farmed fish. This tends to mean they're farmed with higher welfare and environmental standards.
- 'Atlantic fish' and 'UK coastlines' on labelling (eat fish from the rest of the world only occasionally as a treat). The sad truth is that even if we in the UK stopped eating all the endangered fish in the world it would have zero impact on it with China, Japan and Spain's overfishing!

How to know your fish is really fresh:
- Fish should not smell overpowering or unpleasant – it should smell fresh and almost briny.

- Fish eyes should be bright and clear. If they have clouded over, the fish is not at its freshest.

- The gills should be a bright, rich red. If the fish is old, they will have faded and become browner.
- The fresher the fish, the brighter and more metallic the skin.
- When buying shellfish such as mussels, clams and oysters, they should be live to ensure freshness, and should smell fresh, with tightly closed shells. If they are slightly open, give their shells a little tap and they should close. If they do not close, discard.

Vongole

SERVES 2
Preparation time 15 minutes
Cooking time 15 minutes

200g spaghetti
1kg clams, cleaned and rinsed for
    about 10 minutes in cold water
300ml white wine
80ml olive oil
1 head of garlic, cloves peeled and
    thinly sliced
2 dried chillies, crushed
3 vine-ripened tomatoes, chopped
bunch of flat-leaf parsley, finely
    chopped
juice of 1 lemon
sea salt and freshly ground black
    pepper

Clams are my favourite food. Some people can sit and eat ridiculous volumes of oysters (I am also one of those people), and I feel the same about clams. Winey, garlicky clams, with buttery bread to mop up the juices in a hot country like Spain or Portugal and a freezing glass of light white wine are one of the biggest eating pleasures of all. But in Italy you get to have it with the other best food of them all (I may have to broaden my idea of what my actual 'best food' is here) – spaghetti.

Okay, so here's the deal with vongole. I use four techniques to ensure maximum flavour; first, I open the clams early in too much wine, second, I use waaaaay too much garlic (alarming amounts, but go with it, trust me), third, I don't cook the pasta fully, so it finishes cooking in the sauce, and fourth, I use the starchy pasta water to emulsify the sauce.

Bring a large saucepan of heavily salted water to the boil. Add the spaghetti and cook for a minute or two less than the suggested time on the packet so it's al dente and not quite cooked (you will finish cooking the pasta at the end). Get the clams on while the spaghetti is cooking, and when you drain the pasta be sure to save 2–3 ladles of the cooking water as you will add this to the sauce later.

Put a large, dry saucepan over a high heat and let it get really hot. Throw in the clams with the wine and quickly cover to steam the clams for 1–2 minutes, until they have opened. Strain the clams through a sieve (discarding any that remain closed, just as you do with mussels), reserving the liquor in a bowl underneath. Pick the clam meat out of about 80 per cent of the shells, and save the other 20 per cent to serve.

Meanwhile, heat the oil in a large frying pan or wok over a medium heat, add the sliced garlic and crushed chillies and fry for 2–3 minutes until the garlic starts to pick up a little colour. Next, add the chopped tomatoes and fry for a few minutes until they start to break down into the oil. Now pour in the winey clam stock, being careful not to pour in the last bit at the bottom as this can often be a bit sandy or gritty. Whack the heat right up and allow it to reduce to a soupy sauce, then add the spaghetti, the reserved pasta cooking water (start with 2 ladles and add another if you need to), the picked clams and the clams still in their shells. Stir through the parsley and lemon juice and allow the whole lot to boil for 1–2 minutes to finish off cooking the pasta and allow it to absorb the sauce. Season with a good pinch of salt and some freshly ground pepper and serve immediately.

Sumiso Cod Collar

SERVES 4
Preparation time 5 minutes, plus
2–24 hours marinating time
Cooking time 5 minutes

4 cod collars, fins trimmed with
   scissors

FOR THE MARINADE
100ml mirin (if this isn't available
   use a dry sherry or even Chinese
   Shaoxing)
100ml sake
175g caster sugar
400g sweet white miso

The Japanese have been cooking hamachi kama (yellowtail collar) and tuna collar for years, but fish collar has yet to become an ubiquitous cut on these shores. I want to change that! Fish cheeks have become quite fashionable in recent times, so think of the collar as the new cut on the block. It is the same hardworking muscle, but when cooked with care it becomes meltingly tender. Yellowtail and tuna collars are hard to find here, but we do have Atlantic cod and salmon, which are both huge fish with substantial collars that are mighty delicious with these flavours. The collars can look a little intimidating, but you just need to trim off any protruding fins with scissors. The miso marinade was made famous by the exceptionally talented, legendary Japanese Peruvian fusion chef Nobuyuki 'Nobu' Matsuhisa. His Black Cod and Miso dish is something that I've seen on menus for £60 a portion. If you're brave enough to make your own miso (pages 24–25), this is the perfect dish to show it off. It's both elegant and refined, and the marinade could work on lots of different fish (we've tried it on everything from salmon to halibut steaks). These are ideal cooked on the barbecue or in a pizza oven, as the sugars in the marinade begin to caramelise and a slightly charred flavour is key, but you can also cook them under a hot grill.

There are some really cool UK distilleries making Japanese ingredients such as mirin and sake these days – seek them out.

To make the marinade, heat the mirin, sake and sugar in a saucepan until it starts to boil. When the sugar has dissolved, stir in the miso and remove from the heat. Allow it to cool, then coat the collars thoroughly in half the marinade and leave for a minimum of 2 hours (maximum 24 hours) in the fridge, to marinate. Put the rest of the marinade in the fridge too. About 12–15 hours is ideal – the marinade cures the fish a little and starts to break down the sinew and connective tissues. Don't be alarmed if it seeps out loads of water, this is just part of the curing process.

Preheat your barbecue, pizza oven or grill to high (aim for 300°C, if you have a thermometer) – if you're using the barbecue or grill, oil it well. Cook the marinated collars for a couple of minutes on each side. Remove from the grill and set aside on a plate for a few minutes to rest.

Serve with a couple of tablespoons of the remaining room-temperature marinade, and the resting juices from the fish poured over.

Cuttlefish and Courgette Frito

SERVES 4
Preparation time 15 minutes
Cooking time 5 minutes

1 medium cuttlefish (about 600g),
    cleaned, guts and ink sac removed,
    wings trimmed, and outer
    membrane removed (your
    fishmonger can do this for you)
150ml milk
150g rice flour
50g self-raising flour
40g cornflour
1 rounded tsp fine sea salt
¼ tsp finely ground black pepper
1 large courgette, thinly sliced into
    rounds (use a mandoline if you have
    one)
1 lemon, thinly sliced into rounds
    (use a mandoline if you have one)
sunflower or rapeseed oil, for deep-
    frying

TO SERVE
sea salt
lemon wedges
1 quantity Aioli (page 267)

Everyone knows about squid, but cuttlefish tends to only be known for the white cuttlefish 'bones' that budgies love. Cuttlefish meat, however, is really delicious, and in some cases I'd go as far as to say it's more delicious than squid, as it's thicker, firmer and sweeter. They are not just good for deep-frying – they braise really well too. The season is short, but when in season they are in abundance and are really good value. This version of fritti, with very thinly sliced courgettes, resembles the Italian seafood and courgette fritti from Venice, but this has to be served with aioli so I'm taking influence from Spain here.

Ask your fishmonger to prepare the cuttlefish. You can keep the ink sac and whisk the ink into mayonnaise to eat with the cuttlefish (it doesn't work with courgette).

Once you have prepared the cuttlefish, cut through one side of the length of the body with a sharp knife and lay it out flat. Score diagonal lines on the outer side in a diamond pattern, being careful not to cut through the flesh, then cut into 6cm-thick strips.

Heat the oil in a wok or deep-fat fryer to 190°C (use a cooking thermometer or jam thermometer, if you're using a wok) and line two plates with kitchen paper.

Pour the milk into a bowl and mix the flours with the seasoning in a separate bowl. Lay out the cuttlefish strips ready for dredging. Place a handful of strips in the milk for a few seconds then coat them in the seasoned flour. Repeat the process once more, to make sure you get a really good coating on the cuttlefish. Once all the cuttlefish is coated, lay them out on a tray ready for frying. The courgette and lemon only need one coating of milk, then they can just be tossed in whatever's left of the flour mix.

Start by frying the cuttlefish (in three or four batches to stop the oil cooling down too much). Add some of the coated strips to the oil and fry for 1½ minutes maximum, until lightly golden and crisp. Remove from the oil with a spider utensil or slotted metal spoon and transfer to the plate to absorb any excess oil and ensure crispiness.

Fry the lemon and courgette slices for a minute or so until lightly golden and, again, transfer to a plate lined with kitchen paper.

Combine the cuttlefish, courgette and lemon on a serving platter, sprinkle liberally with salt, and serve with lemon wedges and the aioli in a small bowl for dipping.

Chilli con Pesce

SERVES 4
Preparation time 15 minutes
Cooking time 1 hour 20 minutes

3 tbsp olive oil

2 onions, very finely chopped

1 small fennel bulb or ½ large
  one, finely chopped

1 head of garlic, cloves peeled and
  finely chopped

1 tbsp tomato puree

1 tsp regular paprika

1 tsp smoked paprika

¼ tsp ground white pepper

a good grinding of black pepper

pinch of ground cloves

3 tsp ground cumin

2 tsp ground coriander

¼ tsp ground fennel seeds

1 bay leaf

2 tsp chipotle in adobo paste

300g tomatoes, blitzed to a puree

300ml white wine

1 litre fresh prawn stock

FOR THE FISH AND SHELLFISH

glug of oil

700g mixed fish and shellfish (such
  as 175g smoked haddock, 175g
  tuna, 150g shelled prawns, and
  200g mixed white fish, all roughly
  diced)

400g tin aduki or black beans,
  drained and rinsed

1 tsp sea salt

juice of ½ lemon

TO SERVE

sour cream

coriander leaves

grated Cheddar

cooked rice, burrito or soft Tortillas
  (page 167) (optional)

I wanted to write a recipe for this book that showed how to utilise scraps of fish you can pick up from your fishmonger (I use fish bones and prawn shells in the fish or prawn stocks on page 263). While I was thinking about this, Rick Stein's show *The Road to Mexico* was on TV in the background and he was cooking up a fish chilli with a fishmonger from San Diego. They were making it with the most enormous fish I've ever seen (it had jowls bigger than an ox), a little-known, inexpensive fish species that us common folk don't get to hear about and are very unlikely to ever be able to cook with as it's from the Pacific. Inspired by this, I came up with this chilli con pesce. The best way to source the fish for this recipe is to get down to your local fishmonger and ask for any offcuts or tail-ends, or ask them what they have too much of, and you'll likely get it for a good price. What you're looking for is sturdy fish that can stand up to cooking in the chilli, such as monkfish, swordfish, tuna, prawns or hake. Collars or tails of turbot would be ideal. I wouldn't recommend salmon or mackerel, as they are too oily and would make the chilli cloying. Obviously this can be made with finer cuts of fish, but it kind of defeats the object of the dish, and as you cut the fish so small it feels wasteful to use prime cuts. Most people are put off making fish stews as they are expensive and too time-consuming; the opposite is true of this recipe, but it still really delivers the BANG and POW!

Heat the oil in a saucepan over a medium-low heat, add the onions and fennel and sweat for at least 20 minutes until cooked down and golden. Add the garlic, fry for another 5 minutes then add the tomato puree and cook for 2 minutes. Add all the spices, the bay leaf and chipotle paste. Cook for 2 minutes, then tip in the tomatoes and cook for about 15 minutes until reduced down into an emulsified, volcanic mulch. Add the wine and simmer rapidly for about 15 minutes until the sauce has reduced by half and has a soupy consistency. Add the stock and cook for 30 minutes until rich and viscous.

While the sauce is cooking, heat a glug of oil in a frying pan over a high heat until super hot. Fry the fish briefly in batches, for a few minutes per batch, to caramelise. Set aside.

Add the fish and aduki beans to the sauce and cook for a further 10–15 minutes – the fish will break down and flake into the sauce. Add the salt and lemon juice. Serve with a dollop of sour cream, coriander and grated Cheddar, with rice or in a burrito or tortillas.

Wet & Wild Monkfish Kievs

SERVES 4

Preparation time 20 minutes, plus minimum 30 minutes chilling time
Cooking time 1 hour

100g plain flour, seasoned with salt and pepper
2 free-range eggs, beaten with a little milk
300g white or panko breadcrumbs
4 large meaty pieces of monkfish, from the top, wider end of the fish, trimmed into neat pieces (keep the trimmings for later!)
sunflower or rapeseed oil, for deep-frying

FOR THE WILD GARLIC BUTTER

1 head of wet, new season garlic
1 garlic clove, finely grated (use a Microplane grater if you have one)
200g butter, at room temperature
10 wild garlic leaves, thinly sliced, and a handful of wild garlic flowers (if you can find them), with extra flowers to serve
2–3 tablespoons chopped flat-leaf parsley
sea salt flakes and freshly ground black pepper

When you write recipes, sometimes they evolve later on down the line. I wrote a recipe for Wet & Wild Chicken Kievs for *Healthy Appetite* – wet and wild in the vulgar sense (I'm sorry, I know), but also because it included both wet spring (new season) garlic and the leafy wild garlic herb. Looking back (I've written three books since then), I had one problem with it, in that I only used the wild garlic as a shield to hold the butter inside the chicken, and only parsley as the herb. I later kicked myself for not including the finely chopped wild garlic within the butter mix and have since used wild garlic butter in wood-roasted scallops and lobster, and as a bar snack of chicken Kiev bonbons – fish takes to this butter as much as chicken does. One of the chefs whose work with fish I am in awe of is Australian chef and restaurateur Josh Niland, who fills the body of a whole whiting with wild garlic butter before breading and frying it. I tried doing this with monkfish one day and it was absolutely stunning. This book is about sustainability and I have questioned whether it's viable to use monkfish, as it was once being overfished, but I can tell you on good authority that monkfish stocks are on the rise, probably in the same way as cod has been; this is partly because people have been conscientious in their purchasing habits and that they are also fishable from and native to the UK, so I feel that as a treat, it's okay.

Preheat the oven to 220°C/200°C fan/gas mark 7.

Wrap the head of wet garlic loosely in foil and roast it in the oven for 40 minutes, or until the cloves are soft and gooey when squished. Remove from the oven and leave until it's cool enough to handle.

Squeeze out the roasted garlic cloves into a small food processor, add the grated garlic, butter, sliced wild garlic leaves, parsley and plenty of salt and pepper, and blitz until smooth. If you have wild garlic flowers, stir them into the garlic butter. With a spatula, scoop the garlic butter onto a layer of cling film or greaseproof paper in 4 even dollops. Shape the butter into nuggets about the size and shape of your thumb and wrap them individually in the cling film. Put them in the freezer for 20–30 minutes to firm up nicely.

When the butter is hard, take three bowls and put the seasoned flour in one, the beaten eggs in another, and the breadcrumbs in the third, ready to pané (coat the fish).

CONTINUED »

Using a sharp knife, make a deep cut lengthways along the longer side of each monkfish piece, to make a pocket inside. Stick your finger in the pocket and root around a bit to make the hole a little larger. Unwrap the frozen butter parcels and stuff one into each piece of fish. Plug up the hole in each monkfish piece with the reserved fish trimmings so that the butter can't escape.

Reduce the oven temperature to 200°C/180°C fan/gas mark 6.

Heat the oil in either a deep-fat fryer or a deep saucepan or wok to 190°C (a high-quality cooking thermometer or jam thermometer is good for testing, if you're using a wok or pan). Carefully dip each stuffed monkfish piece first in the seasoned flour, then in plenty of the egg, and then in the breadcrumbs, coating them thoroughly and paying particular attention to the end where they've been sealed, preferably double-coating this end with more egg and breadcrumbs. Carefully fry the Kievs in batches in the hot oil for 4–5 minutes per batch, or until they start to turn a light golden colour. Transfer to a baking tray and bake in the oven for 12–15 minutes, until cooked through and nicely crisp and brown. Some of the butter will have leaked out, so be sure to pour that back over the fish when you serve it.

Serve the monkfish Kievs, sprinkled with a few salt flakes and any spare garlic flowers for the top, with buttery mashed potatoes, peas and any excess garlic butter poured over.

Moules à la Crème

SERVES 4
Preparation time 15 minutes
Cooking time 15 minutes

20g butter
1 tbsp oil
5 garlic cloves, very finely chopped
2 banana shallots, very finely
    chopped
2–3 sprigs of thyme, leaves picked
1 bay leaf
1kg mussels, well scrubbed and
    cleaned (discard any open mussels
    that don't close when tapped)
350ml white wine
75ml double cream
juice of ½ lemon
large handful of flat-leaf parsley,
    finely chopped
freshly ground black pepper
French fries, or buttered French
    bread, to serve

Mussels are one of the sea's gifts that keeps on giving. If you found yourself marooned on a British Isle, mussels would be one source of food you could rely upon to keep you alive, as they are everywhere around our coastline. They are available wild or rope farmed. I have to say, although it might seem counterintuitive, I do tend to favour rope farmed as, much like farmed rock oysters, you know where you're at with them: they go through a filtration system, they tend to be plumper, and are just as delicious. For me, they are the safer and more sustainable option. Classically, people love moules marinière and as we're writing this we're debating whether the cream is a good or bad addition. Personally, I think the cream provides a welcome viscosity, but you can leave it out if you'd rather. What you can't do, which most recipes won't tell you, is get away with not reducing your sauce separately. I can spot an inferior moules a mile off and it's always the ones where the sauce hasn't been reduced!

Melt the butter into the oil in a large lidded frying pan or wok over a medium heat, add the garlic, shallots, thyme leaves and bay leaf and sweat for 5–8 minutes until the shallots and garlic have softened and are starting to tinge golden brown. Add the mussels, pour over the wine, cover with a lid and cook for 1–2 minutes to steam them open. Remove the lid and pour the mussels through a large fine sieve with a heatproof bowl underneath to catch the cooking liquor.

If you were to taste the cooking liquor at this stage you would notice it tasted very winey, with a subtle undertone of mussels, so what we want to do now is return it to the pan and reduce it at a rolling boil to concentrate the flavour, along with the bay leaf, until the volume has reduced by a little under half.

Once it's reduced, pour in the cream, lemon juice and a generous grinding of pepper. Return all the garlicky mussels and shallots to the sauce and stir through the parsley. Put the lid back on and bring up to the boil for a further minute. Discard any unopened mussels before serving. You won't need to season the dish with any salt as the salinity from the mussels is more than enough. For me, it's a crime not to serve these with French fries, or some buttered French bread.

Sour Orange Fish Curry

SERVES 4

Preparation time 20 minutes, plus 15 minutes tamarind and chilli soaking time

Cooking time 40 minutes

35g block tamarind
5 tbsp sunflower oil
½ tsp ground turmeric
1 tsp ground coriander
400ml tin coconut milk
500ml fresh prawn stock
1 tbsp fish sauce
½ tbsp light brown muscovado sugar
1 large fish such as grey mullet, wild bass, large (overgrown) mackerel, gutted, scaled and cleaned, then cut into about 6 steaks through the spine
large bunch of Thai basil, leaves picked
cooked rice, to serve

FOR THE SPICE PASTE

5 dried red chillies
2 large fresh chillies (I like to keep the seeds in)
30g piece of fresh ginger, peeled and chopped
1 head of garlic, cloves peeled
100g shallots, peeled
1 tsp shrimp paste
1 stalk of lemongrass, chopped

I had this curry on a boat in Thailand in 2019. I had heard of it before, as I studied David Thompson at catering school. He wrote the first western but truly authentic take on Thai regional cookery, *Thai Food*, and, because of this book (and his restaurant Nahm), had become the oracle of Thai food internationally. I'd read recipes for several orange curries in his book and despite my mother relocating to Thailand for 10 years and my getting to spend many holidays there, I'd never eaten it. So, I was on a boat and our driver had bought it off a passing boat for his lunch. It came in a plastic bag, much like when you win a goldfish at a fair. I leapt on the poor man, who confirmed that it was the illusive sour orange curry. I was in the Phi Phi Islands with a friend of mine who lived there, and everyone on the boat thought it was an island dish, but I had always believed it to be a Northern Thai or jungle curry. This one definitely had coconut in it and possibly pineapple, though I was pretty squiffy from cold beers at this point. Either way, it was delicious and this is my version. It's salty, sour and hot, and a lot fresher than most fish curries. I use a rich prawn stock, but any fresh, light vegetable, fish or chicken stock will work just as well. Using whole fish steaks is preferable to fillets here, as you get the added flavour from the gelatin in the bone.

First, rehydrate the tamarind and the dried red chillies for the spice paste. Put them in separate bowls of hot water and leave to soak for at least 15 minutes, then drain and deseed the chillies and pass the tamarind through a sieve – you should have about 150ml liquid tamarind.

Blitz the ingredients for the spice paste in a food processor. Traditionally, the ingredients are pounded with a pestle and mortar, one at a time, into a puree, however it's a bit of a long and arduous process and while I'm not one to shy away from a bit of elbow grease (some of you may relish the stress relief!), I opt for a food processor.

Heat the oil in a wok over a medium heat, add the paste and fry for about 5 minutes, moving it around the wok to keep it from scorching, then add the turmeric and coriander and cook for a couple more minutes. Add the coconut milk, tamarind and stock and simmer for about 25 minutes so the sauce reduces and intensifies in flavour.

Remove from the heat, transfer the sauce to the food processor and blitz until silky-smooth. Return to the wok and season with the fish sauce and sugar. Add the fish and gently poach in the sauce for 6–8 minutes. Remove from the heat, stir through ripped-up Thai basil leaves, and serve with rice (there'll be enough fish for 4 servings).

Black Pepper Crab

SERVES 4
Preparation time 45 minutes, plus
freezing time
Cooking time 10 minutes

2 large brown cock crabs, bought live
    from the fishmonger
2 tbsp salt
5 garlic cloves, finely chopped
3cm piece of fresh ginger, peeled and
    julienned
1 tbsp black peppercorns, coarsely
    ground
1–2 Thai green chillies, finely
    chopped
2 tbsp sunflower oil
large handful of fresh curry leaves
2 tbsp butter

FOR THE SAUCE

100g oyster sauce
60ml soy sauce
125ml fresh chicken stock
1 tbsp caster sugar

TO SERVE

1 red chilli, thinly sliced
2 spring onions, thinly sliced
handful of coriander, leaves picked
cooked rice or noodles

The first time I had this dish, I had stopped off in Malaysia on my way to Borneo and found myself in Kuala Lumpur. Giddily galivanting around town after way too many beers and cocktails, my companion and I stumbled across the Jalan Alor food market. Having grown up in Bangkok I'm used to these markets, but this one is in another league! It's a sensory blast of lights, noise and delicious smells and the whole place pumps with energy. If you're into food, put this place at the top of your bucket list: you pull up a pew at the roadside restaurants with their sticky tables and order from enormous light-boxed menus, sit back and take in the intense humidity and huge crowds with ice-cold beers and satay. The three most famous dishes at the market are 'chicken fish', butter garlic prawns and black pepper crab. Many will be familiar with Singapore crab but black pepper crab is something else altogether – deep, rich, full of umami and just a bit more 'adult'. I can't ever leave Kuala Lumpur without getting my black pepper crab fix. I have introduced loads of people to the dish in the past 20 years, but it's become extra special as Caroline Flack and I thought of it as 'our dish'. When we travelled around Southeast Asia and stayed at an amazing place called Pankor Laut, we stopped in Kuala Lumpur both ways and couldn't resist a repeat visit to Jalan Alor. Since then, she always talked about the crab and how gross I am when I eat! (You have to eat it with your fingers.) It seems a lovely, fitting tribute a month after her death to finally write down the recipe and dedicate it to her.

Cooking and preparing live crabs is a good afternoon's work if you're a novice, and requires fearlessness and dedication. Live crabs need to go straight into the freezer. Freezing them for an hour or longer sends them to sleep and makes the process of dispatching them a little more humane. It's worth the effort, if not for the flavour, then for the life skill and pride. Cock crabs (as used here) have the meatiest claws, but other crabs or prawns would work well too.

I use quite a few imported ingredients here, but crabs are really sustainable, and you can buy British-made soy and oyster sauces.

Put the live crabs in the freezer for 1 hour or so, so they become dormant.

Fill your largest pot with water and add the salt – you want it heavily salted. Bring to a rolling boil, then lower in one frozen crab, cover and cook for 5 minutes. While

CONTINUED ››

it's cooking, prepare a large bowl of ice-cold water. Remove the crab from the pot, rinse under cold running water and transfer to the ice-cold water. Repeat with the second crab. Now, break down the crab. This bit is great fun for some, and hellish to others. I'm in the fun camp. Remove the claws by pulling firmly at the base joint that connects them to the body then give the claws a firm tap with the back of a knife to crack the shell (this allows the flavours to infuse into the claw meat) but keep the shell on the meat to keep it moist. Lay the main body of the crab on a surface with the underside facing you and the mouth facing away. Using the palm of your hand, push down on the shell and put your fingers into the gap where the body meets the shell around the mouth. Pull firmly towards you and the shell and innards should come away in one piece. Pull out the feathery gills, aka 'dead man's fingers', from around the sides of the body and shell, then scoop out the brown meat and set it aside in the fridge to use another time – simply spread on toast with a bit of lemon is delicious.

Finally, cut the body with its legs into equal quarters, rinse them all under cold running water and leave in the fridge until you are ready to cook.

As with most Asian cooking, it all happens fast and hot, so have everything prepared before you start cooking.

Bash the garlic, ginger, black pepper and chilli in a pestle and mortar or blitz in a blender and transfer to a bowl. Mix all the sauce ingredients in a bowl.

Once you're ready, take a very large wok or large frying pan and heat the oil over a high heat. Add the bashed or blitzed ginger, garlic, chilli and pepper mixture and fry for a minute or so, moving it around to prevent it burning, then throw in the curry leaves and fry until they start to crackle and pop. Pour in the sauce and add the butter. Bring to the boil and cook until the butter has melted and the sauce starts to reduce and thicken, then add all the crab pieces and stir-fry for about 4 minutes (if you feel like you're wrestling with it a bit, pop a lid on and let it cook for a minute, stir, put the lid back on, cook for a minute, give it another hefty stir and so on), making sure it's all well coated and the sauce has thickened a little further.

Transfer everything to a large serving platter, discarding any loose bits of shell, then pour over the sauce. Finally, scatter over the shredded chillies, spring onions and coriander. Serve with rice or noodles. Eating it is an inevitably messy business, but that is one of the real joys of this dish.

ESSENTIALS

Fresh Hand-rolled Pasta

MAKES 4 portions
Preparation time 15 minutes, plus
1 hour resting
Cooking time 3 minutes

300g 00-grade pasta flour
½ tsp salt
3 large free-range eggs (medium eggs
   will make your pasta too dry)
1 tsp olive oil
semolina flour, for dusting

Put the flour, salt, eggs and oil in a food processor and blitz until they form large waxy crumbs. Transfer the mixture to a work surface and knead it for about 3 minutes until it forms a smooth dough. Some recipes say to knead pasta dough for 10 minutes, as you would bread dough, but I tested this recipe numerous times and it made no difference. I also made it in a stand mixer fitted with the dough hook, but I felt that technology didn't actually help the process, and that I had more control kneading by hand. The 00 flour is high in gluten and springs back really quickly, and the kneading is quite a fight – the mixture is totally unlike bread dough. What you're looking for is a smooth dough that's really firm but on the verge of being both silky and springy to the touch. Wrap it tightly in cling film and let it rest for an hour outside of the fridge. Some people suggest 15 minutes, but for hand rolling it needs more time.

When it's time to make your pasta, dust the work surface with semolina flour. This will stop the pasta drying out or the water getting claggy. This requires some muscle but I've had fights with pasta machines in the past and I would recommend hand-rolling your pasta. Cut the pasta dough in half (keep one half covered by a tea towel) and warm the dough between your hands. Lay it on the dusted surface and sprinkle the top with a little more semolina flour. Then just roll. It takes a bit of welly or elbow grease (or whatever you want to call it). And sometimes, if you stop for a few seconds, you will see that it rests again and is easier to roll.

You need to roll it pretty thin – to the thickness of a small coin perhaps. Try to roll it into a neatish rectangle, but you will find that pasta dough has a mind of its own, or at least it does in my case. Roll it out until it's about 50 × 30cm, then roll out the other half to the same dimensions. Cut each rectangle in half and then lay all four pieces on top of one another. Trim the edges to neaten them. You can leave them in sheets if using them for lasagne or cannelloni (see my Pork and Sage Cannelloni on pages 218–19), or roll them all up tightly and cut the rolls into thin strips that look like linguine, fettuccine, tagliatelle or pappardelle.

To cook the pasta, bring a large saucepan of very salty water (1–2 tablespoons per 10 litres) to the boil. Drop the pasta in and cook for a minute, or until it rises to the top. It should be firm to bite, but make sure it's actually cooked through too. Now you're ready to toss it in a sauce. Reserve a little of the pasta cooking water in case your sauce is too dry.

Elevated Hollandaise Sauce, *for asparagus, artichokes, fish and eggs*

MAKES 500g
Preparation time 5 minutes
Cooking time 10 minutes

FOR THE REDUCTION

1 medium banana shallot, very, very finely diced
100ml white wine, rice wine or cider vinegar
3 black peppercorns
1 bay leaf
1 small (4cm) piece of dried kombu seaweed
2 blades of mace

FOR THE SAUCE

4 free-range egg yolks
pinch of salt, plus extra to taste, if needed
225g hot melted unsalted butter
squeeze of lemon juice

When you discover an ingredient that changes how you cook because it's such a flavour elevator, you really don't want to share it. The discovery of kombu seaweed was this ingredient to me. The Japanese have been using it forever but it was only after interviewing chef Massimo Bottura, from the celebrated Osteria Francescana, about how he makes the brodo (broth) for his tortellini brodo with this seaweed, that I started using it. The umami and roundness of its sweet, salty and savoury flavour changes stock and broth making for good. I now use kombu in every stock. Once you've done it, you too will not look back. I have tried it in all kinds of things, and when I was developing recipes for one of my restaurants with my head chef at the time, Phil Smith, I added it to the reduction for a hollandaise sauce. We compared it to a classic hollandaise and the difference was astonishing. Only the Japanese really utilise kombu, but it grows worldwide and in abundance here – buy it dried from health food and fine food stores and Asian supermarkets, or fresh from the fishmonger. (It's worth saying that this recipe does work without the kombu, too.)

Serve with an eggs Benedict or eggs Royale, with blanched asparagus in spring, steamed whole globe artichoke, grilled fish or in my riff on a McMuffin (see below).

To make the reduction, put all the ingredients in a small saucepan and boil until you only have 2 tablespoons of liquid left, then strain into a cold bowl and squeeze all the aromatics in the sieve as they will be plump with liquid (and flavour to boot!).

You can have the swankiest kit in the world, but the most efficient way to make hollandaise is the old-school way. Whisk the yolks with the salt in a heatproof bowl over a pan of simmering water, making sure the water doesn't touch the bowl. Pour in half the reduction, then, whisking continuously, add half the hot butter very, very slowly, 1 teaspoon at a time (purists think you should leave behind the milk solids from the hot butter pan, but I whisk them in). The sauce should be fairly thick. Pour in the remaining butter in a fine stream, whisking constantly, until you have a thick, emulsified sauce. Season with salt, lemon juice and the remaining reduction (if the sauce needs it).

For a McDonalds-style 'McMuffin'

Add a lick of it to a toasted muffin with eggs, smoked salmon and a slice of processed cheese. I accept that using processed cheese is slightly off brand, but sometimes it's okay to make a tiny exception!

Stocks

These stocks will keep in the fridge for up to 2–3 weeks as long as they have become jellied and the containers they are stored in are tightly sealed. Alternatively, they will freeze brilliantly for a few months.

White Chicken Stock

MAKES 1.5 litres
Preparation time 10 minutes
Cooking time 3 hours 15 minutes

3 chicken carcasses (freeze carcasses after roasts in a bag, until you have enough saved up, or buy 3 or 4 raw chicken carcasses from the butcher) or 2kg chicken wings, jointed, or a mixture of both
2–3 onions, quartered
1 head of garlic, halved
2 carrots, chopped into 3 pieces each
2 leeks, chopped into 3 pieces each
2 celery sticks, chopped into 3 pieces each
2 bay leaves
a few parsley stalks
fresh thyme
8 black peppercorns

Place all the ingredients in a large, deep pan and cover with cold water. Slowly bring to the boil, skimming off the scum that forms on the surface with a large metal spoon, along with any fat. This helps to ensure a lovely clear stock. Turn down the heat and let it simmer gently for 3 hours. It's important to make sure that it doesn't boil at this stage, or else the bubbles will knock away at the bone marrow and make the stock cloudy. While it's simmering, keep skimming the scum from the top, especially for the first 30 minutes of cooking time.

As the stock cooks it will begin to reduce. If the water level falls below the ingredients, add more cold water, which will also reveal any scum hiding at the bottom of the pan.

When the 3 hours are up, place a fine sieve over a large saucepan or heatproof bowl and pour the stock through it, collecting all the flavoursome liquid. It goes against classic rules for a perfectly clear stock, but squeeze all the juice out of the veggies through the sieve. If you taste the stock at this stage it may not have much flavour, so the next step is to reduce the liquid to condense the flavour. Pour the stock into a clean saucepan, bring to the boil and slowly allow the liquid to reduce. Taste it every so often as it gently boils, and once you have the right intensity of chicken flavour you can stop. Do not season your stock as you may want to reduce it more when making gravies which will make it too salty. A good rule of thumb is to reduce any stock by about two thirds to develop a good depth of flavour.

Either use the stock straight away or let it cool, transfer it to a container and keep it in the fridge. A good chicken stock will have a really chickeny essence to it and, once refrigerated, will turn to jelly.

This is the basic process for all stock making. Below and opposite are variants on the method, and a separate recipe for Prawn Stock.

Vegetable Stock

Leave out the chicken carcasses and double the quantity of vegetables in the White Chicken Stock recipe, adding 2 parsnips and some of the outer leaves of a cabbage. Cover with cold water and cook gently for 20 minutes. As with fish stock, vegetable stock is much more delicate than chicken or beef stock, and it will develop a school dinner-like stewed veg smell if cooked for too long! Strain and reduce as normal.

Dark Chicken Stock

For a richer stock that's great to use for gravies and meat stews, roast the chicken carcasses or wings and vegetables in a very hot oven for 30 minutes, or until they have become golden and caramelised. Be careful not to burn them, as this will impart an acrid, charred flavour to your stock. Then follow all the steps in the standard White Chicken Stock recipe opposite.

Beef or Veal Stock

This produces a dark stock. Swap the chicken carcasses for 2kg beef or veal shin bones and cook in the same way as the Dark Chicken Stock. It's really important to roast your bones first, to develop a deep, rich flavour. Cook the stock for longer than chicken stock – about 4 hours.

Roast Meat Stock

Use exactly the same procedure as for the Beef Stock, but use 2kg of leftover bones from your roast (any meat). Remove all the excess fat, but leave any hard-to-remove meaty bits for extra flavour and cook in the same way as the Beef or Veal Stock. You can make this stock extra strong by adding any leftover gravy or meat from a roast.

Fish Stock

Swap the chicken carcasses for the raw carcasses of 3 large white fish, or 1kg fish bones, excluding the heads. Salmon or tuna don't make nice stock, so look for sea bass, halibut or haddock. Follow the recipe for White Chicken Stock, but only cook the carcasses for 20 minutes before straining. Don't cook it for too long or it will become muddy and rancid.

Prawn Stock

This stock is brilliant for fish soups, stews and rice dishes.

MAKES 1.5 litres
Preparation time 10 minutes
Cooking time 45 minutes

2 tbsp olive oil
1 onion, chopped
2 carrots, chopped
1 fennel bulb, chopped
2 celery sticks, chopped
1 head of garlic, cut in half
2 bay leaves
a few sprigs of thyme
a few parsley stalks
1 tbsp tomato puree
heads and shells of 24 raw prawns
a good glug of brandy or cognac
1½ litres fresh chicken or fish stock
400ml dry white wine
4 tomatoes, quartered
½ lemon

Heat the oil in a large heavy-based saucepan over a low heat. Add the onion, carrots, fennel, celery, garlic and herbs and sauté for about 20 minutes. You want them to have a little colour, but not too much. Stir in the tomato puree, coating all the vegetables, and cook for 1 minute, then whack up the heat and add the prawn heads and shells (no prawn meat). Sauté until the shells turn bright pink, then douse with the brandy or cognac. Add the stock and wine – you need the liquid to come above the shells, so add water if necessary – add the tomatoes and simmer for 20 minutes.

Pour through a sieve over a saucepan or heatproof bowl, squashing the shells, particularly the heads, so they release all of their juices. Transfer the strained liquid to a frying pan and simmer it until it has reduced by about two thirds and has started to thicken and become intense in flavour. Remove from the heat and add a squeeze of lemon juice to cut through the richness.

Gizzi's Slow Cooked Tomato Sauce

MAKES 6 portions for pasta, or the base for other dishes on pages 46 and 66
Preparation time 15 minutes
Cooking time 1 hour 45 minutes

3 tbsp olive oil
1 head of garlic, cloves peeled and finely chopped
2kg tomatoes (a mixture of varieties – vine, plums, heirlooms and cherry)
2 tbsp sherry or red wine or white wine vinegar
large bunch of basil leaves
sea salt and freshly ground black pepper

This is a classic that I have included in all my books. It forms the base of so many recipes and I really can't do without it.

Heat the olive oil in a heavy-based casserole dish over a medium heat, add the garlic and fry gently for about 10 minutes until lightly golden. This stage is important because if you cook the garlic too fast it will be scorched but still raw. Let the garlic heat up in the oil and watch it cook gently. You want to see it go from raw, to softened, to only just beginning to go golden.

Meanwhile, blitz the tomatoes into a puree in a food processor and when the garlic is ready add the tomatoes to the pan. Season well with salt and pepper, add the vinegar then cook the tomatoes very slowly for about 1 hour 30 minutes to reduce them so they have a really wonderful concentrated flavour. Once the cooking time is up, I like to blitz the sauce in the food processor again to blend the tomato seeds and garlic into the sauce. Transfer back to the casserole dish, check the seasoning, then tear up the basil leaves and add them to the sauce.

Mayonnaise

MAKES 275g
Preparation time 10 minutes

2 free-range egg yolks
1 tsp Dijon or English mustard
¼ tsp white wine vinegar
300ml sunflower or organic rapeseed
   oil
30ml extra-virgin olive oil
squeeze of lemon juice
sea salt and freshly ground black
   pepper

Put the egg yolks in a bowl with a pinch of salt and pepper, the mustard and vinegar and whisk to combine using a balloon whisk.

Pour the sunflower or rapeseed oil into a jug, and very, very slowly add it to the egg yolk, a teaspoon at a time, whisking as you go, until half of the oil is incorporated. The consistency should be fairly thick at this point. Slowly pour the rest of the oil in a fine stream, continuing to whisk, until it is all combined. Now add the olive oil in the same way, until you have a thick, wobbly mayonnaise. Add a squeeze of lemon juice and season to taste.

Aioli

To turn this into aioli, add 2 finely grated garlic cloves at the first stage, along with the egg yolk, mustard, vinegar, salt and pepper, and follow the rest of the method.

Red Wine and Beef Sauce

MAKES 200ml
Cooking time 10–20 minutes

500ml fresh veal or beef stock
500ml red wine
2 tbsp cubed ice-cold butter

Put the stock and wine in a saucepan and reduce at a simmer until four-fifths of the liquid has evaporated, leaving about 200ml of thickened sauce in the pan. Remove from the heat and whisk in the ice-cold butter until melted, resulting in a rich, glossy sauce.

Rice and Peas

SERVES 4
Preparation time 5 minutes, plus overnight soaking
Cooking time 1 hour 30 minutes

250g dried red kidney beans, soaked overnight in cold water
1.5 litres water
400g basmati rice, rinsed
400ml tin coconut milk
a few thyme sprigs
2 garlic cloves, smashed
1 Scotch bonnet chilli
1½ tsp salt

Rice and peas is a stalwart of West Indian cookery, and it frustrates me how most recipes use tinned beans for convenience. You really miss out on the liquor that you get when you cook the beans from dried. I'm guilty of having used tinned beans myself, but I've endeavoured to amend my ways and make it the proper way from now on. This is the perfect accompaniment to my Allotment 'Ital-Style' Stew on page 82.

Drain the beans and add them to a large saucepan with the water. Bring to the boil, skim away any scum that forms on the surface, then reduce the heat and simmer for 45 minutes (skimming further if necessary) until the beans are beginning to soften. Now add the rice, coconut milk, thyme, garlic, Scotch bonnet chilli and salt. Cook for 25 minutes until the rice is cooked through and the beans are soft but still retain a little bite. The liquid will have all but evaporated, so at this stage remove from the heat, cover with a lid and allow to steam for 20 minutes, which will result in puffed-up fluffy rice and peas! Remove the Scotch bonnet before serving.

Vinaigrette

MAKES 150ml
Preparation time 5 minutes

1 tbsp sherry vinegar, wine vinegar,
   cider vinegar or balsamic vinegar
a good squeeze of lemon juice
1 tsp mustard of choice
pinch of sugar
150ml extra-virgin olive oil or
   rapeseed oil
sea salt and freshly ground black
   pepper

Whisk together the vinegar, lemon juice, mustard, sugar, and some salt and pepper in a small bowl. Slowly pour the oil in a fine stream into the bowl, whisking steadily, until the dressing has completely emulsified and thickened. Check for seasoning.

Confit Garlic

MAKES 3 confit garlic heads
Preparation time 20 minutes
Cooking time 30 minutes

3 heads of garlic, cloves peeled
enough good-quality olive oil to
   just cover the garlic
2 sprigs of rosemary (optional)

This has become a staple ingredient in my kitchen and is the foundation for a myriad of recipes. In this book, it's essential for my Broad Bean, Mint and Feta Salad (page 68–9), and my Patlican Salata (page 61). The soft, buttery cloves are also completely delicious just spread on hot toast.

The only slightly fiddly part of this recipe is peeling the garlic cloves, but once that's done it couldn't be simpler.

Put the garlic cloves in a small saucepan and pour over the olive oil until the garlic is just submerged. Rosemary adds an extra flavour note, so if you have some to hand, add it now too. Heat over the smallest, lowest flame as it is very important that the garlic doesn't burn or the whole thing will turn acrid. Allow the garlic to cook very slowly in the oil for about 30 minutes until soft and buttery, then remove from the heat and leave to cool. This will keep submerged in oil for weeks.

Sourdough Starter

minimum 550g rye flour (or a
combination of rye/wholemeal/
spelt/white/whatever you have
to hand to use up), depending how
many times you wish to feed your
starter
550ml water

You will need a sterilised 1-litre jar
and a thermometer.

A sourdough starter is a commitment. It's like having a child, and you need to persist with it for the first few days – the load lightens up a bit once it's all up and running. I find it hard to keep a plant alive and I've killed many a sourdough starter in my time. I'm not great at commitment, but I am good at admitting when I'm not good at something, so now me and my neighbour share the job (burden) of looking after it. This is also handy as you have to be as keen to make things with the starter as you are to make the starter, otherwise you waste money on flour to feed it without using it. This method is from my good friend Edd Kimber (aka 'The Boy Who Bakes' and 2010 winner of *Great British Bake Off*). He posted it online at the beginning of lockdown. It's more in depth than the recipe Justin Gellatly taught me (Justin is former head baker at St John and co-founder of Bread Ahead, it was my job to feed the sourdough when I was at St John Bread and Wine on stagiaire) and it makes for a feisty starter that is really great for the home cook.

Day 1

Put 50g of your flour/flour blend in a sterilised 1-litre jar. You need the water to be lukewarm to give the fermenting process a head-start: boil some water in a kettle, measure out 50ml and test the water with a thermometer, adding it to the flour in the jar when it has cooled to 26°C (lukewarm). Mix well with a spatula so that the water has been completely absorbed by the flour and there are no air pockets. Cover loosely with a lid so the air can get to it and leave at room temperature in a cupboard.

Day 2

Repeat the steps from Day 1, adding another 50g of flour mix and another 50ml of water at 26°C, mixing into the original mixture until well combined. Leave it in the same place for another 24 hours. At this stage of the first feed there won't be much action, maybe just a bubble or two.

Day 3

Spoon out the starter until you just have about 25g (just under 1 tablespoon) remaining, and repeat the feeding process with 50g of flour mix and 50ml of water at 26°C. Leave it in the same place for another 24 hours. (You can use the excess starter for my Sourdough Flatbreads on page 166 or Sourdough Doughnuts on pages 148–49.)

Day 4

Now we are going to ramp up the feeding to twice a day, 12 hours apart, so it makes sense to do this when you get up and before going to bed. Do the same as Day 3, discarding all but 25g of the starter and feeding the 25g starter with 50g of flour mix and 50ml of water at 26°C, both morning and night. By this point you should be seeing lots of activity in the form of bubbles, and possibly a vaguely unpleasant smell as the natural yeasts and bacteria begin to cultivate. Don't worry, just persevere!

Days 5–7

Repeat the Day 4 process, feeding the starter twice a day. After Day 4 the starter should grow in size every time you feed it. You can check its progress by marking a line on the outside of the jar where the starter comes up to each time you feed it. You may need to continue with the process for about 10 days before you see a regular doubling in size.

Once you've seen this occur for a few days you will have an active starter that can be used to bake with. The more you feed it, the more fermented, active and sourer the starter becomes, improving your bread exponentially. Keeping it in the fridge will slow the fermenting right down, and mean that you only need to feed it occasionally (up to once every 2 weeks).

If you're planning to store it in the fridge, wait an hour or two after feeding it, so that it is at the start of the curve for growth before it's chilled. When you want to bake with it, remove it from the fridge and give it one or two more feeds to bring it back to life before you bake with it (for example: feed it the morning and evening before the day you want to bake). If you leave a starter lingering in the fridge for a while, you will see a thin layer of liquid appear on the surface which will have a kind of nail polish smell. This is known as hooch, and is simply the alcohol produced from the fermenting process. You can just pour it off and give the starter a few more feeds: before you know it, it will have returned to its former health with that nice yeasty smell and will be good for baking.

Cook's Notes

Butter
Always unsalted unless otherwise specified.

Deep-frying
Never fill a deep-fryer or wok above the halfway line (otherwise you risk it boiling over) and always allow for weight to volume ratios increasing once you add the ingredient for frying.

Eggs
All eggs are large unless otherwise specified.

Lemons
All lemons are unwaxed.

Meat and fish
Allow meat and fish to reach room temperature before cooking.

Oils and fat for cooking
See page 147 for more on which oils and fats to use for what purposes.

Preserving jars
I like to use Kilner preserving jars, but any that have a tight seal and are easy to clean will do.

A note about mould on ferments and preserves
If you detect any white mould on the surface of your ferments or preserves, don't be scared. Just scrape it off with a clean knife (in the case of a ferment, ensure any ingredients are immersed in the liquid and clean the sides of the jar with a cloth dipped in alcohol).

Sterilising instructions
The easiest way to sterilise your jars is to fill them with boiling water and allow it to tstand for 3 minutes, then pour out the water and allow the jar to air-dry before filling. Alternatively, preheat your oven to 180°C/ 160°C fan/gas mark 4, wash your jars in soapy water then rinse them and place them on a tray in the preheated oven for 15 minutes just before filling (the heat will dry them).

Environmentally friendly packaging
As incredibly useful as cling film can be, I've made a conscious effort to reduce disposable plastics in the kitchen in exchange for eco-friendly alternatives, including beeswax wrap, greaseproof paper and reusable super-airtight clip-and-click Tupperware boxes.

Index

A

Accelerated Gochujang **14**

aduki beans: Chilli con Pesce **246**

agriculture

  fruit and vegetable **38–41**

  greenhouse gas emissions in pastoral
    farming **198**

  regenerative farming **193–5**

Aioli **267**

Allotment 'Ital-style' Stew **82**

almond milk **171, 172**

anchovies: Celeriac Holstein **89**

Antipasto, English Garden **43–4**

apples

  Celeriac Remoulade **93**

  Cheats' Activated Kimchi **15**

  Fermented Fruit Vinegar **17**

  Fridge-raid 'not quite Branston's' Pickle
    30–1

  Miso and Apple Pork Rib-eye Steaks **211**

  Rainbow Slaw **94**

  spiced apple filling for fruit pies and
    crumbles **105**

artichokes

  Globe Artichokes with Real Salad Cream
    54

  Roasted Violet Artichokes **43**

aubergines

  grilled aubergines **44**

  Patlican Salata **61**

  Ratatouille **46**

avocados **48**

B

bacon

  Egg and Bacon Potato Salad **62**

  Jerusalem Artichoke and Bacon Gratin **95**

Banana Cream Pie **157**

Barbecue Sauce **199**

Barley and Mushroom Risotto with Pan-
  roasted King Oyster **139**

beans **114–15**

beansprouts: Bibimbap **140**

beef **195–6, 198**

  Beef Stock **263**

  Bibimbap **140**

  Braised Beef Shin with Barbecue Sauce
    199

  Red Wine and Beef Sauce **268**

  24-hour Beef Tail and Rib Pho **216–18**

beef dripping **146**

beetroot

  Black Lentil and Beetroot Larb **119**

  Chrain **94**

  Roasted Beetroot, Beluga Lentil and
    Watercress Salad with Goat's Cheese
    Croute **116**

  Sri Lankan Beetroot and Coconut Curry
    85

Bibimbap **140**

biscuits: Banana Cream Pie **157**

black pepper: strawberry and black pepper
  filling for apple pie and crumble **105**

Black Pepper Crab **253–5**

blackberries: a Delicious Port and Blackberry
  Sauce for Game **186**

Boulangère, Parsnip, Miso, Oat and Shallot
97

bread

  Celeriac Bread Sauce **92**

  Rye Tortillas **167**

  Sourdough Flatbreads **166–7**

  Sourdough Starter **270–1**

broad beans

  Broad Bean, Mint and Feta Salad **68–9**

  Peas, Broad Beans and Lettuce Gratin **58**

brown ale: Braised Beef Shin with Barbecue
  Sauce **199**

bulgar wheat: Root Vegetable Bulgar Wheat,
  'Cous cous' style, with Merguez Sausages **78**

Burnt Basque Country Cheesecake with
  Gooseberries in Green Wine **154**

butter

  Honey Butter **69**

  Wild Garlic Butter **247–8**

butternut squash

  Fridge-raid 'not quite Branston's' Pickle
    30–1

  grilled butternut squash **43–4**

buying food **40, 238–9**

C

cabbage

  Cheats' Activated Kimchi **15**

  Quick Pickled Red Cabbage **126–7**

  Rainbow Slaw **94**

  Sauerkraut **20**

cake

  Chocolate School Cake with Chocolate
    Custard **160**

  Jam and Coconut Sponge **160**

  Leftover Juicing Cake **107–9**

  Vanilla School Cake and Custard **159–60**

Cannelloni, Pork and Sage **221–2**

carbon footprints

  avocados **48**

  coconuts **173**

  eggs **158**

  meat **194, 198**

  milks **170, 171**

  poultry **176**

Carlin Pea and Pumpkin Massaman **123**

carrots

  Punchy Piccalilli **33**

Rainbow Slaw **94**

Roast Carrots with Queso Fresco, Coriander and Jalapeño Oil, and Pumpkin Seeds **81**

cashews

Korma Wings **187**

Nut Milks **172**

Sour Cashew Cream **172**

cauliflower

Fridge-raid 'not quite Branston's' Pickle **30–1**

Punchy Piccalilli **33**

Roasted Cauliflower, Preserved Lemon and Chilli Pasta **77**

celeriac

Celeriac Bread Sauce **92**

Celeriac Cordon Bleu **90**

Celeriac Holstein **89**

Celeriac Remoulade **93**

Rainbow Slaw **94**

Salt-baked Celeriac **86**

chard: Gözleme **162**

Chashu Pork Belly **212**

Tonkotsu Ramen **213–14**

Cheats' Activated Kimchi **15**

cheese

Broad Bean, Mint and Feta Salad **68–9**

Celeriac Cordon Bleu **90**

Cheese Ends Soufflé Omelette **168**

Cheese Semolina Grits **130**

Cheesy Scones **135–6**

Elote **69**

Gözleme **162**

Queso Fresco **161**

Roast Carrots with Queso Fresco, Coriander and Jalapeño Oil, and Pumpkin Seeds **81**

Roasted Beetroot, Beluga Lentil and

Watercress Salad with Goat's Cheese Croute **116**

cheesecake: Burnt Basque Country Cheesecake with Gooseberries in Green Wine **154**

cherries

sour cherry filling for apple pie and crumble **105**

Sourdough Doughnuts with White Chocolate Custard and Sour Cherry Jam **148–9**

chicken **176–9, 197, 198**

Chicken in Weeds 2020 **181**

Dark Chicken Stock **263**

Korma Wings **187**

making the most of a bird **177–8**

portioning **179**

White Chicken Stock **262**

chillies

Chilli con Pesce **246**

Chilli Sauces **34–5**

Fauzu Kosho **16**

Guinea Fowl alla 'Diavolo' **182**

Lemon and Lime Pickle **25**

Roasted Cauliflower, Preserved Lemon and Chilli Pasta **77**

Sriracha **35**

Turkish Chilli Sauce **126–7**

Vegan XO Sauce **23**

West Indian Hot Sauce **34**

Chinese napa cabbage: Cheats' Activated Kimchi **15**

chocolate

Chocolate School Cake with Chocolate Custard **160**

Garbage Pail Cookies **153**

Sourdough Doughnuts with White Chocolate Custard and Sour Cherry Jam

148–9

Chrain **94**

clams: Vongole **240**

clementines: Fauzu Kosho **16**

climate change **6–7, 194, 236**

cocoa powder: Pumpkin Seed and Cocoa Mole Sauce **52–3**

coconut **173**

Jam and Coconut Sponge **160**

coconut milk **171**

Allotment 'Ital-style' Stew **82**

Rice and Peas **268**

Sri Lankan Beetroot and Coconut Curry **85**

coconut oil **145, 173**

cod: Sumiso Cod Collar **244**

Confit Garlic **269**

Cookies, Garbage Pail **153**

Cordial, Summer Fruit **111**

coriander

Chicken in Weeds 2020 **181**

Coriander and Jalapeño Oil **81**

corn on the cob: Elote **69**

courgettes

Braised Courgettes **64**

Cuttlefish and Courgette Frito **245**

grilled courgettes **44**

Linguine alla Courgette Aglio e Olio **68**

Ratatouille **46**

Court Bouillon **54**

crab: Black Pepper Crab **253–5**

cream

Banana Cream Pie **157**

homemade non-dairy **172**

cream cheese: Burnt Basque Country Cheesecake with Gooseberries in Green Wine **154**

creams

Oat Cream **172**

Index

Sour Cashew Cream **172**

crumble filling and toppings **105, 106**

cucumber: Summer Salad Soup **55**

curry

    Carlin Pea and Pumpkin Massaman **123**

    Jamaican Goat Curry Patties **207–8**

    Korma Wings **187**

    Mutton Nihari **219**

    Sour Orange Fish Curry **252**

    Sri Lankan Beetroot and Coconut Curry **85**

curry leaves: Lemon and Lime Pickle **25**

custard

    Chocolate School Cake with Chocolate
        Custard **160**

    Vanilla School Cake and Custard **159–60**

    White Chocolate and Vanilla Pâtissière
        Custard **148–9**

Cuttlefish and Courgette Frito **245**

D

dates

    Fridge-raid 'not quite Branston's' Pickle
        30–1

    Leftover Juicing Cake **107–9**

Devilled Kidneys **226**

Dhal, Tarka **125**

doughnuts: Sourdough Doughnuts with
    White Chocolate Custard and Sour Cherry
    Jam **148–9**

Dressing, Salsa Verde **116**

drinks

    Summer Fruit Cordial **111**

    Tepache **19**

duck: Roast Mallard Duck **185**

E

eggs **158, 198**

    Celeriac Holstein **89**

Cheese Ends Soufflé Omelette **168**

Egg and Bacon Potato Salad **62**

Green Shakshuka **50**

Marinated Eggs **213–14**

Egyptian Fava Bean Falafels and Sauces
    126–7

Elote **69**

English Garden Antipasto **43–4**

Ethiopian Lentil Stew **122**

F

Faggots **228–9**

falafels: Egyptian Fava Bean Falafels and
    Sauces **126–7**

farming

    fruit and vegetable **38–41**

    greenhouse gas emissions in pastoral
    farming **198**

    regenerative **193–5**

fats **144–7**

    rendering from meat **145**

Fauzu Kosho **16**

fava (broad) beans: Egyptian Fava Bean
    Falafels and Sauces **126–7**

ferments and fermenting **10–11**

    Accelerated Gochujang **14**

    Cheats' Activated Kimchi **15**

    Fauzu Kosho **16**

    Fermented Fruit Vinegar **17**

    Fish Sauce **24**

    health benefits of **11**

    how fermenting works **10–11**

    Lacto-fermented Watermelon Rind **27**

    Quick Ferments **14–20**

    Sauerkraut **20**

    Slow Ferments **21–4**

    Tepache **19**

    Vegan XO Sauce **23**

Watermelon Juice Vinegar **27**

White Miso **21–2**

feta

    Broad Bean, Mint and Feta Salad **68–9**

    Gözleme **162**

fish **234–57**

    Celeriac Holstein **89**

    Chilli con Pesce **246**

    Fish Sauce **24**

    Fish Stock **263**

    freshness of **239**

    native British fish **238–9**

    Sour Orange Fish Curry **252**

    Sumiso Cod Collar **244**

    Wet & Wild Monkfish Kievs **247–8**

    when to buy fish **238–9**

flat beans: Braised Flat Beans in Slow
    Cooked Tomato Sauce **66**

Flatbreads **166–7**

    Rye Tortillas **167**

    Sourdough Flatbreads **166–7**

Fridge-raid 'not quite Branston's' Pickle **30–1**

Frito, Cuttlefish and Courgette **245**

fruit **98–111**

    fruit agriculture **38–41**

    fruit pie and crumble fillings and toppings
    105–6

    a Glut of Jams **110**

    Leftover Juicing Cake **107–9**

    Summer Fruit Cordial **111**

Fruit Vinegar, Fermented **17**

frying oils **144, 147**

G

game **178**

    a Delicious Port and Blackberry Sauce for
        Game **186**

Garbage Pail Cookies **153**

garlic
  Allotment 'Ital-style' Stew **82**
  Braised Beef Shin with Barbecue Sauce **199**
  Burnt Garlic Oil (Mayo) **213–14**
  Chicken in Weeds 2020 **181**
  Chilli con Pesce **246**
  Confit Garlic **269**
  Ethiopian Lentil Stew **122**
  Garlic Sauce **126–7**
  Goat Ragu, with its Offal **232**
  Green Tomato Salsa **49**
  Guinea Fowl alla 'Diavolo' **182**
  Jamaican Goat Curry Patties **207–8**
  Linguine alla Courgette Aglio e Olio **68**
  Patlican Salata **61**
  Pork and Sage Cannelloni **221–2**
  Pumpkin Seed and Cocoa Mole Sauce
    52–3
  Rabbit à la Moutarde **188**
  Sriracha **35**
  Three Ways with Mexican Braised Pinto
    Beans **131**
  Vegan XO Sauce **23**
  Vongole **240**
  see also wild garlic
genetic modification **114–15**
ghee **144**
ginger
  Cheats' Activated Kimchi **15**
  Mutton Nihari **219**
  Vegan XO Sauce **23**
Gizzi's Slow Cooked Tomato Sauce **264**
Globe Artichokes with Real Salad Cream **54**
a Glut of Jams **110**
goat **197, 198**
  Goat Herder's Pie **206**
  Goat Ragu, with its Offal **232**
  Jamaican Goat Curry Patties **207–8**

goat's cheese: Roasted Beetroot, Beluga
    Lentil and Watercress Salad with Goat's
    Cheese Croute **116**
Gochujang, Accelerated **14**
  Cheats' Activated Kimchi **15**
gooseberries
  Burnt Basque Country Cheesecake with
    Gooseberries in Green Wine **154**
  a Glut of Jams **110**
Gözleme **162**
grains **114–15**
gratins
  Jerusalem Artichoke and Bacon Gratin **95**
  Parsnip, Miso, Oat and Shallot Boulangère
    97
  Peas, Broad Beans and Lettuce Gratin **58**
green beans: Punchy Piccalilli **33**
Green Shakshuka **50**
greengages: a Pistachio Tart for Soft Fruit
    100–1
greenhouse gas emissions in pastoral farming
    198
Greenhouse Romesco Sauce with
    Chargrilled Spring Onions **57**
grouse **178**
  roast grouse **185**
guinea fowl **178**
  Guinea Fowl alla 'Diavolo' **182**

H
ham: Celeriac Cordon Bleu **90**
hogget **196, 198**
Hollandaise Sauce **261**
Honey Butter **69**

J
jalapeños
  Coriander and Jalapeño Oil **81**

Green Tomato Salsa **49**
jam
  a Glut of Jams **110**
  Jam and Coconut Sponge **160**
  Sour Cherry Jam **148–9**
Jamaican Goat Curry Patties **207–8**
Jerusalem Artichoke and Bacon Gratin **95**

K
kalettes, roasted **44**
Kidneys, Devilled **226**
Kievs, Wet & Wild Monkfish **247–8**
Kimchi, Cheats' Activated **15**
kombu: White Miso **21–2**
Korean red pepper flakes: Accelerated
    Gochujang **14**
Korma Wings **187**

L
labels, meat **197**
Lacto-fermented Watermelon Rind **27**
lamb **196–7, 198**
  Faggots **228–9**
  a Really Great Lamb Neck Stew **202–5**
  Roasted Lamb Belly and Ribs **223**
lamb's kidneys: Devilled Kidneys **226**
Larb: Black Lentil and Beetroot **119**
lard **145–6**
late summer fruit filling **105**
Lebanese cucumber: Summer Salad Soup **55**
leeks, roasted **44**
Leftover Juicing Cake **107–9**
lemons
  Lemon and Lime Pickle **25**
  Roasted Cauliflower, Preserved Lemon and
    Chilli Pasta **77**
lentils
  Black Lentil and Beetroot Larb **119**

Index

Ethiopian Lentil Stew **122**

Puy Lentils, a Big Red and Roasted Toulouse Sausage **120**

Roasted Beetroot, Beluga Lentil and Watercress Salad with Goat's Cheese Croute **116**

lettuce

Peas, Broad Beans and Lettuce Gratin **58**

Summer Salad Soup **55**

limes

Fauzu Kosho **16**

Green Tomato Salsa **49**

Lemon and Lime Pickle **25**

Linguine alla Courgette Aglio e Olio **68**

local food **40**

M

McDonalds-style 'McMuffin' **261**

Mallard duck, roast **185**

Marmite: Onion and Roast Root Vegetable Stew with Cheesy Scones **135–6**

marrows: Stuffed Marrows and Tomatoes with Mushrooms and Orzo **65**

Massaman, Carlin Pea and Pumpkin **123**

Mayonnaise **267**

meat

ethical meat eating **192–8**

greenhouse gas emissions **198**

labelling **197**

rendering fat from **145**

Roast Meat Stock **263**

see also beef; lamb; etc

Merguez sausages, Root Vegetable Bulgar Wheat, 'Cous cous' style, with **78**

Mexican Braised Pinto Beans, Three Ways with **131**

Mexican-Spiced Pickled Watermelon Rind **26**

milk, dairy **170**

Queso Fresco **161**

milks, non-dairy **170–3**

almond milk **171**

coconut milk **171**

homemade **172**

oat milk **171**

rice milk **171**

soy milk **170**

mint: Broad Bean, Mint and Feta Salad **68–9**

miso

Accelerated Gochujang **14**

Miso and Apple Pork Rib-eye Steaks **211**

Parsnip, Miso, Oat and Shallot Boulangère **97**

White Miso **21–2**

mole: Pumpkin Seed and Cocoa Mole Sauce **52–3**

monkfish: Wet & Wild Monkfish Kievs **247–8**

monoculture agriculture **39**

Moules à la Crème **251**

mushrooms

Barley and Mushroom Risotto with Pan-roasted King Oyster **139**

Bibimbap **140**

roasted mushrooms **44**

Stuffed Marrows and Tomatoes with Mushrooms and Orzo **65**

Vegan XO Sauce **23**

mussels: Moules à la Crème **251**

mustard: Rabbit à la Moutarde **188**

mutton **196, 198**

Mutton Nihari **219**

Wild Garlic Stuffed Mutton **201**

N

Nam Prik Ong with Allotment Vegetables **71**

Nihari Masala, Mutton **219**

noodles: Tonkotsu Ramen **213–14**

nori seaweed: Vegan XO Sauce **23**

Nut Creams **172**

Sour Cashew Cream **172**

Nut Milks **172**

O

oat milk **171**

oats

Garbage Pail Cookies **153**

Oat Cream **172**

Parsnip, Miso, Oat and Shallot Boulangère **97**

offal

Devilled Kidneys **226**

Faggots **228–9**

Goat Ragu, with its Offal **232**

oils **144–7**

coconut oil **145, 173**

Coriander and Jalapeño Oil **81**

frying **144–5, 147**

olive oil **145**

palm oil **146–7**

rapeseed oil **145**

which to use **147**

Omelette, Cheese Ends Soufflé **168**

onions

Faggots **228–9**

Marmite, Onion and Roast Root Vegetable Stew with Cheesy Scones **135–6**

Punchy Piccalilli **33**

Sage and Onion Stuffing **186**

Szechuan Onion Flower **74**

organic food **40, 197**

Orzo, Stuffed Marrows and Tomatoes with
Mushrooms and 65

P

palm oil 146–7

Parsnip, Miso, Oat and Shallot Boulangère
97

pasta
Fresh Hand-rolled Pasta 260
Linguine alla Courgette Aglio e Olio 68
Pork and Sage Cannelloni 221–2
Roasted Cauliflower, Preserved Lemon and
Chilli Pasta 77
Stuffed Marrows and Tomatoes with
Mushrooms and Orzo 65
Vongole 240

pastries: Gözleme 162

Pastry, Sweet Shortcrust 106

Patlican Salata 61

Patties, Jamaican Goat Curry 207–8

pearl barley: Barley and Mushroom Risotto
with Pan-roasted King Oyster 139

peas
Carlin Pea and Pumpkin Massaman 123
Peas, Broad Beans and Lettuce Gratin 58
Summer Salad Soup 55

peppercorns
Black Pepper Crab 253–5
strawberry and black pepper filling for
crumbles and pies 105

peppers
Accelerated Gochujang 14
Green Shakshuka 50
Greenhouse Romesco Sauce with
Chargrilled Spring Onions 57
Patlican Salata 61
roasted peppers 44

pheasant 178

Roast Pheasant 184–5

Pho, 24-hour Beef Tail and Rib 216–18

pickles 25–33
Fridge-raid 'not quite Branston's' Pickle
30–1
Lemon and Lime Pickle 25
Mexican-Spiced Pickled Watermelon Rind
26
Punchy Piccalilli 33
Quick Pickled Red Cabbage 126–7

pies
fruit pie fillings and toppings 105–6
Goat Herder's Pie 206

Pigeon, Roast Wood 185

pig's trotters: Tonkotsu Ramen 213–14

pineapple
Tepache 19
West Indian Hot Sauce 34

Pinto Beans, Three Ways with Mexican
Braised 131

pistachios: a Pistachio Tart for Soft Fruit
100–1

pluck
Faggots 228–9
Goat Ragu, with its Offal 232

pork 197
Chashu Pork Belly 212
greenhouse gas emissions 198
Miso and Apple Pork Rib-eye Steaks 211
Nam Prik Ong with Allotment Vegetables
71
Pork and Sage Cannelloni 221–2
Tonkotsu Ramen 213–14

port: a Delicious Port and Blackberry Sauce
for Game 186

potatoes
Egg and Bacon Potato Salad 62
Goat Herder's Pie 206

a Really Great Lamb Neck Stew 202–5

poultry 176–9
see also chicken

Prawn Stock 263

preserving 10–11

prunes: Fridge-raid 'not quite Branston's'
Pickle 30–1

pulses 114–15

pumpkin
Carlin Pea and Pumpkin Massaman 123
grilled pumpkin 43–4

pumpkin seeds
Pumpkin Seed and Cocoa Mole Sauce
52–3
Roast Carrots with Queso Fresco,
Coriander and Jalapeño Oil, and Pumpkin
Seeds 81

Punchy Piccalilli 33

Q

Queso Fresco 161
Roast Carrots with Queso Fresco,
Coriander and Jalapeño Oil, and Pumpkin
Seeds 81

R

rabbit 178
Rabbit à la Moutarde 188

radishes: Rainbow Slaw 94

ragu: Goat Ragu, with its Offal 232

Rainbow Slaw 94

Ramen, Tonkotsu 213–14

rapeseed oil 145

Ratatouille 46

red kidney beans: Rice and Peas 268

red wine: Puy Lentils, a Big Red and Roasted
Toulouse Sausage 120

regenerative farming 193–5

Index

Remoulade, Celeriac **93**

rhubarb filling for crumbles and pies **105**

rice

    Bibimbap **140**

    Black Lentil and Beetroot Larb **119**

    Rice and Peas **268**

rice koji: White Miso **21–2**

rice milk **171**

risotto: Barley and Mushroom Risotto with
    Pan-roasted King Oyster **139**

Romesco Sauce: Greenhouse Romesco Sauce
    with Chargrilled Spring Onions **57**

Root Vegetable Bulgar Wheat, 'Cous cous'
    style, with Merguez Sausages **78**

rye flour

    Rye Tortillas **167**

    Sourdough Starter **270–1**

S

sage

    Pork and Sage Cannelloni **221–2**

    Sage and Onion Stuffing **186**

Salad Cream **54**

salads

    Broad Bean, Mint and Feta Salad **68–9**

    Chrain **94**

    Egg and Bacon Potato Salad **62**

    Patlican Salata **61**

    Rainbow Slaw **94**

    Roasted Beetroot, Beluga Lentil and
      Watercress Salad with Goat's Cheese
        Croute **116**

    Summer Salad Soup **55**

salsa

    Green Shakshuka **50**

    Green Tomato Salsa **49**

    Salsa Verde Dressing **116**

salt

Salt-baked Celeriac **86**

Salty Miso **21–2**

sauces

    Barbecue Sauce **199**

    Celeriac Bread Sauce **92**

    Chilli Sauces **34–5**

    a Delicious Port and Blackberry Sauce for
      Game **186**

    Egyptian Fava Bean Falafels and Sauces
      126–7

    Elevated Hollandaise Sauce **261**

    Fish Sauce **24**

    Garlic Sauce **126–7**

    Gizzi's Slow Cooked Tomato Sauce **264**

    Greenhouse Romesco Sauce with
      Chargrilled Spring Onions **57**

    Pumpkin Seed and Cocoa Mole Sauce **52–3**

    Red Wine and Beef Sauce **268**

    Sriracha **35**

    Turkish Chilli Sauce **126–7**

    West Indian Hot Sauce **34**

Sauerkraut **20**

sausages

    Puy Lentils, a Big Red and Roasted
      Toulouse Sausage **120**

    Root Vegetable Bulgar Wheat, 'Cous cous'
      style, with Merguez Sausages **78**

Scones, Cheesy **135–6**

seafood, buying **239**

seasonal eating **40–1**

semolina: Cheese Semolina Grits **130**

Shakshuka, Green **50**

shallots: Parsnip, Miso, Oat and Shallot
    Boulangère **97**

shellfish **236–9**

    Chilli con Pesce **246**

    see also individual types of shellfish

shiitake mushrooms: Vegan XO Sauce **23**

Slaw, Rainbow **94**

Slump topping **106**

Soufflé Omelette, Cheese Ends **168**

Soup, Summer Salad **55**

Sour Cashew Cream **172**

sour cherries

    sour cherry filling for crumbles and pies
      105

    Sourdough Doughnuts with White
      Chocolate Custard and Sour Cherry Jam
      148–9

sour cream: Elote **69**

Sour Orange Fish Curry **252**

Sourdough

    Sourdough Doughnuts with White
      Chocolate Custard and Sour Cherry Jam
      148–9

    Sourdough Flatbreads **166–7**

    Sourdough Starter **270–1**

soy industry, veganism and the **39–40**

soy milk **170**

soybeans: White Miso **21–2**

spatchcocking **185**

spiced apple filling for crumbles and pies **105**

spinach

    Bibimbap **140**

    Chicken in Weeds 2020 **181**

    Green Shakshuka **50**

split green peas: Mushy Peas **138**

split yellow peas: Tarka Dhal **125**

spring onions

    Greenhouse Romesco Sauce with
      Chargrilled Spring Onions **57**

    Summer Salad Soup **55**

squash

    Fridge-raid 'not quite Branston's' Pickle
      30–1

    grilled squash **43–4**

Sri Lankan Beetroot and Coconut Curry **85**

Sriracha **35**

stews

Allotment 'Ital-style' Stew **82**

Ethiopian Lentil Stew **122**

Marmite, Onion and Roast Root Vegetable
Stew **135–6**

a Really Great Lamb Neck Stew **202–5**

stocks **262–3**

strawberries

strawberry and black pepper filling for
crumbles and pies **105**

Summer Fruit Cordial **111**

Stuffing, Sage and Onion **186**

suet: Faggots **228–9**

Sumiso Cod Collar **244**

Summer Fruit Cordial **111**

Summer Salad Soup **55**

sustainable eating **6–7**

sweet miso **21–2**

Sweet Shortcrust Pastry **106**

sweetcorn: Elote **69**

Szechuan Onion Flower **74**

T

Tarka Dhal **125**

tart: a Pistachio Tart for Soft Fruit **100–1**

Tepache **19**

Three Ways with Mexican Braised Pinto
Beans **131**

tomatoes

Braised Beef Shin with Barbecue Sauce **199**

Braised Flat Beans in Slow Cooked
Tomato Sauce **66**

Chilli con Pesce **246**

Ethiopian Lentil Stew **122**

Gizzi's Slow Cooked Tomato Sauce **264**

Goat Ragu, with its Offal **232**

Green Tomato Salsa **49**

Greenhouse Romesco Sauce with
Chargrilled Spring Onions **57**

Guinea Fowl alla 'Diavolo' **182**

Nam Prik Ong with Allotment Vegetables
71

Pork and Sage Cannelloni **221–2**

Pumpkin Seed and Cocoa Mole Sauce
52–3

Ratatouille **46**

roasted tomatoes **44**

Stuffed Marrows and Tomatoes with
Mushrooms and Orzo **65**

Tonkotsu Ramen **213–14**

Tortillas, Rye **167**

Turkish Chilli Sauce **126–7**

24-hour Beef Tail and Rib Pho **216–18**

V

Vanilla School Cake and Custard **159–60**

veal **196, 198**

Veal Stock **263**

Vegan XO Sauce **23**

Carlin Pea and Pumpkin Massaman **123**

veganism **7, 38, 192, 193**

and the soy industry **39–40**

vegetables **38–41**

Allotment 'Ital-style' Stew **82**

autumn to winter **72–97**

Leftover Juicing Cake **107–9**

Marmite, Onion and Roast Root Vegetable
Stew with Cheesy Scones **135–6**

Nam Prik Ong with Allotment Vegetables
71

Root Vegetable Bulgar Wheat, 'Cous cous'
style, with Merguez Sausages **78**

spring to summer **36–71**

Vegetable Stock **262**

see also individual types of vegetable

venison **178**

Vinaigrette **269**

vinegar

Fermented Fruit Vinegar **17**

Watermelon Juice Vinegar **27**

Vongole **240**

W

walnuts: Leftover Juicing Cake **107–9**

waste **38, 195**

watercress: Roasted Beetroot, Beluga Lentil
and Watercress Salad with Goat's Cheese
Croute **116**

watermelon **26–7**

Lacto-fermented Watermelon Rind **27**

Mexican-Spiced Pickled Watermelon Rind
26

Watermelon Juice Vinegar **27**

West Indian Hot Sauce **34**

Wet & Wild Monkfish Kievs **247–8**

wheat **114–15**

White Miso **21–2**

wild garlic

Wild Garlic Butter **247–8**

Wild Garlic Stuffed Mutton **201**

wine

Burnt Basque Country Cheesecake with
Gooseberries in Green Wine **154**

Goat Ragu, with its Offal **232**

Puy Lentils, a Big Red and Roasted
Toulouse Sausage **120**

Red Wine and Beef Sauce **268**

Wood Pigeon, roast **185**

X

XO sauce, Vegan **23**

Carlin Pea and Pumpkin Massaman **123**

Acknowledgements

You'd think that by book six this would all start getting a little easier, but it never does. This time has been particularly hard. While commissioned two years ago, it always takes bit of time to get going on these things and I really wanted to live this book. Writing a book about environmental issues is no mean feat, especially when one of the core reasons for wanting to write it is the constant feed of 'broad facts' and misinformation.

I hijacked the life of one of my great friends and producers, Matt Chatfield from the Cornwall Project and Cull Yaw (both of which you will have read about in this book). You see, Matt is like no one else I know. He has been my guru on agricultural sustainability issues pretty much since I first met him about 14 years ago, when he delivered the freshest Cornish seasonal fish, caught that day, to my door. Matt just wants a better world. He, like me, cannot accept the economic benefits and agricultural destruction of mass production. He is a meat producer, yes, but he is one who (like me) fully acknowledges the impact the meat industry has had on not just the environment, but the soil itself and it's that soil that we need more than anything. There we were, both frustrated about the new narrative of sustainability, and Matt made maximising his knowledge not just his vocation but also his hobby, and he took me on this journey with him. Produce is my passion, but soil health is now my geek-out subject and it goes without saying that Matt has been THE key figure in this so THANK YOU Matt… what we have learnt (and endured) on this path, ey?!

I have also been able to utilise friendships and contacts within the wider fields of agriculture, farming, environmental science and the government. I need to thank Henry Dimbleby at DEFRA, David Boules at the RSPCA, Tracy Worcester at Farms not Factories, Ben Goldsmith, Greenpeace, Fred at Gothelney Farm, and Chris Jones for being a huge inspiration for silvopasture and farming for nature; Peter Hannan at Hannan Meats Ltd, Ben White at Coombeshead Organic, Mark Hayward at Dingley Dell Pork and Rewilding centre, James George and Richard Turner at Turner and George butchers, fish chef and conservationist Mitch Tonks, Jace Bowden from Wild Harbour and Sean O'Neil from Keveral biodynamic farm; the head of sustainability science at Bolton University, Emma Gardner; and my good friend and business partner nutritionist Rosemary Ferguson for all of your nutritional advice on biodiversity. This book has strengthened my relationship with ALL my producers and if you haven't been thanked please know that there is little space and so, SO many of you, but the progressive way you work is a huge inspiration to so many of us. Thank you for pushing against the system.

Next up I need to offer a heartfelt thank you to my team at HQ at HarperCollins. First and foremost to the deputy publishing director Kate Fox. Your patience with me, ability to allow me to get into a tizz and then soothe it, your fantastic eye and way with words, and how fantastic you are at managing people are so valued. You know I'm HQ 4 lyfe now – bad luck!!! Laura Nickoll you absolute KING. I salute your calmness and every single bit of advice was taken, which I'm not sure has ever happened in my whole career. We'll always have that weird Zoom from when I was drunk in Croatia… Thanks also to the Head of Design Kate Oakley HQ team, the sales team fronted by Fliss Porter, Halema Begum in Production and the bloody BRILLIANT Joe Thomas in PR – the best book PR in the UNIVERSE. You are my book family.

Now for the art and design team. Thanks to the art director of all my projects and my great friend Dean Martin. Another smasher, even later than usual. I know you love it. Your work gets better and better. Thanks for less moans than normal! Issy Croker, thanks for your incredible photos once again. There really isn't a talent like you anywhere. And thanks too to your assistant, the glorious Steph McLeod. Emily Ezekiel – WE MADE IT THROUGH the Zoom shoots. Look, I know I'm your number 1 pain in the arse, but I also know that when we work together we create magic. This was really hard as the shoot was socially distanced, but this is the best book we've done. I hope you agree. The shots I was a shithead on are some of my best. I love you always for persevering. Our motto – we are friends first! I love you for that. Truly. Thanks also to Joe Denison Carey, Laurie Perry, Kitty Coles and Dom.

My personal thanks need to start with my team. They say loyalty is the key to real success and we have all stuck together since Day One. Severine Berman and Tim Beaumont, you guys are as much a part of my success as me – I literally couldn't have done it without you. What a year we have had and just look at us all grown up. Thanks to my mother Maria, sisters Heni and Cora, my brothers-in-law Matt and Kieron, and my nieces and nephews Edie, Sholto and Beacan; to Phil Smith, my professional cooking sidekick, for working so hard with me always; and my darling Vic, thank you for always being there, getting me and my brain on track – your sisterly friendship, organisational skills and compassion mean the world. My Mickey: fucking hell! – the bane of my life, fast becoming the love of it; Jess and Benny, the best neighbours: you set me up with Mickey and we got to spend lockdown together on our brilliant mews (SHOUT OUT TO THE MEWS CREW: Lauren, Michael, Jade, Jordon and Gen), and Jessie (my secret weapon) helped me with the fermenting chapters and gave me such fresh insight. Benny, your portraits are some of the best I've ever had and the one for this book is the best picture of me of all time. To my closest friends, Stephen and Karima, Sydney, Lou, Ciara, Jack, Haydon, Olivia, Sophie, Candice and Neil – thanks for the respite and fun.

Finally, to Caroline. My WORD I miss you. I think of you every day. I'm not entirely sure how any of us are expected to get over you. We won't, but I swear I will keep your light alive.

HQ
An imprint of HarperCollinsPublishers Ltd
1 London Bridge Street
London SE1 9GF

10 9 8 7 6 5 4 3 2 1

First published in Great Britain by HQ
An imprint of HarperCollinsPublishers Ltd 2020

ISBN 9780008375690

Our policy is to use papers that are natural, renewable and recyclable products and made from wood grown in sustainable forests. The logging and manufacturing processes conform to the legal environmental regulations of the country of origin.

For more information visit: www.harpercollins.co.uk/green

Photographer: Issy Croker
Art Director, Props and Food Stylist: Emily Ezekiel
Food Assistant and Researcher: Rose Dougal
Designer: Dean Martin
Editorial Director: Kate Fox
Project Editor: Laura Nickoll
Author photo credit: Ben Robinson

Printed and bound in Great Britain by Bell & Bain Ltd, Glasgow